Sustainability and Small and Medium-Sized Enterprises

Industrialisation has brought great benefits to humankind but now, after 200 years of fossil fuel use, land clearance and pollution, the planet's boundaries are being stretched to their limits. Going beyond these confines would have severe consequences for humankind. To prevent this from happening, government, corporate and community initiatives must focus on reducing the environmental impact of approximately 400 million small and medium-sized enterprises (SMEs), given that they produce approximately 70% of the world's pollution, 60% of carbon emissions and have a significant impact on land. To date, research shows that SMEs have been environmental laggards and more needs to be understood to improve sustainability in the SME sector. Broadening the researcher's methodological focus, beyond traditional singular approaches, improves knowledge generation and better informs policy and practice. This book paves the way by showing the reader that a mixed method research design is able to provide a deep, diverse and holistic understanding of sustainability and SMEs. Importantly, the book also provides an in-depth mapping of mixed method sustainability and SME research at a regional level.

As this book is about environmental sustainability framed in a business context, it will be of interest to researchers, academics, students and those in industry who are enquiring about the environmental sustainability of SMEs.

Aharon Factor is an MBA educator with Southern Cross University, NSW, Australia, and operates his start-up research and consulting company – Sustainable SME Consulting.

John Parm Ulhøi is Professor of Organization and Management Theory at the School of Business and Social Sciences, University of Aarhus, Denmark.

Sustainability and Small and Medium-Sized Enterprises

Lessons from Mixed Methods Research

Edited by Aharon Factor and John Parm Ulhøi

Routledge
Taylor & Francis Group

LONDON AND NEW YORK

First published 2021
by Routledge
2 Park Square, Milton Park, Abingdon, Oxon OX14 4RN

and by Routledge
605 Third Avenue, New York, NY 10158

Routledge is an imprint of the Taylor & Francis Group, an informa business

British Library Cataloguing-in-Publication Data
A catalogue record for this book is available from the British Library

Library of Congress Cataloging-in-Publication Data
Names: Factor, Aharon, 1965- editor. | Ulhøi, John P., editor.
Title: Sustainability and small and medium-sized enterprises: lessons from mixed methods research / edited by Aharon Factor and John Parm Ulhøi.
Description: Abingdon, Oxon; New York, NY: Routledge, 2021. | Includes bibliographical references and index.
Identifiers: LCCN 2020046823 (print) | LCCN 2020046824 (ebook) | ISBN
9781138387270 (hbk) | ISBN 9780429426377 (ebk)
Subjects: LCSH: Small business. | Sustainability. | Sustainable development.
Classification: LCC HD2341 .S875 2021 (print) | LCC HD2341 (ebook) | DDC 338.9/27--dc23
LC record available at https://lccn.loc.gov/2020046823
LC ebook record available at https://lccn.loc.gov/2020046824

ISBN: 978-1-138-38727-0 (hbk)
ISBN: 978-0-367-75141-8 (pbk)
ISBN: 978-0-429-42637-7 (ebk)

Typeset in Sabon
by MPS Limited, Dehradun

Contents

List of Figures

List of Tables

Editors' Preface

The book is about environmental sustainability framed in a business context. Effective attempts at building a sustainable world are unlikely to happen without the active involvement of the business sector. With the majority of businesses being small and their response to environmental sustainability lagging behind their corporate counterparts, there is a real need both for the research community and society as a whole, to address this issue. Particularly, considering that the adjective 'small' hides the aggregative effects on sustainable development of approximately 400 million small and medium-sized enterprises (SMEs) across the globe.

Building knowledge around environmental sustainability in SMEs becomes a complex endeavour, however, considering that SMEs differ from larger enterprises in many ways; especially with regards to the central focus on the owner/manager in decision-making and the unstable and diverse SME business environment. Furthermore, an arrangement of scientific aspects of sustainability and competing moral, economic and regulatory tensions exacerbate complexities involved in understanding this phenomenon. Notably, it is this complexity, that provides the rationale of this book which draws on a distinct and growing knowledge production methodology which mixes quantitative and qualitative approaches through a concerted design known as mixed method research (MMR). Quite an MMR field has emerged and has provided excellent guidance on 'why to choose' and 'how to conduct' mixed method studies. Where this book makes a contribution is that it fills a gap where there has been significantly less information available regarding the added value and challenges associated with undertaking MMR in the context of sustainability and SMEs.

The journey that led to the idea of this book included the authors' own experiences of using MMR and the realisation of an emerging interest in mixed methods research in the field of sustainability and business studies. We also recognised a real opportunity that we were part of a small global research community with an important contribution to be made. By reaching out to this community, we are now able to present this book's research rationale which uses MMR to examine the book's main idea from a global perspective. This has also allowed for the presentation of many chapters that focus on specific studies undertaken by experts, along with exemplars of their particular viewpoints and choices. In addition to this solid empirical grounding, an engagement with the MMR community as well as the non-academic community has broadened reflections on the possible added value and/or challenges associated with MMR design.

Overall, the book recognises that researching sustainability spans a broad range of academic and non-academic players. In response, we intend for this book to serve different purposes and related audiences, and have tried to limit scientific jargon and use of referencing in this book, as much as possible, without jeopardizing its authenticity. We believe this book will especially be of use to those aiming at:

1　Evidencing state-of-the-art knowledge in environmental sustainability
2　Contributing to increasing an understanding of the importance of methods when facing complex problems of sustainability and business activities
3　Making decisions concerning sustainability strategy and policy
4　Engaging with executive and postgraduate education
5　Offering a 'boundary spanning and/or transgressing' sourcebook

During the writing of the book, attendance at the Mixed Method International Research Association's conferences in Vienna, Austria, in 2018, and Wellington, NZ, in 2019, expanded the authors' insights as regards the existence of a broader MMR community, especially in the areas of health and social sciences. MMR has enriched these disciplines, and it is our hope and aspiration that our book will not only promote and add value to researchers in our field, but will also be successful in meeting the global challenges that we all face.

Acknowledgements

When we reached out to recognised experts in the field, we were soon impressed by the positive response we received from all contributors. We appreciate their willingness to share their time and insights in the book. It has been a privilege and a pleasure to work with such committed and insightful experts.

We would also like to thank Routledge, particularly Rebecca Marsh, Kristina Abbotts, Brianna Ascher, Lauren Ellis and Naomi Round Cahalin, for their excellent cooperation in the preparation of the book. For supporting the development of the book, we would like to thank all our families and friends for their continued support. In particular, we would also like to recognise the contributions of Gina Milgate, Alex Baker and Catherine Moore, for their professionalism and assistance with administrative, technical and editorial functions.

About the Editors

Dr Aharon Factor is an MBA educator at the Southern Cross University, NSW, Australia. He teaches executives in the areas of Strategy, Sustainable Business and Project Management. He also operates a start-up company – Sustainable SME Consulting. He has undertaken research for the Australian Environment Ministry and contributed to the Theo Murphy Think Tank on Climate Change (organised jointly by the Royal Society of London and the Australian Academy of Sciences) He undertook his PhD research at the Aarhus School of Business in Denmark with Professor John Ulhøi, building into the school's successful Danish Environmental Barometer Programme.

Dr John P. Ulhøi is Professor of Management in the Department of Management at Aarhus University. He is Vice-President of the European Doctoral Programmes Association in Management and Business Administration. He has been in the field of business and sustainability since the 1990s. His interdisciplinary research has been sponsored by Danish, Nordic as well as European funding bodies. He has been the recipient of various awards and honours, including being decorated as Knight of the Order of Dannebrog.

List of Contributors

Dr Jennifer Moss Breen is Associate Professor and Programme Director of the interdisciplinary leadership programme at Creighton University in the US. Her scholarly focus is to promote exceptional leadership that will empower people to thrive. Her ongoing research interests include leader humility, Ignatian leadership, leader resilience, complexity in higher education and VUCA.

Dr Alessandro Bressan is a Lecturer and researcher at the University of Notre Dame Australia where he teaches undergraduate and postgraduate management courses. Alessandro's area of research is in social and environmental responsibility, entrepreneurship and innovation. From 2005 to 2008, he was also an expert member of the International Standard Organization (ISO) Committee for developing ISO 26000 International Guidelines on Environmental and Social Responsibility.

Dr Elizabeth G. Creamer is Professor Emerita with the educational research programme at Virginia Polytechnic Institute and State University in the US. She is the author of the 2018 SAGE textbook, *An Introduction to Fully Integrated Mixed Methods Research,* and has an up-coming textbook with Routledge, UK, *Advancing Grounded Theory with Mixed Methods.* She is the Editor-in-chief of the mixed method research stream in the Methods in Psychology journal.

Dr Mark Gagnon is Harbaugh Entrepreneur and Innovation Faculty Scholar and Associate Teaching Professor of Agribusiness at Penn State University in the US. His scholarly interests lie within entrepreneurship and small business, specifically addressing challenges in food, agriculture and bio-renewables. His current research examines new technology value proposition development and strategy implementation.

Dr Timothy C. Guetterman is a methodologist and Associate Director of the mixed methods programme at the University of Michigan in the US. His methodological interest is to advance approaches to integrative analysis and to the intersection of qualitative designs with mixed methods research. His interdisciplinary NIH-funded research focuses on health services and education.

Dr Ralph Hamann is Professor at the UCT Graduate School of Business in South Africa, where he works on business sustainability and social entrepreneurship and innovation. Among his other roles, he is co-founder of the South African leg of the Embedding Project and the Southern Africa Food Lab, two award-winning initiatives bridging research and practice.

Dr Steve Harris is Senior Researcher and project manager at IVL Swedish Environmental Research Institute. He has a PhD in Industrial Ecology (University of Edinburgh) and 20 years' experience in sustainability research, in academic and consultancy positions, spanning life cycle assessment, circular economy, policy assessment and sustainable urban development.

Dr Ruth Hillary is a consultant and widely published author with over 25 years' experience in sustainability and EMS. Her multi-disciplinary research in the EU and UK was among the first to investigate the Eco-management and Audit Scheme/ISO 14001 and SMEs. She is a UK expert on international and British standards. Her current interest is blockchain and its sustainability impacts.

Dr Maria D. Lopez-Gamero is Associate Professor in the Department of Management at the University of Alicante, Spain. Her Ph.D. dissertation was an analysis of the relationship between environmental management and firm performance. Her current research includes sustainable tourism, environmental management and its relationship with quality management and organisational design.

Dr Jose F. Molina-Azorin is Professor in the Department of Management at the University of Alicante, Spain. His research focuses on strategic management, environmental management, sustainability, quality management and organisational design, mainly in the tourism industry. His current research interests are also focused on mixed methods. He is Co-editor of the Journal of Mixed Methods Research.

Dr Jorge Pereira-Moliner is Professor in the Department of Management at the University of Alicante, Spain. His Ph.D. dissertation was an analysis of strategic groups in the hotel industry. His current research includes strategic management, quality management, environmental management and sustainability in the tourism industry.

Dr Eva M. Pertusa-Ortega is Associate Professor in the Department of Management at the University of Alicante, Spain. Her Ph.D. dissertation was an analysis of the relationship between organisational design and competitiveness. Her current research includes organisational design and its relationship with environmental and quality management, and also the topic of organisational and individual ambidexterity.

Dr Bradley Pettitt was elected Mayor of Freemantle, Australia, in 2009, and re-elected in 2017. His expertise includes climate change, international policy and sustainability planning. He was previously the Dean of the School of Sustainability at Murdoch University and was appointed to the Heritage Council of WA in 2014.

Dr Norma Romm (DLitt et Phil) is Research Professor in the Department of Adult Education at the University of South Africa. She has published four sole-authored books, three co-authored ones and five co-edited ones, plus over 100 research articles on the links between social research and social and ecological existence.

Dr Eustathios Sainidis is Senior Lecturer in Strategic Management at Northumbria University and Deputy Director of the Northumbria University London Campus. He is an experienced academic and has taught extensively at undergraduate and postgraduate levels, and has supervised and been examiner to a number of doctoral candidates. Eustathios is an active researcher in the subject of manufacturing strategy in SMEs and has a particular interest in the application of mixed methods in business and management research.

Dr Juan Jose Tari is Professor in the Department of Management at the University of Alicante, Spain. His Ph.D. dissertation was an analysis of quality management. His current research includes total quality management and its relationship with sustainability, environmental management, organisational design, innovation and higher education.

Part A

Sustainability, SMEs and mixed methods

1 Key roots and approaches to sustainability

Aharon Factor, John Parm Ulhøi, and Norma Romm

1.1 Introduction: The roots and meaning of sustainable development

The roots of contemporary environmentalism go back to more than half a century. During the 1960s, Carson (1962) drew attention to the uncontrolled accumulation of pesticides in the food chain. Her book not only paved the way for the early development of contemporary environmentalism, but it also set about a political debate (e.g., Shrivastava and Berger, 2010; Ishwaran, 2012; Magill, 2018).

Rachel Carson's book also brought to the fore, the concept of an 'ecological ethic', challenging the pervading economic logic of limitless growth. This was also purported by Hardin, by accentuating the conflict between individual rationality and shared resources (Hardin, 1968). While Hardin's overpopulation thesis may be contestable, it is his ecological narrative that has captivated global audiences (Ells, 2008). Hardin traces the roots of this narrative back to the work of Oxford political economist William Forster Lloyd (1833) and also derives from James Madison's insight in 1788 as to how self-interested individuals seeking competitive advantage leads to the overuse of resources (Dershowitz et al., 2019). Weber-Blaschke et al. (2005) suggest that this was also recognised as early as the 16th century, with forestry management practices suggesting the recognition of limits to resource usage, and also historically contextualises sustainability as a concept that goes back several centuries.

The proponents of the limits to natural resource exploitation might, thus, be long-standing, but it was not until authors such as Carson and Hardin set the modern context, that of the downside to economic growth becoming more broadly recognised in Western thought. Following their work, the early 1970s then became an important and fertile period, especially in terms of the work undertaken by international institutions. On a global level, two important events at the beginning of the 1970s, in particular, deserve a mention; namely, 'The United Nations (UN) Conference on the Human Environment' (held in Stockholm, 1972) and the Club of Rome's report (1972). The report presented the results of computer modelling undertaken by researchers from the Massachusetts Institute of Technology (MIT). It showed that the golden age of capitalism (1951 to 1973) that had done so much to re-establish the world economy, and social development following World War II, was on a road leading to collapse in the 21st century. The report claimed that an expansive ideology aligning strong economic growth with natural resource usage would not be sustainable by the middle of the 21st century (Meadows et al., 1972, 2005).

The 1972, UN Conference on the Human Environment, held in Stockholm was the first prominent international event that directed its focus on the relationship between economic development and the natural environment. The conference led to the first international action plan with specific recommendations (United Nations, 1972). These events arguably fertilised the soil for important follow-ups (Ulhøi, 1995). The former UNEP Deputy Executive Director, Dr Mushtafa Tolba, for example, introduced the concept of 'Development without destruction' in his book from 1982. He presented this concept during a series of UNEP speeches and reports in the late 1970s and early 1980s. Shortly thereafter, Repetto, in 1985, also published a book that helped to lay the foundation for what a few years later was successfully introduced as 'sustainable development'.

It was not until 1987, however, that as part of the World Commission on Environment and Development, the concept of sustainable development became more evident. The Commission published its report (1987), thereby recognising the urgency for a more expansive sustainable development that sought a more harmonious balance between economic, social and environmental interests. This report laid down the basis for the 1992 Rio Conference and the 2002 World Summit on Sustainable Development in Johannesburg, both ratified by some 190 countries. By 2015, the UN had strengthened these earlier efforts and adopted a new initiative, Agenda 2030 which placed 17 key sustainable development goals (SDGs) at the centre of its sustainable development strategy. This was adopted through a political declaration at the United Nations 2019 summit (United Nations, 2019).

1.2 Critique and developments

Without the unification of interests defining sustainable development, the concept of sustainability has become a semantic quagmire. Since the year 2000, there have arisen, some 300 definitions of 'sustainability' and 'sustainable development' that are mainly related to environmental management and associated disciplines (Johnston et al., 2007, p. 60). Planning for change, though, demands an understanding of the problem at hand, one that is difficult as the very concept of sustainable development is frequently contested. A plurality of interpretations and definitions, thus, brings forth an array of descriptive, normative and instrumental philosophical assumptions. This situation is, among others, related to the affinity of the concept of sustainability with other concepts, which implies that the concept cannot be interpreted in isolation from discussions around economic and social structures and ecological boundaries. As Ramsey (2015) describes, words and their meanings are contextually set within defined social structures and attempts to impose interpretations without recognising the necessity and importance of those structures 'most definitions of sustainability are doomed to failure' (Ramsey, 2015, p. 1078).

This broader semantic for speaking about sustainable development is well captured by Fergus and Rowley (2005) who suggest that while sustainable development offers the opportunity for an ethical discourse concerning society's future development, and one that is based on values that are inclusive, diverse and integrative, 'The importance of philosophical context within which the term is used influences the definitional process of meaning' and has been dominated by the scientific-economic discourse (2005, p. 17). The presiding scientific-economic approach, it can be argued, still serves to frame prevalent discourses for addressing sustainability challenges. It postulates scientific-technological solutions for economic development, thereby suggesting that somehow science can lead to the creation of 'green' growth paths in a sustainable fashion. Pearce and Turner (1990b) reflect on how economics might reconcile environmental protection with economic growth. They posture a sustainability continuum by which the scientific-economic approach fosters a weak response to sustainability at one end of the continuum and a stronger sustainability approach at the other end. In the next section, we explore, in a little more detail, the concepts and voices along this continuum.

1.2.1 The scientific-economic approach to sustainability and some critiques

Since the so-called Age of Enlightenment (1685 to 1815) in Western cultural discourses (Peters, 2019), a great shift has occurred, elevating logical reason to the centre of a new scientific era (McIntyre-Mills, 2006; Bausch, 2016). Following this shift, knowledge creation was deemed to be a process of logical deduction that focused on explaining observable cause and effect relationships and has contributed significantly to the technical development of our society today. The transformation of theoretical science to applied technology then came to dominate how the world is understood and treated, as an object for manipulation (Habermas, 1984; Bud et al., 2018). This experimental mode of positivistic science, (Gibbons et al., 1994) labelled as Mode 1 science, has also laid down the basis for an economic paradigm which McCloskey (1983) refers to as 'modernism'. She describes how the classical economics of the 1930s and 1940s came to be dominated by the underpinning logical positivism and hypothetical-deductive model of science that was central to 19th century physics. Caldwell and Coats (1984) expand on McCloskey's argument that the scientific approach is inadequate as a methodology for economics, and they suggest that a more inclusive methodology of knowledge generation is needed; one that brings in other academic disciplines. In response, a more pluralistic and open field of economics has emerged (Angner, 2019), one that is more tolerant, reflective (Tomer, 2007) and better able to tackle the complexities associated with sustainability.

Evidence of this shift is indicated in the works of Aronsson and Schöb (2018) who describe how economic modelling around climate change adaptation needs to venture beyond a techno-centric approach to adaptation, to one that can gain insights into the psychology of adaptation. Nonetheless, the positivistic nature of psychological economics tends to minimise qualitative enquiry (Tomer, 2007). Instead, Milne (2017) identifies that the inclusion of qualitative, subjective elements needs to be incorporated in a far more holistic trade-off between economics, environment and social considerations; one that systematically interconnects psychology, philosophy, science and ethics within a sustainability framework.

Although the sentiments of Brundtland's (1987) World Commission on Environment and Development was to bring a more holistic and integrative approach to sustainable development, since its first induction, the terminology around the concept has become radically colonised by the modernity paradigm with its technology-based interests across economic, environmental and societal spheres. The institutions that control this era of modernity use both media (Diprose et al., 2018; Yacoumis, 2018) and corporate rhetoric (Zyglidopoulos and Fleming, 2011) to legitimise their own interpretation of sustainability. In this new world, 'corporate responsibility' is about shaping legitimacy through controlling the scientific-economic discourse, theoretical constructions as well as practices and standards (Castelló and Lozano, 2011). For Zyglidopoulos and Fleming (2011), this allows corporations to hide their malpractices and provides a purposeful ambiguity and protective 'smoke screen' for organisations with greater stakeholder visibility (Meyer and Höllerer, 2016, p. 394). This shift in corporate focus from profit maximisation (as proposed by 20th century neoclassical thinkers such as Stigler and Friedman, see Morgan, 2015) to legitimising corporate activities (Castelló and Lozano, 2011) is also captured by Schaltegger and Hörisch (2017).

Fergus and Rowley (2005) and (Romm, 2001) use Habermas's arguments to explore how the scientific-economic approach came to dominate the meaning of sustainable development, at the centre stage, and allowed influential business interests to hijack the environmental agenda (Welford, 1997, 1998; Cerin, 2003; McIntyre-Mills, 2014; Stokols, 2018). A well-known example of the latter is the influential industrialist Stephen Schmidheiny's and the World Business Council for Sustainable Development's entrance into the sustainability debate, which sought to maintain economic functions in line with the Earth's carrying capacity. Stephan Schmidheiny has persistently argued that sustainable development was achievable through free market forces and the integration of the 'polluter pays' principle (Schmidheiny, 1992), and seeking a term beyond sustainable development, he took the opportunity at the Rio de Janeiro Conference to coin the expression 'eco-efficiency' as a concept of 'doing more with less' (Dobers and Wolff, 1999, p. 33).

This was an extension of the concepts of pollution control and 'end-of-pipe' approaches of the 1960s to 1980s that sought to maintain business stakeholder legitimacy. For example, the legitimacy process of modernity is rooted in what Whittaker and Likens (1975) have referred to as a 'quick-fix approach' to complex problems. Biely et al. (2018) describe how this quick-fix is a weak form of sustainability, politically driven with significant support from economists. This weak response to addressing before, as purported to earlier in this chapter, may be envisaged as the continuum of weak to strong sustainability (Pearce and Turner, 1990a; Landrum and Ohsowski, 2018). This continuum gives rise to a spectrum of perspectives and alternative approaches which we illuminate upon, further into the chapter.

The weak and very weak form of sustainability maintains economic growth through 'increases in production and consumption, economic growth, valuation and utilization of natural resources, and technocratic solutions to environmental problems' (Landrum and Ohsowski, 2018, p. 130). This has created a linear model that emphasises waste minimisation, recycling and reduction of pollution and downstream production and consumption rather than putting in place a value chain approach that can adequately deal with the inputs and outputs (Sauvé et al., 2016). A linear conceptualisation of sustainable development in a linear economic model of production is likely to cause other problems too. Krysiak (2006), in his formal modelling approach, for example, uses the second law of thermodynamics to investigate if the production and consumption of products has limits. The findings reveal that weak sustainability coupled with economic growth becomes constrained by increasing resource limitations.

Victor (2012) supports this finding and demonstrates that while de-growth economics (in the context of his Canadian study) would cut greenhouse gas (GHG) emissions by 88%, it would also see a dramatic decrease in GDP, while low growth/no growth strategies would maintain GDP levels to 80% of business-as-usual approaches and GHGs would only be cut to 56% by 2035. Such considerations are, therefore, postured to be accounted for if high consumption societies aim for steady state and de-growth strategies. For Groen (2019), however, only degrowth and zero growth strategies can address the ecological and economic challenges of the 21st century.

The belief that all problems can be solved by new (and better) technology (the techno-fix approach) also extenuates the belief of continuing and expanding present lifestyles indefinitely, without causing economic, social or environmental collapse (Huseman and Huseman, 2011). It also builds on the premise of the weak sustainability camp, that of the needs of the World Commission and the Bruntland report, that future generations can inherit an equitable stock of capital through the efficient conversion of natural resources into financial capital, as long as this is within the carrying capacity of the Earth. Aimed at enhancing the eco-efficiency principle, the concept of industrial ecology arose in the 1990s whereby environmental impacts could be reduced through symbiotic relationships between organisations. It was argued that industrial wastes could become another company's raw material and thus marked the emergence of a new perspective on organising (Ulhøi et al., 2000), based on mutual interdependence and cooperation. This was an early development that laid the foundations for the decoupling concept. This concept recognises that eco-efficient uses of resources still draw from natural capital stock. This is due to linear organisational value chains that extract natural resources through an open system. Closing the system so that organisational value is gained through resources that already exist inside a closed system has been at the centre of research (Ünal et al., 2019; Werning and Spinler, 2020) and is gaining increasing traction in the 21st century.

This decoupling of the economy from the natural environment, proponents posit, will allow for sustainable economic growth and preservation of natural capital. This idea has become central to the United Nations Sustainable Development Goals (SDGs, 2015) and the European Investment Bank (EIB, 2020). Since 2015, when this was presented at that UN Sustainability Conference, these goals had become the cornerstone of corporate social responsibility practice for many leading organisations. Scoones (2016), nonetheless, describes how there is much disagreement around the SDG concepts. The concept of decoupling by the UN in 2015, has, for example, been criticised by Fletcher and Rammelt (2017, p. 463) as a 'smokescreen to continue business as usual' and propagate environmental devastation into the future. They also describe that not only is decoupling a poorly understood concept and lacks empirical rigour, its aspirations to reconcile poverty alleviation with environmental sustainability and corporate development have, instead, been entrapped in the growth doctrine of neoliberal economics. Accordingly, the UN SDGs seek an intensification of economic growth, the antithesis of ecological sustainability, and they pit sustainable development against notions of sustainability (Hannis, 2017).

Assumptions that continual economic growth has its limits (e.g., Limits to Growth Report: Meadows, 1972; Meadows et al., 1992) was supported by a 2014 research investigation at the University of Melbourne's Melbourne Sustainable Society Institute. The researchers showed the limits to growth modelling to be alarmingly accurate with economic and population collapse forecasted for 2030 (Turner, 2012, 2014). The Melbourne-based research team suggests that the global financial crisis may be an indication of the early stages of collapse and stress and that a rapid switch to renewable energy resources and changes in societal behaviours is essential. Butler (2017), furthermore, shows how the signs of limits to growth are playing out in the early part of the 21st century, such as climate change-induced aquifer depletion in Syria which has been implicated as a driver of the growing refugee crisis.

Even though the Melbourne-based team finds accord with the original Limits to Growth report findings, there has been a significant split over the findings by members of the Club of Rome to which the MIT researchers belonged. At the time, the Club of Rome was a newly-founded and prominent group of industrialists, economists, scientists and technologists. Not all members were so pessimistic about the future, and believed that science and technology would enable both continued economic growth and protection of the Earth's ecological systems. Blanchard (2010) finds that in the counter modelling to the pessimistic forecasts of Limits to Growth, considerable political bias favoured methodologies with research outcomes favourable to existing philosophical positions. Significant change had, nonetheless, occurred at the Club of Rome since 1972, and in September 2019, the Club of Rome published its Planetary Emergency Plan which recognises that economic growth and human behaviours now threaten Earth's life-support systems (The Club of Rome, 2019).

Against this backdrop, Turner (2014) concludes with the caveat that the Limits to Growth model holds true under the assumption that humans do not make the choice to change. They discuss how the unknown is the human reaction. This is supported by the work of Forsyth and Levidow (2015, p. 143) who suggest that a behavioural element needs to accompany Limits to Growth investigations, which otherwise are limited themselves by 'rational' assumptions that humans will not intervene to better manage resource scarcities as well as to reduce consumption. Sachs (2017), however, suggests that expansive modernity will decline as Agenda 2030 seeks to overcome the domination of the economic-scientific approach to sustainable development. In its place, Agenda 2030 urges for more ethically inclined action whereby a new socio-green economic world order arises. The very notion of 'development' used in 2015 and the Paris agreement, Sachs believes, will give way to the new cooperative economics Agenda 2030.

1.3 Transformative approaches to sustainability

The linear paradigm that underpins the weak sustainability approach is criticised by Thatcher and Yeow (2016) for inadequately applying linear relationships to discrete parts of what they describe as an interconnected world. Instead, they call for emancipation beyond bounded rationality to a broader systems framework. This is a framework also supported by scholars such as Chilisa (2017), McIntyre-Mills et al. (2017) and Stokols (2018). Modernism, however, acts to protect the paradigm of linearity, as experts who have developed social capital within the paradigm may have vested interests in the type of knowledge created through this paradigmatic approach (Haugaard, 2018). This has been described by Flood and Romm (2018) as theoretical isolation. This eventuates when strong ontological and epistemological beliefs protect against the knowledge creation approach of other paradigms. This leaves only a singular approach to knowledge building, instead of a richer, more pluralistic knowledge creation process, as demanded by the complexities faced with understanding sustainability phenomena.

While this mono-paradigmatic approach to knowledge generation has been central to the growth of modern economies and technological and scientific advancement, this has also created a significant impact on socio-ecological systems. With increasingly complex challenges surfacing, such as climate change and COVID 19, a new way forward is needed whereby a more holistic view is developed, based on dialogue and pluralism, language and culture (Colucci-Gray et al., 2013). COVID 19, for example, may have consequences as to how we think and redefine sustainability, especially in terms of human health (Hakovirta and Denuwara, 2020), which is especially important in developing countries, as sustainability becomes the focus after the COVID pandemic is contained (Barbier and Burgess, 2020). In the present COVID-19 situation, Barreiro-Gen et al. (2020) urge organisations to regain a positive focus towards environmental issues that had been generated in the previous three decades and use the pandemic as an opportunity to drive forward the sustainability agenda. Another key area of a post-COVID world will be to recognise that the adherence to the UN SDGs will be an important driver of building a sustainable world, particularly in resolving global inequalities which are inextricably linked to sustainability outcomes (Ashford et al., 2020).

While COVID and climate change are representative of a whole complexity of concerns that are bound up in the sustainability phenomenon, specialisation of knowledge across business, social science, technology and natural sciences (cf. Stokols, 2018) may create a barrier to understanding sustainability as a multidimensional and integrating concept. Instead, Kudo and Mino (2020) meld economic, social, cultural and environmental issues together – emphasising that sustainability cannot be adequately captured and understood by mono-disciplinary approaches alone (Allen and Giampietro, 2006; Hadorn et al., 2006). Different and integrated approaches that can engage with multifaceted and complex sustainability problems is, thus, warranted.

In short, the complexity, uncertainty and urgency that sustainability issues bring, requires engagement in cross-disciplinary enquiry into human behaviour and interactions with the ecological world (Colucci-Gray et al., 2013; Stokols, 2018). As Hulme (2009, p. 28) emphasises, sustainability 'exists as much in the human mind and in the matrices of cultural practices as it exists as an independent objective physical category'. Sustainability solutions are, therefore, just as much about people than adherence to relying on technology as the sole solution (Maguire et al., 2009). These more complex patterns of interaction, however, make attributing specific causes and effects anything but straightforward (Romm, 2017). Even in the natural sciences, the limitations of linear approaches which try to identify 'causes' of effects without appreciating the confluence of interconnected factors that make up the web of life, are being questioned. Researchers studying the Amazon rainforest have, for example, recognised the need to go beyond linear modelling to studying complex non-linear problems (Menck et al., 2013).

Within such a debate, many advocates of sustainability science call for inter-disciplinary and inter-paradigmatic collaboration, including dialogue between experts and non-experts in the construction of new scientific knowledge. Chilisa (2017) points out that this implies not only inter-disciplinary collaboration between professionals (academics/scientists), but also collaboration with practitioners in the field (which she considers as a *transdisciplinary* endeavour). She is concerned that there still seems to be prevalent across the globe, the notion that 'knowing' has to be validated through formal academic processes (Sillitoe, 2010). This means that co-generating workable knowledge with practitioners gets ruled out as the way forward for sustainability science (Sillitoe, 2010).

This means that during the 1970s and 1980s, interdisciplinary fields emerged such as human ecology, ecological economics and technology assessment. Yet, Kastenhofer et al. (2011, p. 835) describe how these have, for the most part, remained siloed within the scientific mono-paradigm and have been unable to address sustainability as a truly holistic concept. Ecological economics has, for example, been through a 'normalisation' phase that has seen a strong focus on quantitative and reductionist studies. Studies by Kastenhofer et al. (2011) have also observed that sustainability research has been found to be strongly represented by the environmental sciences but has been lagging in participatory research and socio-political enquiry. This is indeed the argument as expressed by Chilisa (2017), who suggests that a transdisciplinary approach is defined by it being *participatory* as well as taken into account (and trying to shift) the power dynamics within the knowledge-production process, so that the ways of knowing of academics does not come to dominate the social discussion.

Paradigmatic differences are also seen by other authors as central to interdisciplinary (and potentially transdisciplinary) exchange (e.g., Lowe and Phillipson, 2009). Evans and Marvin (2006, p. 1172), for example, describes how a 'radical interdisciplinarity' was originally encouraged by various research councils for a strategic commitment to inter-disciplinary collaboration. This was intended to bring together the social, natural and engineering sciences but failed due to underlying disciplinary philosophies and knowledge building approaches.

In this regard, it is the transformative capacity of Gibbons' Mode 2 post-modernist science (Gibbons et al., 1994; Gibbons et al., 2011), therefore, that is crucially important for allowing sustainability researchers to be able to critically reflect beyond the confines of the linear disciplines. Gibbons et al. (1994) use the concept of the Greek forum, or *agora*, whereby participants possessing multiple perspectives are able to solve pragmatic problems in situ. In this agora, participants are able to break free from the myopic constraints of mono-paradigmatic approaches to avoid standing 'as deer in the headlights of oncoming complexity' as Allen and Giampietro (2006, p. 614) put it. This is also the argument developed by Christakis (2004) and Flanagan and Christakis (2009) who propound the value of a redefined agora in the current era. Another knowledge production mode as propounded by the Institute for 21st century Agoras is based on a community approach. This approach builds on community 'understanding-making' and involves century Agoras is based on a community century Agoras is based on a community century Agoras is based on a community 'individuals and organizations who take front line positions in civic engagement' (Institute for 21st Century, 2020).

Transformative science also builds on the work of Jantsch (1972) who recognised that knowledge creation runs beyond disciplines, not just between disciplines, while opening a new mode of enquiry known as 'transdisciplinarity', as discussed above. Instead of being theory-driven, the transdisciplinary approach seeks solutions through the investigation of complex phenomena and interaction with societal stakeholders and multiple disciplines (Christakis, 2004; Kakoulaki et al., 2017). That is, citizens become involved in deliberating together with professional natural and social scientists about the social and ecological crises (as experienced) – so that systemic understanding of leverage points for effective and ethical action can be devised.

This underpins the concept of systems thinking which breaks down the silos of the mono-paradigmatic approach and provides a more holistic approach to sustainability, which is geared to an inclusive human and planetary well-being (McIntyre-Mills, 2014; Williams et al., 2017; McIntyre-Mills and Romm, 2019). It also places human responsibility at the centre of pre-occupation of Mode 2 science and is, therefore, more socially accountable and opens possibilities for a more pragmatic and transformative approach (Popa et al., 2015). Especially as 'it includes a wider, more temporary and heterogeneous set of practitioners, collaborating on a problem identified in a specific, localised context' (Gibbons et al., 2011, p. 362). This alternative approach to knowledge creation emancipates sustainability researchers from traditional disciplinary silos and allows new modes of interdisciplinary and transdisciplinary knowledge generation, and has significant implications for researching sustainability.

As Knaggård et al. (2018), notes that, for sustainability research to help enhance society's ability to interact [between humans and between humans and nature] more sustainably 'the processes of knowledge production for sustainability should be interdisciplinary or even transdisciplinary' (p. 20). Knaggård et al. (2018) note, along with authors such as Chilisa (2017) and Stokols (2018), that while interdisciplinarity refers to research that cuts across boundaries of academic disciplines or institutions, *transdisciplinary* research involves a 'critical and self-reflexive research approach that relates societal and scientific problems; it produces new knowledge by integrating different scientific and extrascientific insights' (p. 20).

1.4 Reimagining sustainability

Malone et al. (2017) invite readers to think about sustainability in the light of new contexts, new questions and new ways of conducting research. At the same time, novel ethical dilemmas and questions of fairness are also seen to emerge in a renewed vision of sustainability. One aspect of re-inventing sustainability is to first recognise the effect of human-induced planetary change as discussed by a leading team of international researchers, driven by the Climate Change Institute at the Australian National University and Germany's Max Planck Institute for Chemistry (Steffen et al., 2011). They explain how the Industrial Revolution is affecting geological and climatic cycles so significantly that the geological era known as the Holocene is being reformed into a human-centred epoch known as the Anthropocene. This refers to a period in which 'humankind has become a global geological force in its own right' (Steffen et al., 2011, p. 843). That is, the human footprint on resources now matches any other geological forces in terms of the functioning of the Earth's system. Steffen et al. (2011) associate this change in the Earth's reconstruction with humankind's GHG emissions, as well as broader environmental impacts.

Further insight into this phenomenon can be analysed using Ehrlich's renowned IPAT equation model, defined as: I (Environmental Impact of Humans) = P (population) + A (affluence) and T (Technology) (Fischer-Kowalski et al., 2014). It describes how the right-hand side of the equation driven by fossil fuels, has greatly accelerated technological development, affluence and growing populations, and that is now pushing the planet beyond its limits (Meadows et al., 1972, 1992). A re-balancing of the IPAT equation in the Anthropocene period is, therefore, suggested whereby humankind may connect more with nature, and reduces environmental impact as denoted as I on left-hand side of the IPAT equation.

In this new world order, the great technical acceleration created during the industrial period, as described by Fischer-Kowalski et al. (2014), needs to be replaced by a more ecologically focused, less consumer and politically fragmented (Blühdorn, 2017; Colocousis et al., 2017) and more resilient society (Benson and Craig, 2014). In this new re-imagined world, although challenges may exist to both preserve nature and support humans, a plurality of ideas and perspectives around sustainability may instigate a new wave of human ingenuity and creativity (Romm, 2017).

At the turn of the 21st century, Bryson's (2003) account of the works of science writers Rachel Carson and Loren Eisely, underpins this sense of re-imagining sustainability. Bryson (2003) explains how these writers were wary of 'Big Science' and the preoccupation with humankind's control over nature, and instead, urged for an ethically driven 'Good Science'. For Carson and Eisely, this more reflective, morally centred scientific approach rejects anthropocentrism and recognises an appreciation of nature as something to be cared for, grounded in its social context (Bryson, 2003, p. 386). While this non-anthropocentric approach finds accord with McIntyre-Mills (2014) in redefining sustainability and reshaping the future, Spahn (2018) describes how Western preoccupations with sustainable development within a human rights framework places Western individualism above the rights of nature. This is why, as Spahn (2018) continues to explain that while the UN's Agenda 2030 might have aspirations to protect nature, the dominating framework prioritises human rights.

In the United Nations (2019) report on global sustainable development, the scientific expert panel emphasises that the nature of Western economic growth can no longer sustain the planet. The report captures the essence of Steffen et al. (2011, p. 843) and their insight of the skewed benefits which accrue to different countries, in terms of the Western-powered approach to 'growth'. This point has previously been expressed somewhat more sharply by Victor (2012), suggesting that only degrowth can sustain the planet. Haapanen and Tapio (2016), in their critique of growth, nonetheless suggest that while growth cannot continue unabated, solutions need to be better formulated; ones that balance economic, environmental and social considerations.

Insights into redressing the growth debate could be developed more around the indigenous understandings of *balance* as propagated in some indigenous communities, which arguably kept a 'steady state', more in balance with nature. In this respect, many authors argue that indigenous worldviews prior to colonialism in many indigenous cultural contexts contained a recognition that economics had to be tied to conservation of the environment, for the sake of both humans and the environment (Edington, 2017; Quan-Baffour, 2017; Magill, 2018; Osuji, 2018). According to these authors, indigenous communities arguably managed to keep a steady state in their relations with the environment (to which they felt spiritually connected), which means, they were in balance with nature. Smith (1999, 2012) avers that balance is a central concept in indigenous thought. Edington points out that, in contrast, the Western world currently produces and consumes to provide a growth rate that is unsustainable (2017, p. 205).

The importance, therefore, of the inclusion of indigenous voices into growth debates is critical for humankind as indigenous populations seek more pluralistic and harmonious existence with nature, which is in stark contrast to the dominant, exclusive and exploitative Western cultures (Harris and Wasilewski, 2004). Furthermore, indigeneity is 'a very ancient global paradigm of sustainability, spiritual interconnectedness and coexistence – of *convivencia*[1] – of living together. This is a worldview that up until now has been undervalued' (Harris and Wasilewski, 2004, p. 494). The argument, here, is that modernism sets the social structures by which the dominant scientific-economic order maintains hegemony over sustaining nature through instrumental goals bound by the rationality of its own boundaries (Pontus, 2003). In this anthropocentric view, humankind is elevated over the interests of nature. Harris and Wasilewski express the alternative indigenous understanding which they see as advanced in much of indigenous thought as follows:

> Relationship is the kinship obligation, the profound sense that we human beings are related, not only to each other, but to all things, animals, plants, rocks—in fact, to the very stuff the stars are made of. This relationship is a kinship relationship. Everyone/everything is related to us as if they were our blood relatives. We, thus, live in a family that includes all creation, and everyone/everything in this extended family is valued and has a valued contribution to make (2004, p. 492).

This implies a radical critique of reductionist scientific construction whereby humans assume that they have no direct responsibility towards nature. Jakobsen (2017) delineates further on how the reductionist approach segregates knowledge generation from value and belief concepts as if knowing can be a value-free enterprise. Instead, Arko-Achemfuor and Dzansi, (2015, p. 63) make the point that in efforts to collaboratively find solutions for more sustainable ways of living (including recognising our essential connectedness with 'nature'), all ways of knowing should become part of the discussion. They add that this implies offering critiques of economic efficiencies and profit maximisation associated with economic globalisation. They suggest that this focus is premised on the notion that 'human beings are just economic beings' (2015, p. 63). They point out that this Western-oriented model tends to view efficiency as the only value of importance – and other issues, such as the need to protect the environment and humans, become secondary.

As such, Sillitoe (2010) posits that indigenous knowledge systems, instead, are relegated to 'non-science' and hence, are not taken seriously. She, therefore, pleads for recognising a variety of ways of justifying processes of knowing, including those advanced within what she calls the indigenous paradigm for research. Arko-Achemfuor and Dzansi (2015) and Sillitoe (2010) present an argument that is consistent with Chilisa's point that it is necessary to take indigenous paradigms for sustainability research seriously, while recognising the need to also be cross-disciplinary across boundaries which separate out fields of knowledge and to be transdisciplinary to the concerns and ways of knowing of lay people.

1.5 Business and sustainability

It was in the aftermath of the Brundtland Report in the late 1980s, that the academic business community began taking an interest in the interrelationships between business activities and the natural environment, and if or how this important interplay was addressed by business managers. The earliest studies can be traced back to the 1970s. Welles (1973), for example, examined how environmental concerns were to affect MNCs. The author already foresaw that unless executives acknowledged the necessity to incorporate environmental considerations into their strategy activities, nothing was going to happen. A seminal paper by Gladwin and Walters (1976) introduced an interesting framework for analysing the responses of MNCs to social issues. Later in the 1990s, a variety of international guidelines and integrated environmental management systems such as the European EMAS and the international ISO 14001 emerged. Following these guidelines and management systems, the authors, identified an increasing number of scholarly studies involving normative recipes on the art of environmental management. It was not until the later 1990s, that the field of environmental management began to scrutinise and expose the rhetorics (Welford, 1997) and spin (Beder, 2001) associated with much of the debate on corporate sustainability. The vast majority of scholarly studies in the field were focussing on large firms. It was not until the late 2000s and early 2010s that the focus on the importance of small and medium-sized enterprises (SMEs) surfaced (Aragón-Correa et al., 2008; Reyes-Rodríguez et al., 2016).

Triple Bottom Line (TBL) terminology came into vogue when John Elkington sought to integrate environmental and social considerations into business strategies (Elkington, 1997). TBL has since been the focus of some debate amongst sustainability proponents but it is not without its critics. A review of the recent literature in the field (2007–2017), for example, found that despite a high number of sustainability indicators that are available (144), many of these (49) have been only used once (Ahmad et al., 2019). It has been further evidenced that sustainability indicators were more commonly used at the product level (rather than at other levels). While there are obvious reasons for this (e.g., increasing complexity), there are a few notable exceptions. Veiga et al. (2018), for example, performed a hybrid input-output life cycle analysis to analyse the TBL aspects of sugarcane production in Sao Paulo state. A recent study of the TBL of 746 firms Walker et al. (2020) provided compelling evidence, rejecting the notion that the three dimensions are not mutually exclusive. Rather, they tend to move in tandem, and thus represent a stronger interrelationship than previously assumed.

Despite the measuring challenges associated with TBL, it has also to be emphasised that the TBL leaves capitalism unchallenged (Jeong et al., 2018). Arko-Achemfuor and Dzansi (2015) offer a somewhat different reading of the TBL which does try to challenge the capitalist focus on profit at the expense of human and ecological well-being. As they aver: 'Viewing businesses from a purely economic perspective has given rise to a number of challenges for humanity, the environment and the sustainability of some organizations' (p. 56). Others have been more irreconcilable in their vocabulary. Norman and MacDonald (2015) have recently argued that the TBL paradigm, for conceptual as well as practical reasons, has nothing new to add to the field. Based on an analysis and redefinition of the concept of capital and resource, framed in an ecological context, Rambaud and Richard (2015) have deconstructed the TBL concept and proposed to replace it with a 'triple bottom depreciation line'. From the point of view of knowledge development, this situation not only indicates complexity but further also suggests that the field is still evolving and rather unsettled.

1.6 Conclusion

Key contributions and major events from the late 1960s and early 1970s that fertilised the soil have been identified. Despite the sentiments of the World Commission and its holistic and integrative approach to sustainable development, the concept was soon to be 'taken over' by the modernity paradigm with its technology-based interests across economic, environmental and societal spheres. The weight of the economic dimension of the sustainability concept has been reinforced, among others, by an intensified globalisation and focus on efficiency over the past few decades. Along with the predominance of the techno-economic approach to economic development and sustainability, an increasing specialisation tendency has taken place, with little scope for including trans-paradigmatic knowledge production.

The sustainability discourses, however, are not immune to societal norms. Sustainability discourses may be designed to keep the focus on an increasing demand for social values (such as equity, justice and fairness). Societal norms have been adding the binding ingredients in the mortar of social structures by which decisions are made in firms as well as institutions, thereby implying that norms are not fixed. Rather, they will lend meaning to the concept of sustainability.

The very notion of what sustainability represents, however, is a complex maze of a scientific, economic and cultural web of competing tensions and aspirations. Set against this, the UN has set ambitious SDGs which aim to redefine societal norms so that the planet can live within its ecological means. Many global institutions and MNCs have been realigning their operations in accordance with the UN's 17 SDGs. The challenge will be whether this set of hegemonic powers can make the shift from a scientific-economic approach to a more inclusive, holistic dynamic which values nature and all humans in a more ethical and sustainable manner.

Significantly though, the key players that will best define whether the planet can remain sustainable are the millions of SMEs that represent the mainstay of most global economies. Getting these companies to become more sustainable is another critical dimension to sustainability endeavours.

Note

1 *Convivencia* is Spanish for living together.

References

Ahmad, S., Wong, K. Y., and Srithar, R. (2019). Sustainability indicators for manufacturing sectors. *Journal of Manufacturing Technology Management*, 30(2), 312–334.

Allen, T. F. H., and Giampietro, M. (2006). Narratives and transdisciplines for a post-industrial world. *Systems Research and Behavioral Science*, 23, 595–615.

Angner, E. (2019). We're all behavioral economists now. *Journal of Economic Methodology*, 26(3), 195–207.

Aragón-Correa, J. A., Hurtado-Torres, N., Sharma, S., and García-Morales, V. J. (2008). Environmental strategy and performance in small firms: A resource-based perspective. *Journal of Environmental Management*, 86(1), 88–103.

Arko-Achemfuor, A., and Dzansi, D. Y. (2015). Business doing well by doing good in the community: The case of Sedikong sa Lerato in South Africa. *The Journal of Commerce*, 7(2), 53–68.

Aronsson, T., and Schöb, R. (2018). Climate change and psychological adaptation: A behavioral environmental economics approach. *Journal of Behavioral and Experimental Economics*, 74, 79–84.

Ashford, N. A., Hall, R. P., Arango-Quiroga, J., Metaxas, K. A., and Showalter, A. L. (2020). Addressing inequality: The first step beyond COVID-19 and towards sustainability. *Sustainability*, 12(13), 1–37.

Barbier, E. B., and Burgess, J. C. (2020). Sustainability and development after COVID-19. *World Development*, 135, 1–4, doi.org/10.1016/j.worlddev.2020.105082.

Barreiro-Gen, M., Lozano, R., and Zafar, A. (2020). Changes in sustainability priorities in organisations due to the COVID-19 outbreak: Averting environmental rebound effects on society. *Sustainability*, 12(12), 1–13, doi:10.3390/su12125031.

Bausch, K. (2016). *Back stories for robust postmodern living*. ISCE, United States.

Beder, S. (2001). Global spin. In R. Starkey and R. Welford (Eds.), *Business and sustainable development* (242–267). Earthscan, London.

Benson, M. H., and Craig, R. K. (2014). The end of sustainability. *Society and Natural Resources*, 27(7), 777–782.

Biely, K., Maes, D., and Van Passel, S. (2018). The idea of weak sustainability is illegitimate. *Environment, Development and Sustainability*, 20(1), 223–232.

Blanchard, E.V. (2010). Modelling the future: An overview of the 'Limits to Growth' debate. *Centaurus*, 52(2), 91–116.

Blühdorn, I. (2017). Post-capitalism, post-growth, post-consumerism? Eco-political hopes beyond sustainability. *Global Discourse*, 7(1), 42–61.

Bryson, M. A. (2003). Nature, narrative, and the scientist-writer: Rachel Carson's and Loren Eiseley's critique of science. *Technical Communication Quarterly*, 12(4), 369–387.

Bud, R., Greenhalgh, P., James, F., and Shiach, M. (2018). *Being modern: The cultural impact of science in the early twentieth century*. UCL Press, London.

Butler, C. D. (2017). Limits to growth, planetary boundaries, and planetary health. *Current Opinion in Environmental Sustainability*, 25, 59–65.

Caldwell, Bruce J., and Coats, A. W. (1984). The rhetoric of economists: A comment on McCloskey. *Journal of Economic Literature*, 22(2), 575–578.

Carson, R. (1962). *Silent Spring*. Houghton Mifflin Company, Boston.

Castelló, I., and Lozano, J. M. (2011). Searching for new forms of legitimacy through corporate responsibility rhetoric. *Journal of Business Ethics*, 100(1), 11–29.

Cerin, P. (2003). Sustainability hijacked by the sociological wall of self-evidence. *Corporate Social Responsibility and Environmental Management*, 10(4), 175–185.

Chilisa, B. (2017). Decolonising transdisciplinary research approaches: An African perspective for enhancing knowledge integration in sustainability science. *Sustainability Science*, 12(5), 813–827.

Christakis, A. N. (2004). Wisdom of the people. *Systems Research and Behavioral Science*, 21(5), 479–488.

Colocousis, C. R., Rebellon, C. J., Smith, N., and Sobolowski, S. (2017). How long can we keep doing this? Sustainability as a strictly temporal concept. *Journal of Environmental Studies and Sciences*, 7(2), 274–287.

Colucci-Gray, L., Perazzone, A., Dodman, M., and Camino, E. (2013). Science education for sustainability, epistemological reflections and educational practices: From natural sciences to trans-disciplinarity. *Cultural Studies of Science Education*, 8(1), 127–183.

Dershowitz, A., Hamilton, A., Madison, J., and Jay, J. (2019). *The federalist papers*. Racehorse, New York.

Diprose, K., Fern, R., Vanderbeck, R. M., Chen, L., Valentine, G., Liu, C., and McQuaid, K. (2018). Corporations, consumerism and culpability: sustainability in the British press. *Environmental Communication*, 12(5), 672–685.

Dobers, P., and Wolff, R. (1999). Eco-efficiency and dematerialization: scenarios for new industrial logics in recycling industries, automobile and household appliances. *Business Strategy and the Environment*, 8(1), 31–45.

Edington, J. (2017). *Indigenous environmental knowledge*. Springer, Cham.

Elkington, J. (1997). *Cannibals with forks - Triple bottom line of 21st century business*. New Society Publishers, Stoney Creek, CT.

Ells, K. (2008). Ecological rhetoric through vicarious narrative: The enduring significance of Garrett Hardin's Ecological Rhetoric through Vicarious Narrative: The Enduring Significance of Garrett Hardin's The Tragedy of the Commons. *Environmental Communication*, 2(3), 320–339.

Evans, R., and Marvin, S. (2006). Researching the sustainable city: three modes of interdisciplinarity. *Environment and Planning A: Economy and Space*, 38(6), 1009–1028.

Fergus, A. H. T., and Rowley, J. I. A. (2005). Sustainable development: Lost meaning and opportunity? *Journal of Business Ethics*, 60, 17–27.

Fischer-Kowalski, M., Krausmann, F., and Pallua, I. (2014). A sociometabolic reading of the anthropocene: Modes of subsistence, population size and human impact on Earth. *Anthropocene Review*, 1(1), 8–33.

Flanagan, T. R., and Christakis, A. N. (2009). *The talking point: Creating an environment for exploring complex meaning*. Information Age, Charlotte.

Fletcher, R., and Rammelt, C. (2017). Decoupling: A key fantasy of the post-2015 sustainable development agenda. *Globalizations, 14*(3), 450–467.

Flood, R. L., and Romm, N. R. A. (2018). A systemic approach to processes of power in learning organisations: Part I – literature, theory, and methodology of triple loop learning. *The Learning Organization, 25*(4), 260–272.

Forsyth, T., and Levidow, L. (2015). An ontological politics of comparative environmental analysis: The green economy and local diversity. *Global Environmental Politics, 15*(3), 140–151.

Gibbons, M., Limoges, C., Nowotny, H., Schwartzman, S., Scott, P., and Trow, M. (1994). *The new production of knowledge: The dynamics of science and research in contemporary societies.* Sage, London.

Gibbons, M., Limoges, C., and Scott, P. (2011). Prometheus: Critical studies in innovation revisiting Mode 2 at Noors Slott. *Prometheus: Critical Studies in Innovation, 29*(4), 361–372.

Gladwin, N. T., and Walter, I. (1976). Multinational enterprise, social responsiveness, and pollution control. *Journal of International Business Studies, 7*, 57–74.

Gladwin, N. T., and Welles, J. G. (1976). Multinational corporations and environmental protection: Patterns of organizational adaptation. *International Studies of Management and Organization, 6*(1-2), 160–184.

Groen, M. (2019). Zero growth: A grand challenge for the Asia-Pacific region. *Australian Journal of Management, 44*(4), 632–647.

Haapanen, L., and Tapio, P. (2016). Economic growth as phenomenon, institution and ideology: A qualitative content analysis of the 21st century growth critique. *Journal of Cleaner Production, 112*, 3492–3503.

Habermas, J. (1984). Reason and rationalization of society. *Theory of communicative action* (vol. 1). Beacon Press, Boston.

Hadorn, G. H., Bradley, D., Christian, P., Stephan, R., and Wiesmannd, U. (2006). Implications of transdisciplinarity for sustainability research. *Ecological Economics, 60*, 119–128.

Hakovirta, M., and Denuwara, N. (2020). How COVID-19 redefines the concept of sustainability. *Sustainability, 12*(9), 10–13.

Hannis, M. (2017). After development? In defence of sustainability. *Global Discourse, 7*(1), 28–38.

Hardin, G. (1968). Tragedy of the commons. *Science, 162*(3859), 1243–1248.

Harris, L. D., Wasilewski, J. (2004). Indigeneity, an alternative worldview: Four R's (relationship, responsibility, reciprocity, redistribution) vs. two P's (power and profit). Sharing the journey toward conscious evolution. *Systems Research and Behavioral Science, 21*(5), 489–503.

Haugaard, M. (2018). Justification and the four dimensions of power. *Journal of Political Power, 11*(1), 93–114.

Hulme, M. (2009). *Why we disagree about climate change: Understanding controversy, inaction and opportunity.* Cambridge University Press, Cambridge.

Huseman, M. and Huseman, J. N. S. P. (2011). Techno-fix. *Why technology won't save us or the environment.* New Society Publishers, Gabriola Island.

Institute for 21st Century Agoras. (2020). The agoras. http://globalagoras.org/. Accessed: 29/09/2020.

Ishwaran, N. (2012). Science in intergovernmental environmental relations: 40 Years of UNESCO's man and the biosphere (MAB) programme and its future. *Environmental Development, 1*(1), 91–101.

Jakobsen, T.G. (2017). Environmental ethics: Anthropocentrism and non-anthropocentrism revised in the light of critical realism. *Journal of Critical Realism, 16*(2), 184–199.

Jantsch, E. (1972). Towards interdisciplinarity and transdisciplinarity in education and innovation Paris: OECD. In E. Jantsch (Ed.), *In: Interdisciplinarity: Problems of teaching and research in universities* (97–121). OECD, Washington DC.

Jeong, S., Britton, S., Haverkos, K., Kutner, M., Shume, T., and Tippins, D. (2018). Composing new understandings of sustainability in the Anthropocene. *Cultural Studies of Science Education, 13*(1), 299–315.

Johnston, P., Everard, M., Santillo, D., and Robèrt, K. H. (2007). Reclaiming the definition of sustainability. *Environmental Science and Pollution Research, 14*(1), 60–66.

Kakoulaki, M. Alexander, N. Christakis, A. N. (2017). Demoscopio: The demo-sensual [r]evolutionary eutopia. In N. Romm, Y. Corcoran-Nantes, and J. McIntyre–Mills (Eds.), *Balancing individualism and collectivism: Social and environmental justice* (429–460). Springer, Cham.

Kastenhofer, K., Bechtold, U., and Wilfing, H. (2011). Sustaining sustainability science: The role of established inter-disciplines. *Ecological Economics, 70*(4), 835–843.

Knaggård, Å., B. Ness, and D. H. (2018). Finding an academic space: reflexivity among sustainability researchers. *Ecology and Society, 23*(4), 20–35.

Krysiak, F. C. (2006). Entropy, limits to growth, and the prospects for weak sustainability. *Ecological Economics, 58*(1), 182–191.

Kudo, S., and Mino, T. (2020). *Framing in sustainability science.* Springer, Singapore.

Landrum, N. E., and Ohsowski, B. (2018). Identifying worldviews on corporate sustainability: A content analysis of corporate sustainability reports. *Business Strategy and the Environment, 27*(1), 128–151.

Lowe, P., and Phillipson, J. (2009). Barriers to research collaboration across disciplines: Scientific paradigms and institutional practices. *Environment and Planning A: Space and Economy, 41*(5), 1171–1184.

Magill, G. (2018). Pivotal perspectives on integral ecology. In G. Magill and J. Potter (Eds.), *Integral ecology: Protecting our common home* (2–7). Cambridge Scholars Publishing, Newcastle upon Tyne.

Maguire, S., Ojiako, U., and Robson, I. (2009). The intelligence alchemy and the twenty-first century organization. *Strategic Change, 18*, 125–139.

Malone, K., Truong, S., and Gray, T. (2017). *Reimagining sustainability in precarious times.* Springer, Singapore.

McCloskey, D. (1983). The rhetoric of economics. *Journal of Economic Literature, 21*(2), 481–517.

McIntyre-Mills, J. J. (2006). *Rescuing the enlightenment from itself.* Springer, Boston.

McIntyre-Mills, J. J. (2014). *Transformation from Wall Street to wellbeing.* Springer, Boston.

McIntyre-Mills, J. J., and Romm, N. R. A. (2019). Conclusion: Potential for transformative research to address risks. In N. R. A. Romm, Y. Corcoran-Nantes, and J. J. McIntyre-Mills (Eds.), *Democracy and governance for resourcing the commons* (461–472). Springer, Cham.

McIntyre-Mills, J. J., Wirawan, R., Laksmono, B. S., Widianingsih, I., and Sari, N. H. (2017). Pathways to wellbeing: Low carbon challenge to live virtuously and well: Participatory design and education on mitigation, adaptation, governance and accountability. In N. R. A. Romm, Y. Corcoran-Nantes, and J. J. McIntyre-Mills (Eds.), *Balancing individualism and collectivism: Social and environmental justice* (37–73). Springer, Cham.

Meadows, D. H., Meadows, D. L., and Randers, J. Behrens, W. (III). (1972). *The limits to growth: A report for the club of Rome's project on the predicament of mankind.* Universe Books, New York.

Meadows, D. H., Meadows, D. L., and Randers, J. (1992). *Beyond the limits: Confronting global collapse, envisioning a sustainable future.* Chelsea Green, Post Mills.

Meadows, D. H., Randers, J., and Meadows, D. L. (2005). *Limits to growth: The 30-year update.* Earthscan, London.

Menck, P. J., Heitzig, J., Marwan, N., and Kurths, J. (2013). How basin stability complements the linear-stability paradigm. *Nature Physics, 9*(2), 89–92.

Meyer, R. E., and Höllerer, M. A. (2016). Laying a smoke screen: Ambiguity and neutralization as strategic responses to intra-institutional complexity. *Strategic Organization, 14*(4), 373–406.

Milne, B. T. (2017). Elements of a holistic theory to meet the sustainability challenge. *Systems Research and Behavioral Science, 34*(5), 553–563.

Morgan, J. (2015). Introduction: The meaning and significance of neoclassical economics. What is Neoclassical Economics?: *Debating the origins, meaning and significance.* Routledge, London.

Norman, W., and MacDonald, C. (2015). Getting to the bottom of "triple bottom line". *Business Ethics Quarterly, 14*(2), 243–262.

Opoku, A., and Fortune, C. (2011). Organizational learning and sustainability in the construction industry. *The Built and Human Environment Review, 4*(1), 98–107.

Osuji, P. (2018). Laudato si' and traditional African environmental ethics. In G. Magill and J. Potter (Eds.), *Integral ecology: Protecting our common home* (184–208). Cambridge Scholars Publishing, Newcastle upon Tyne.

Pearce, D. W., and Turner, R. K. (1990a). *Economics of natural resources and the environment.* Harvester Wheatsheaf, London.

Pearce, D. W., and Turner, R. K. (1990b). *Economics of natural resources and the environment.* The Johns Hopkins University Press, Baltimore.

Peters, M. (2019). The enlightenment and its critics. *Educational Philosophy and Theory, 51*(9), 886–894.

Pontus, C. (2003). Sustainability hijacked by the sociological wall of self-evidence. *Corporate Social Responsibility and Environmental Management, 10,* 175–185.

Popa, F., Guillermin, M., and Dedeurwaerdere, T. (2015). A pragmatist approach to transdisciplinarity in sustainability research: From complex systems theory to reflexive science. *Futures, 65,* 45–56.

Quan-Baffour, K. P. (2017). A systemic view of the value of environmental conservation: The case of Bono Takyiman, Ghana. In N. R. A. Romm, Y. Corcoran-Nantes and J.J. McIntyre-Mills (Eds.), *Balancing individualism and collectivism: Social and environmental justice* (211–220). Springer, Switzerland.

Quinn, L., and Baltes, J. (2007). Leadership and the triple bottom line: bringing sustainability and corporate social responsibility to life. A CCL Research White Paper.

Center for Creative Leadership. https://cclinnovation.org/wp-content/uploads/2020/03/quinn_leadership-and-the-triple-bottom-line.pdf. Accessed September 25 2020.

Rambaud, A., and Richard, J. (2015). The "triple depreciation line" instead of the "triple bottom line". Towards a genuine integrated reporting. *Critical Perspectives on Accounting, 33,* 92–116.

Ramsey, J. L. (2015). On not defining sustainability. *Journal of Agricultural and Environmental Ethics, 28*(6), 1075–1087.

Reyes-Rodríguez, J. F., Ulhøi, J. P., and Madsen, H. (2016). Corporate environmental sustainability in Danish SMEs: A longitudinal study of motivators, initiatives, and strategic effects. *Corporate Social Responsibility and Environmental Management, 23*(4), 193–212.

Romm, N. R. A. (2001). Critical theoretical concerns in relation to development. In G. W. J. K. Coetzee, J. Graaff, and F. Hencdricks (Eds.), *Development theory, policy and practice* (141–153). Oxford University Press, Oxford.

Romm, N. R. A. (2017). Foregrounding critical systemic and indigenous ways of collective knowing towards (re)directing the Anthropocene. In N. R. A. Romm, J. J. McIntyre-Mills and Y. Corcoran-Nantes (Eds.), *Balancing individualism and collectivism: Social and environmental justice* (1–18). Springer, Cham.

Sachs, W. (2017). The sustainable development goals and Laudato si': Varieties of post–development? *Third World Quarterly, 38*(12), 2573–2587.

Sauvé, S., Bernard, S., and Sloan, P. (2016). Environmental sciences, sustainable development and circular economy: Alternative concepts for trans-disciplinary research. *Environmental Development, 17,* 48–56.

Schaltegger, S., and Hörisch, J. (2017). In search of the dominant rationale in sustainability management: legitimacy- or profit-seeking? *Journal of Business Ethics, 145*(2), 259–276.

Schmidheiny, S. (1992). The business of sustainable development. *Finance and Development, 29*(4), 4–27.

Scoones, I. (2016). The politics of sustainability and development. *Annual Review of Environment and Resources, 41,* 293–319.

Shrivastava, P., and Berger, S. (2010). Sustainability principles: A review and directions. *Organization Management Journal, 7*(4), 246–261.

Sillitoe, P. (2010). Trust in development: some implications of knowing in indigenous knowledge. *Journal of the Royal Anthropological Institute, 16*(1), 12–30.

Smith, L. T. (1999). *Decolonising methodologies: Research and Indigenous peoples.* Zed Books, New York.

Smith, L. T. (2012). *Decolonising methodologies: Research and Indigenous peoples.* Zed Books, New York.

Spahn, A. (2018). "The first generation to end poverty and the last to save the planet?" - Western individualism, human rights and the value of nature in the ethics of global sustainable development. *Sustainability, 10*(6), 1–16, doi:10.3390/su10061853.

Steffen, W., Grinevald, J., Crutzen, P., and Mcneill, J. (2011). The anthropocene: Conceptual and historical perspectives. *Philosophical Transactions of the Royal Society A: Mathematical, Physical and Engineering Sciences, 369*(1938), 842–867.

Stokols, D. (2018). *Social ecology in the digital age.* Academic Press, London.

Thatcher, A., and Yeow, P. H. P. (2016). A sustainable system of systems approach: A new HFE paradigm. *Ergonomics, 59*(2), 167–178.

The Club of Rome. (2019). About the club of Rome. https://clubofrome.org/about-us/. Accessed: 29/09/2020.

Tomer, J. F. (2007). What is behavioral economics? *Journal of Socio-Economics*, 36(3), 463–479.

Turner, G. (2014). 'Is global collapse imminent?', MSSI Research Paper No. 4, *Melbourne Sustainable Society Institute*. The University of Melbourne, Melbourne.

Turner, G. M. (2012). On the cusp of global collapse? Updated comparison of the Limits to Growth with historical data. *GAIA - Ecological Perspectives for Science and Society (GAIA)*, 21, 116–124.

Ulhøi, J. P. (1995). Corporate environmental and resource management: In search of a new managerial paradigm. *European Journal of Operational Research*, 80(1), 2–15.

Ulhøi, J. P., Gattiker, U. E., Bojsen, I. (2000). A new perspective on organizing in industry. In R. Golembiewski (Ed.) *Handbook of organizational behavior* (2nd ed., 725–736). Marcel Dekker, New York.

Ünal, E., Urbinati, A., and Chiaroni, D. (2019). Managerial practices for designing circular economy business models: The case of an Italian SME in the office supply industry. *Journal of Manufacturing Technology Management*, 30(3), 561–589.

United Nations. (1972). United Nations conference on the human environment (Stockholm Conference). https://sustainabledevelopment.un.org/milestones/humanenvironment. Accessed: 29/09/2020.

United Nations. (2015). Sustainable development goals kick off with start of new year. https://www.un.org/sustainabledevelopment/blog/2015/12/sustainable-development-goals-kick-off-with-start-of-new-year/. Accessed: 29/09/2020.

United Nations. (2019). SDG Summit 24–25 September. https://sustainabledevelopment.un.org/sdgsummit. Accessed: 29/09/2020.

Veiga, J. P. S., Malik, A., Lenzen, M., de Souza, J. B., Filho, F., and Romanelli, T. L. (2018). Triple-bottom-line assessment of Sao Paulo state's sugarcane production based on a Brazilian multi-regional input-output matrix. *Renewable and Sustainable Energy Reviews*, 82, 666–680.

Victor, P. A. (2012). Growth, degrowth and climate change: A scenario analysis. *Ecological Economics*, 84, 206–212.

Walker, K., Yu, X., and Zhang, Z. (2020). All for one or all for three: Empirical evidence of paradox theory in the triple-bottom line. *Journal of Cleaner Production*, 275, 1–12.

Weber-Blaschke, G., Mosandl, R., Faulstich, M. (2005). History and mandate of sustainability: From local forestry to global policy. In P. A. Wilderer, E. D. Schroeder, H. Kopp (Eds.) *Global sustainability: The impact of local cultures, a new perspective for science and engineering, economics and politics* (pp. 5–19). Wiley-VCH Verlag, Weinheim.

Welford, R. (1997). *Hijacking environmentalism: Corporate responses to sustainable development* (1st ed.). Earthscan, Abingdon.

Welford, R. J. (1998). Editorial: Corporate environmental management, technology and sustainable development: Postmodern perspectives and the need for a critical research agenda. *Business Strategy and the Environment*, 7(1), 1–12.

Welles, J. G. (1973). Multinationals need new environmental strategies. *Columbia Journal of World Business*, 11–18.

Werning, J. P., and Spinler, S. (2020). Transition to circular economy on firm level: Barrier identification and prioritization along the value chain. *Journal of Cleaner Production*, 245, 118609. doi.org/10.1016/j.jclepro.2019.118609.

Whittaker, R. H., and Likens, G. E. (1975). The biosphere and man. In H. Lieth and R. H. Whittaker (Eds.), *Primary Productivity of the Biosphere. Ecological Studies (Analysis and Synthesis)*, vol. 14, Springer-Verlag, Berlin.

Williams, A., Kennedy, S., Phillip, F., and Whiteman, G. (2017). Systems thinking: A review of sustainability management research. *Journal of Cleaner Production, 148*, 866–881.

World Commission on Environment and Development. (1987). *Our common future*. Oxford University Press, Oxford.

Yacoumis, P. (2018). Making progress? Reproducing hegemony through discourses of "Sustainable Development" in the Australian news media. *Environmental Communication, 12*(6), 840–853.

Zyglidopoulos, S., and Fleming, P. (2011). Corporate accountability and the politics of visibility in "late modernity." *Organization, 18*(5), 691–706.

2 Research on small and medium-sized enterprises and sustainability

Aharon Factor, John Parm Ulhøi, and Norma Romm

2.1 Introduction

The environmental impacts associated with the activities of larger organisations have been on a scale that has attracted society's attention and has subsequently stimulated a movement towards improving corporate environmental performance. In consequence, larger organisations have legitimised their operations (Schaltegger and Hörisch, 2017; Naidoo and Gasparatos, 2018) as they respond to reputational, customer and legislative pressures (Lozano, 2015), and thus, are inclined to invest in green research and development aimed at contributing to environmental efficiency and sustainability (Corrocher and Solito, 2017). Particularly, companies in resource-intensive sectors have been seen as drivers of change in addressing and improving various climate-related problems Lampikoski (2012), while at the same time having the resources needed for securing external communication and reporting about their environmental performance (Baumann-Pauly et al., 2013).

It makes, however, perfect sense to see large enterprises being among the early adopters of green practices as most of these companies have learned the lesson of being one step ahead rather than risking the negative effects of stringent regulations on production, and/or corporate branding being the campaign target of international environmental movements. In the United States, for example, since the 1960s and 1970s, the oil and chemical industries came under societal pressure for strict regulation of environmental pollution. Notably, the American chemical manufacturing giant Du Pont, that previously had an appalling environmental record has, since 1989, transformed the organisation into a sustainable business front-runner (Rome, 2019).

Today, sustainable policies and a focus on corporate environmental business have come to be broadly acknowledged across the corporate sector, and environmental commitment is now a strategic issue for all companies (Lubin and Esty, 2010) and their stakeholders such as investors, consumers, NGOs and society at large (Radhouane et al., 2018). As a result, environmental issues have gone mainstream (Lyon et al., 2018). In

China, for example, media coverage of major environmental pollution oc-
currences has impacted corporate boardrooms (Jia et al., 2016). Increasing
evidence associating humankind's greenhouse gas emissions and climate
change in particular, has also heightened society's concern for the environment (Lee and Lee, 2018) and has challenged businesses to respond
with new sustainable products and services. This is particularly demanding
for the largest carbon emitters as the regulatory environment changes (York
et al., 2018). Such developments have, therefore, been rapidly gaining pace,
with increasing calls for business to act responsibly with respect to the
environment, as well as to social issues (Leavy, 2016; Bhattacharya, 2020).

Nonetheless, governments around the world, however, have been responding to sustainability with policies targeted toward larger organisations (Blundel et al., 2013). This has driven the development of
sophisticated environmental policies that have steered change throughout
corporations. As Tukker's (2006, p. 1) portrayal of the last decades of the
20th century emphasises, 'in the last 40 years, one can see that the emphasis
of environmental policy has almost literally crept its way down, through the
smokestacks and effluent pipes, toward the processes that finally drive the
generation of environmental impacts.' As a result, larger companies have
been prompted to engage in environmental initiatives such as EMAS (Ulhøi
et al., 1996) and ISO 14001 (Reverdy, 2006), as the 21st century develops
to recognise the need for corporate action to address more broadly political,
economic, social as well as environmental considerations (Ararat et al.,
2018; Odongo and Wang, 2018).

2.2 SMEs and sustainability

While multinational enterprises (MNEs) are under increasing public scrutiny regarding their sustainability impacts, the effect of the roughly 400
million small and medium-sized enterprises (SMEs), the mainstay of global
business and critical to shaping a sustainable planet, have been largely
overlooked (Reyes-Rodríguez et al., 2016; Global Reporting Initiative,
2018). SMEs represent a fundamental component of society, composing
approximately 90% of all private sector companies in most industrialised
nations (OECD, 2017), and they also provide half of a nation's employment and GDP (Vives, 2010, p. 419; World Bank, 2020). Breaking that
down in the European and US context, in the European Union, 99.8% of
non-financial business sector companies are SMEs, 93.1% are micro firms
with less than 10 employees whilst two-thirds (66.4%) of EU-28 employees
are employed in SMEs (Muller et al., 2018, p. 13). Similarly, in the US,
SMEs (with less than 500 employees) comprise 99.7% of all firms with paid
employees (US Small Business Administration, 2018).

The sheer number of 'small businesses' also means that approximately
half of all business energy use in many developing nations is by SMEs
(Fawcett and Hampton, 2020). This aggregated affect is also evident in

their overall high environmental footprint (Koirala, 2018, p. 4). For example, in 1995, Hillary used estimates that SMEs may produce approximately 70% of global pollution. While Hillary (2000) suggested that the estimate might be speculative, a research study (Calogirou et al., 2010) revealed that SMEs actually produce 64% of the EU's industrial pollution. Furthermore, other authors too show that SMEs cannot only produce up to 70% of societal pollution [e.g., 50-70% in Brazil (Vives, 2010) and more than 50% in Asia-Pacific (Parker et al., 2009)] but that they also contribute to 60% of CO_2 emissions (Parker et al., 2009).

Despite the SME sector being vast in size and contributing significantly to global pollution, 'small is attached to almost no significance'; it means that being too small, these enterprises are simply not noticed (Chadwick et al., 2003). Thus, what has not caught society's attention, to the same extent as the pollution from larger enterprises, is that a vast number of SMEs, although small in number, together have considerable environmental impact (European Commission Enterprise and Industry (ECEI), 2010; Revell et al., 2010; Lynch-Wood and Williamson, 2014). A highly significant business sector both to the community and in its environmental impact, therefore, comes under disproportional pressures for organisational greening, when compared to larger organisations (Chadwick et al., 2003; Graafland and Smid, 2016) and presents a significant barrier to sustainable development (Miller et al., 2011).

As a result, environmental practices that have mostly originated in large private sector organisations may not necessarily be applicable to SMEs. As will be elaborated in the next section, SMEs are structurally and culturally different entities when compared with larger enterprises. The planning and change processes of larger organisations, therefore, cannot necessarily be applied to SMEs in a less formal manner or on a smaller scale (Löfving, et al., 2014; Samuelsson et al., 2016). Historically too, SMEs have not been subject to the same regulatory oversight to the same extent as larger firms (Petts, 2000) and so, there has been less pressure for SMEs to curb environmental pollution (Blundel et al., 2013; Graafland and Smid, 2017). This is partly because SMEs have less individual power than that of larger companies that are also more internationally heterogeneous and able to exert greater control over regulatory frameworks than SMEs (Kusyk and Lozano, 2007), and also due to the limited consumer pressure that SMEs face (Drake et al., 2004). Another key limitation that still exists is the ability of SMEs to invest in eco-innovations due to high costs and difficulties in accessing capital (Koirala, 2018). Given the important role SMEs will play, not only in reducing global carbon emissions but in also contributing to meeting the United Nations SDG's access to appropriate finance for SMEs is critically important (Andries et al., 2018).

The beginning of this century has seen an interest in improving the environmental performance of SMEs (Blundel et al., 2013; Eweje, 2020). Accordingly, institutional pressures for greening SMEs have been gaining ground (Ayuso and Navarrete-Báez, 2018). At the supranational level, for example, through the EUs' Green Action Plan, it has committed itself to the green transformation of SMEs, targeting resource efficiencies, green entrepreneurship, green value in supply chains and access to markets (Doranova et al., 2018) as well as to promote the benefits of the circular economy (European Commission, 2020a). The EU and the OECD also recognised that SMEs face considerable regulatory difficulties and are working together to ease understanding and relevancy in regulating the sector. This builds on the EU's Small Business Act 2008 to drive environmental improvements into business opportunity (European Commission, 2009) and collaboration between the OECD's 2019-2020 GREEN Action Task Programme and the United Nations (Secretariat, 2018). Greener outcomes for SMEs from such programmes will be essential for Europe as it strives to achieve its ambitious greenhouse gas reductions by 2050 (KPMG, 2018; European Investment Bank, 2020).

The European Union not only recognise the need for SMEs to take advantage of greater resource efficiencies and engagement with the circular economy but it also understands that SMEs find the regulatory environment complex and confusing. The EU, thus, engages with SMEs not only to achieve better compliance but also with standards and other requisites (European Commission, 2020a). New funding opportunities have also emerged to assist European SMEs with regulatory compliance (European Commission, 2020b) notably through COSME – the EU Programme for the Competitiveness of Enterprises and SMEs.

2.3 Environmental responsibility and SMEs

The SME sector is comprised of a vast range of business organisations, spread globally across multiple regions. This brings together a wide range of heterogeneous factors that impinge on the way SMEs engage with environmental issues (Hillary, 2000; Patton and Worthington, 2003). Moreover, environmental responsiveness may be as diverse as the owners/managers and company characteristics that constitute the SME sector (De Steur et al., 2020). In particular, a complexity of company size, turnover, perceptions, motivations, local context (Uhlaner et al., 2012; Dey et al., 2018), organisational cultures (Studer et al., 2006) and resource capabilities (Baranova and Paterson, 2017) have been shown to be critically important barriers or catalysts. This broad variation represents a challenge to researchers and policymakers in defining their environmental behaviours and influencing the sector.

One overarching feature that does, however, unify SME environmental behaviour is the role of the owner/manager. Consisting of fewer personnel, and shorter communication channels than larger companies, SMEs encapsulate ownership and managerial functions in a single individual (Blackburn, 2007, p. 421) rather than ownership being absent as with corporate entities (Williamson, 1963, pp. 238-239). This enables a more informal and ad hoc internal structure that will determine environmental behaviours differently to those of larger corporate organisations. Muñoz-Pascual et al. (2019), for example, show that this can enable SMEs to better implement environmental management due to greater mobility, stronger communications and motivation. This is partly also because, in SMEs, rather than the divergence of decision-making between groups of individuals in larger organisations, decision-making is more convergent in the owner/manager. This presents a decision-making style strikingly different from the corporate contexts.

In this setting, although SME owners/managers are free of being incentivised to adopt a short-term focus and the shackles of command and control structures reminiscent of larger organisations, and are better placed to impart their consciousness and intent on the organisation, they also face significant resource capabilities and constraints compared to larger organisations. This has been shown to have both positive and negative influences on the way SME owners/managers engage with environmental issues. Although there has been limited research examining this phenomenon when compared to scholarly enquiry into the sustainability activities of corporations, a growing body of research has been establishing itself since the early 1990s. Much of the research has focused on the perceptions and attitudes of SME owners/managers (Petts et al., 1998) and the level of research has been growing rapidly since the advent of the century (Collins et al., 2010; Papagiannakis and Lioukas, 2012; Aguado and Holl, 2018).

For researchers exploring SMEs and their sustainability behaviours, capturing perceptions is critically important as they provide insights to the way SME owners/managers identify and connect with the world, and is the causative and knowledge-base that drives cognition. In other words, 'perception is *the* input to cognition' and shapes the way we think about and act about the world (Cahen and Tacca, 2013, p. 144) and it influences what people value (Wang and Kim, 2018). Conceptually, values are defined by Schwartz (1994, p. 21) as 'a guiding principle in the life of a person or other social entity.' They are deeply rooted in people's culture, ideology and are what provides meaning in people's lives and has been shown to influence the way people identify with environmental issues (Wang and Kim, 2018). Furthermore, values are also deeply engrained through a socialisation process that brings together our awareness of the world around us, our emotions and the way we think and act (Zsóka, 2008) and this, in turn, influences our environmental attitudes (Yapici et al., 2017). This is because the cognitive element of our values provides the consciousness which allows us to become aware of facts and knowledge about the world around us and forms our beliefs and attitudes about them and determines how we emotionally behave and act on them.

In the main, societal awareness of environmental issues and concern about the future of the planet has been rising (cf. e.g., The Lancet Plantary

Health, 2019). In particular, there has been an extra emphasis on climate change in society (Hughes, 2020) and this has put pressure on business to act on climate change (Cadez et al., 2019). Certainly, there is growing evidence of environmental awareness amongst SMEs globally. For example, Walker and Redmond (2015) have shown that a clear majority of surveyed Australian SMEs believed in climate change, reported interest in environmental issues and understood that their business did have detrimental impacts on the environment.

Translating environmental awareness into action, however, is quite a challenge for many SMEs. While a few SME early movers can be found amongst some of the first companies to be DS7750 and EMAS certified studies, such cases still represent exceptions to the rule. A more general pattern shows that having environmental awareness does not necessarily result in pro-environmental behaviour (Steg et al., 2014; Markle's, 2019). This is borne out in SME and environmental literature. Tilley's (1999) extensive study of SMEs and the environment, for example, exposed a rhetorical gap that existed between SME owners/managers' perceptions of environmental issues and environmental practice within their companies. Furthermore, a study of Melbourne-based SMEs from 2008 to 2020 initially reported moderate to high environmental interest with 83% of surveyed companies reporting significant concern for future generations and the state of the planet (Factor, 2010). In addition, longitudinal interviews with respondents for more than a decade have found that overall environmental responsiveness has not matched increasing environmental concern. Cassells and Lewis (2011) describe how this is due to the manner in which environmental responsibility is perceived. Individually, the owner/ manager may be concerned for the environment, but once in the business setting, a different set of responsibilities exists which may work against the owner/manager's consciousness and emotions (Zsóka, 2008; Yapici et al., 2017).

Another key consideration is that while many SME owners/managers may be environmentally aware, they may also have different ways by which they frame decisions (Spence and Rutherfoord, 2001) and this is the key to understanding the decision-making process in SMEs. Decision-making is essential to management (Longenecker, 1969, p. 141; Laroche, 1995) and with the SME owner/manager being so involved with all aspects of organisational functioning, the manner in which demographics, scientific and religious beliefs, political views, culture, personal traits, attitudes and values come together impinge on SME environmental behaviours (Yapici et al., 2017). In particular, values have been closely associated with transformational leadership (Groves, 2020) and they influence organisational CSR responses (Groves, 2014). In SMEs in particular, the individual values of owners/managers also constitute a critical element of the leadership process in SMEs, and are essential for creating responsible business (Grayson and Dodd, 2007; Lee et al., 2016).

Schaefer et al. (2020), for example, has shown how values are important in shaping culture and in driving environmental performance. A study by Markle (2019), in particular, documents culture to be a central component in determining environmental outcomes. She describes how three cultural representations may influence environmental behaviours. The first are Egalitarians who seek a fairer and more equal world. They recognise the immediate need for collective action to tackle an existential environmental crisis and are found to be more likely to display pro-environmental behaviours. Individual SME owners/managers fitting this representation may feel a 'warm glow' from contributing to the good of society (Graafland and Gerlagh, 2019, p. 1105). Markle's second cultural representation pertains to the individualistic types who are aware of environmental threats but will only act in accordance with free market solutions. Reyes-Rodríguez et al. (2016), for example, found that the prospects of lower cost and competitive advantage have particularly driven SMEs' strategic intent and engagement with sustainability. Markle's third cultural representation is particularly relevant in understanding SME owner/manager's responsiveness to environmental issues; the conformists to society's expectations who are driven by rules and regulations. It is this last representation that is largely identifiable in the SME sector (Lynch-Wood and Williamson, 2014).

Markle's (2019) findings that environmental proactivity was primarily driven, in US respondents, by market and regulatory drivers finds strong accord with Graafland and Bovenberg's (2020) pan-European investigation. They found that roughly half of SME owners/managers had not taken any voluntary measures to tackle environmental initiatives due to low levels of internal or regulatory-driven motivations. For Schaefer et al. (2020, p. 1), however, overcoming this lack of engagement is critically a function of aligning self-enhancing with self-trandscending values, meaning that when business and altruistic values align, SMEs are far more likely to improve their environmental performance. And this finds accord with commonly known approaches to sustainability such as win-win solutions and people, planet and profit.

While the work of Schaefer et al. (2020), therefore, reveals that environmental responsiveness in the SME sector is dependent on a complexity of personal factors aligning, Graafland and Bovenberg's (2020) work also shows that a regulatory framework that does not restrict egalitarian and individualistic behaviours or overburdens conformists can allow for SMEs to improve their environmental responsiveness. Although these studies present signposts to drive the SME sector towards environmental responsiveness, research undertaken in the UK suggests that SMEs are beginning to identify with the sustainability business case (Revell et al., 2010; Dey et al., 2018) while longitudinal studies in Denmark have shown that environmental engagement has increased over time (Madsen and Ulhøi, 2016).

The trend of environmentally aware SMEs may also be showing its roots in China. Liu and Bai (2014), for example, provide insights from a Chinese

2008 survey (undertaken by the Bureau of Zhejiang) showing that SMEs are becoming more aware of environmental issues, particularly concerning the need to reduce consumption of resources. Liu and Bai (2014) compare this study with their more recent investigation revealing a strong awareness of the circular economy, even though actual behaviours still lag behind awareness. In Africa too, there is a newly emerging interest in researching the SME and environmental field. Countries such as Ghana, for example, has seen researchers such as Afrum et al. (2020) and Ahinful et al. (2019) lead the way in a new wave of studies across the continent.

A study by the European Commission on 'SMEs, resource efficiency and green markets' also reveals that 28% of companies across Europe place the environment as one of the top priorities for taking action to be more re-source efficient (TNS Political and Social, 2012). Even more so, the Commission study also reports that US SMEs are almost twice more likely to be ready to engage with resource efficiency measures than their European counterparts. This consideration is borne out by a study of Spanish auto-motive suppliers that showed that the environment is a top priority for surveyed companies and that managerial intentions concerning the en-vironment are influential in developing environmental strategies, manage-rial training programmes and a suite of practices, including the manufacture of environmentally benign products and processes (Martín-Peña, et al., 2010, 2014). This may, in part, be driven by the pressures on the auto-mobile industry to improve engine efficiency and reduce greenhouse gas emissions (Lee, 2011).

Furthermore, environmental business performance can be improved when business leaders make a transformational commitment to 'greening' their organisations but this also requires building appropriate 'green' dy-namic capabilities and developing a culture that promotes 'green creativity' (Chen and Chang, 2013, p. 107). Some researchers (Aragón-Correa et al., 2008; De Steur et al., 2020) for example, describe how internally unique organisational characteristics also support innovation and capabilities for environmental management. Externally to the organisation, Tantalo et al. (2012, p. 146) have shown how the 'managerial perception of the firm as a social actor' is key to placing sustainability at the strategic centre of SME decision-making.

With increasing media and government interest around environmental issues, this 'social actor' role is suggested to have played a prominent role in elevating the importance of environmental issues within SMEs (Baden et al., 2011). The role of external stakeholders does not only play a critical role in driving pro-environmental behaviour in SMEs but also adds a heightened role in creating legitimacy when SMEs' environmental impacts are more visible (Marco-Fondevila et al., 2018). Lewis et al. (2015), in particular, build on their longitudinal survey work in New Zealand and strengthen their insight that even when SME owners/managers harbour pro-environmental attitudes, they are fundamentally shaped by societal influences. For example, they show that in New Zealand, SME owners/ managers may want to act on climate change but that this should be driven by government and other nation states.

2.4 Barriers to environmental improvement in the SME sector

Another important barrier to improving the environmental performance of SMEs is the logic of economic reasoning that society benefits from economic growth without accounting for the considerable environmental and social costs. This economic logic is challenged by the economist Herman Daly. He describes how ecological economists identify with the economic logic as a quantitative rationalisation of resources, from raw materials through an economic system and ending with pollution (Daly, 2013). This also provides a frame within SMEs that if they use resources in a rational manner, they can maintain and grow their businesses within the boundaries of certainty and known knowledge of the world. In essence, it provides a sense of reality to the owner/manager (Laroche, 1995).

Sustainability challenges this realm, with a more complex behavioural reality that places the SME owner/manager's decision-making in the middle ground between logical reasoning and the unknown (Langley et al., 1995). Decision-making, thus, becomes a function of the individual's cognitive limits (Cyert and March, 1963). In addition, with only one person often being the decision-maker in SMEs, this can itself be a hindrance (Mintzberg, 1971), especially when resources are limited (Baranova and Paterson, 2017). As a consequence, many SMEs often struggle to run their business (Everett and Watson, 1998) as they are already working to full capacity (Taylor et al., 2012) and do not have the time to attend to improving their environmental performance (Campos, 2012; Bevan and Yung, 2014).

Another compounding factor is that with a lack of resource capabilities and knowledge about environmental management, there can be a perception that environmental management is costly (Vives, 2010). As a result, due to these critical resource constraints, many companies remain as environmental laggards (Granly and Welo, 2014; Boiral et al., 2019). This sets a cultural context within which decisions are made and may conspire to bring uncertainty to tackling sustainability (Seidel et al., 2008). Instead, many owners/managers are still likely to operate within the confines of the traditional economic imperative, resulting in significant caution towards environmental action (Revell et al., 2010). Adding to the difficulties in promoting environmental proactivity in the SME sector, many SME owners/managers may also be 'un-sensitised' to their environmental impact (Friedman and Miles, 2001, p. 207).

Overall, a diversity of perceptions and actions exists within the SME sector, creating a sector of business that generally tends to react to, rather than anticipate, change (Gadenne et al., 2009). In consequence, small business management is crystallised in managerial attitudes that may often bring a negative slant to decision-making (Levy and Powell, 2005), especially where there is considerable uncertainty surrounding environmental issues (Lin and Ho, 2010).

This also means that although there is sufficient evidence that SMEs can achieve cost savings and profit from increased productivity (Henriques and Catarino, 2016), many SME owners/managers do not perceive the benefits of investing in this area (Brammer et al., 2012; Sáez-Martínez et al., 2016). This is exemplified by the work of Howgrave-Graham and van Berkel (2007), revealing a low level of uptake of cleaner production practices even though there are significant benefits. Where SMEs do take up initiatives, they are usually the low-hanging fruits rather than higher level strategic initiatives (Howgrave-Graham and van Berkel, 2007). This practice is not that typical in the SME sector and finds synergy with the behaviours of larger enterprises.

Picking these lower-hanging fruits may also be identified as a 'natural' step in the direction of a more concerted effort towards greening across the business community. The heterogeneous nature of the SME sector also meant that a range of more proactive actions and an environmental focus had been reported, such as the potential for reducing greenhouse gas emissions and solid wastes (Côté et al., 2008; Côté and Liu, 2016), and sustainability innovations (Bos-Brouwers, 2010). Meanwhile, Cassells and Lewis (2011) reported that 80% of their surveyed companies in New Zealand understood environmental risks from their activities. Not only the reduction of energy, water emissions and usage, but also green products and packaging, and design for the environment provided significant environmental responsiveness by the SMEs.

These experiences suggest that SMEs can invest to make changes to specific operations so that they can reduce waste and other environmental impacts and that these are likely to be more direct and effective and easier to accept (Arend, 2014). Going beyond this transformation to promote a broader set of environmental initiatives across the company is difficult, as many SMEs are weary that investments in improving their environmental performance adds extra cost without any clear guarantee for a financial reward. As Lee (2009) describes it, environmental transformation in organisations requires investments in technological development, employee training, and new organisational architecture. In contrast, larger enterprises are more likely to mitigate these costs by achieving economies of scale and through being more financially capable of investment and reaping financial benefits.

The size of SMEs may also explain, to some extent, why managerial perceptions may differ considerably from larger multinational companies. In the larger SMEs, for example, Rahbauer et al. (2018) have shown that they could more easily achieve economic benefit through switching to green energy while smaller SMEs relied on altruistic measures. Santos (2011, p. 492), for example, has shown how the personal values of owners/managers of SMEs underpinned basic motivations and that direct perceptions improved CSR performance in SMEs and could drive beneficial actions that ventured beyond a profit maximisation approach. SMEs may, therefore, not benefit financially from practicing CSR but are doing so for the sake of their own beliefs and values. They may also identify with being good to society as they are consuming society's resources for their work. But as we have seen earlier in this chapter, the majority of SME owners/managers respond to market and regulatory drivers, and as Schaefer (2020) highlights, only when altruistic and market forces combine are SMEs really driven to improve their environmental performance.

Structurally too, there are barriers. Even though pressures for SMEs to engage in environmental issues by regulators, customers and consumers is mounting (Madsen and Ulhøi, 2016; Sáez-Martínez et al., 2016), many SMEs are not able to take advantage of the loose or 'organic' business framework (Jennings and Beaver, 1997) even if, potentially, these explorative capabilities may be balanced with structurally managing organisational resources to improve business responsiveness (Chang and Hughes, 2012). As the findings of Redmond et al. (2008) show, the different organisational arrangements in an SME compared to a corporate structure may present a barrier to implementing environmental management.

2.5 Discussion and conclusion

While it makes perfect sense to see large enterprises being among the early adopters of green practices, the effect of SMEs, representing the vast majority of all businesses around the world, has largely been overlooked. SMEs, however, are structurally and culturally different entities in relation to larger enterprises, such that the planning and change processes of larger organisations cannot necessarily be applied to SMEs in a less formal manner or on a smaller scale.

One overarching feature does, however, add contradictory characteristics to SME environmental behaviour. Although SME owners/managers are free of being forced to adopt a short-term focus and the shackles of command and control structures are better placed to impart their consciousness and intent on the organisation, they still face significant resource capabilities and constraints compared to larger organisations. Furthermore, the attitudes of SME owners/managers are residual within their consciousness and emotions and it is these two value components that will determine the manner in which they engage with environmental issues. The values that underpin these cultural typologies are critical in shaping the environmental behaviours of the SME owner/manager. The SME sector, however, remains highly heterogeneous, with differing motivations, belief systems, psychological characteristics as well as differing capabilities.

SME owners/managers seem more inclined to identify narrowly with a customer-focused stakeholder that may not demand for environmental criteria to be part of their business operations. This, in turn, may shape a narrow market focus and stifle more visionary and enlightened strategic initiatives. Nonetheless, as we have highlighted in this section, there may be a broad range of views that are likely to shape the SME owner/manager's worldview and the way they identify with, understand and perceive environmental issues (Markle, 2019). With increasing societal awareness and interest in environmental issues as well as greater attention by the business community to act on key environmental considerations such as climate change, biodiversity and waste management there can be greater optimism that SMEs owner/managers can make a significant contribution to achieving a more sustainable planet.

References

Afrum, E., Osei-Akenkan, V. Y., Agyabeng-Mensah, Y., Owusu, A. J., Kusi, Y. L., and Ankomah, J. (2020). Green manufacturing practices and sustainable performance among Ghanaian manufacturing SMEs: The explanatory link of green supply chain integration. *Management of Environmental Quality*, 1477–7835. doi:10.1108/MEQ-01-2020-0019.

Aguado, E., and Holl, A. (2018). Differences of corporate environmental responsibility in small and medium enterprises: Spain and Norway. *Sustainability*, *10*(6). doi:10.3390/su10061877.

Ahinful, G. S., Tauringana, V., Essuman, D., Boakye, D. J., Sha'ven, W. B. (2019). Stakeholders pressure, SMEs characteristics and environmental management in Ghana. *Journal of Small Business and Entrepreneurship*, 1–28. doi: 10.1080/08276331.2018.1545890.

Amaeshi, K., Adegbite, E., Ogbechie, C., Idemudia, U., Kan, K. A. S., Issa, M., and Anakwue, O. I. J. (2016). Corporate social responsibility in SMEs: A shift from philanthropy to institutional works? *Journal of Business Ethics*, *138*(2), 385–400.

Andries, A. M., Marcu, N., Oprea, F., and Tofan, M. (2018). Financial infrastructure and access to finance for European SMEs. *Sustainability*, *10*(10), 1–15. 10.3390/su10103400.

Aragón-Correa, J. A., Hurtado-Torres, N., Sharma, S., and Garcia-Morales, V. J. (2008). Environmental strategy and performance in small firms: A resource-based perspective. *Journal of Environmental Management*, *86*(1), 88–103.

Ararat, M., Colpan, A. M., and Matten, D. (2018). Business groups and corporate responsibility for the public good. *Journal of Business Ethics*, *153*(4), 911–929.

Arend, R. J. (2014). Social and environmental performance at SMEs: Considering motivations, capabilities, and instrumentalism. *Journal of Business Ethics*, *125*(4), 541–561.

Ayuso, S., and Navarrete-Báez, F. E. (2018). How does entrepreneurial and international orientation influence SMEs' commitment to sustainable development? Empirical evidence from Spain and Mexico. *Corporate Social Responsibility and Environmental Management*, *25*(1), 80–94.

Baden, D., Harwood, I. A., and Woodward, D. G. (2011). The effects of procurement policies on 'downstream' corporate social responsibility activity: Content-analytic insights into the views and actions of SME owner-managers. *International Small Business Journal, 29*(3), 259–277.

Baranova, P., and Paterson, F. (2017). Environmental capabilities of small and medium-sized enterprises: Towards transition to a low carbon economy in the East Midlands. *Local Economy, 32*(8), 835–853.

Barbosa, M., Castañeda-Ayarza, J. A., and Lombardo Ferreira, D. H. (2020). Sustainable strategic management (GES): Sustainability in small business. *Journal of Cleaner Production, 258*, 1–11. doi.org/10.1016/j.jclepro.2020.120880.

Baumann-Pauly, D., Wickert, C., Spence, L. J., and Scherer, A. G. (2013). Organizing corporate social responsibility in small and large firms: Size matters. *Journal of Business Ethics, 115*(4), 693–705.

Bevan, E. A. M., and Yung, P. (2014). Implementation of corporate social responsibility in Australian construction SMEs. Engineering. *Construction and Architectual Management, 22*(3), 295–311.

Bhattacharya, C. B. (2020). *Small actions, big difference: Leveraging corporate sustainability to drive business and societal value.* Routledge, Abingdon.

Blackburn, W. R. (2007). Approach to sustainability for small and struggling companies. In *The sustainability handbook: The complete management guide to achieving social, economic and environmental responsibility.* Earthscan, Washington.

Blundel, R., Monaghan, A., and Thomas, C. (2013). SMEs and environmental responsibility: A policy perspective. *Business Ethics, 22*(3), 246–262.

Boiral, O., Ebrahimi, M., Kuyken, K., and Talbot, D. (2019). Greening remote SMEs: The case of small regional airports. *Journal of Business Ethics, 154*(3), 813–827.

Bos-Brouwers, H. E. J. (2010). Corporate sustainability and innovation in SMEs: Evidence of themes and activities in practice. *Business Strategy and the Environment, 19*(7), 417–435.

Brammer, S., Hoejmose, S., and Marchant, K. (2012). Environmental management in SMEs in the UK: Practices, pressures and perceived benefits. *Business Strategy and the Environment, 21*(7), 423–434.

Burivalova, Z., Butler, R. A., and Wilcove, D. S. (2018). Analyzing Google search data to debunk myths about the public's interest in conservation. *Frontiers in Ecology and the Environment, 16*(9), 509–514.

Cadez, S., Czerny, A., and Letmathe, P. (2019). Stakeholder pressures and corporate climate change mitigation strategies. *Business Strategy and the Environment, 28*(1), 1–14.

Cahen, A., and Tacca, M. C. (2013). Linking perception and cognition. *Frontiers in Psychology, 4*, 144. doi.org/10.3389/fpsyg.2013.00144.

Calogirou, C., Sørensen, S. Y., Larsen, B. P., Alexopoulou, S. et al. (2010). SMEs and the environment in the European Union. Main Report. PLANET S.A. and Danish Technology Institute, Published by European Commission, DG Enterprise and Industry. https://op.europa.eu/en/publication-detail/-/publication/aa507ab8-1a2a-4bf1-86de-5a60d14a3977. Accessed 26/09/2020.

Campos, L. M. S. (2012). Environmental management systems (EMS) for small companies: A study in Southern Brazil. *Journal of Cleaner Production, 32*, 141–148.

Cassells, S., and Lewis, K. (2011). SMEs and environmental responsibility: Do actions reflect attitudes? *Corporate Social Responsibility and Environmental Management, 18*(3), 186–199.

Chadwick, M., Fussler, C., Htun, N., Khosla, A., Mansfield (III), W. H., Mattos de Lemos, H., Retzsch, W., de Rosen, L., and Trinidade, S. C. (2003). Big challenge for small business: sustainability and SMEs. *Industry and Environment*, 26(4), 1–50. http://www.uneptie.org/media/review/vol26no4/IE26_4-SMEs.pdf. Accessed: 26/09/2020.

Chang, Y. Y., and Hughes, M. (2012). Drivers of innovation ambidexterity in small- to medium-sized firms. *European Management Journal*, 30(1), 1–17.

Chen, Y. S., and Chang, C. H. (2013). The determinants of green product development performance: Green dynamic capabilities, green transformational leadership, and green creativity. *Journal of Business Ethics*, 116(1), 107–119.

Collins, E., Roper, J., and Lawrence, S. (2010). Sustainability practices: Trends in New Zealand businesses. *Business Strategy and the Environment*, 19(8), 479–494.

Corrocher, N., and Solito, I. (2017). How do firms capture value from environmental innovations? An empirical analysis on European SMEs. *Industry and Innovation*, 24(5), 569–585.

Côté, R. P., and Liu, C. (2016). Strategies for reducing greenhouse gas emissions at an industrial park level: A case study of Debert Air Industrial Park, Nova Scotia. *Journal of Cleaner Production*, 114, 352–361.

Côté, R. P., Lopez, J., Marche, S., Genevieve, P., and Ramsey W. (2008). Influences, practices and opportunities for environmental supply chain management in Nova Scotia SMEs. *Journal of Cleaner Production*, 16(15), 1561–1570.

Cyert, R. M., and March, J. G. (1963). *A behavioral theory of the firm.* Prentice-Hall, Englewood Cliffs.

Daly, H. (2013). A further critique of growth economics. *Ecological Economics*, 88, 20–24.

De Groot, J. I. M., and Steg, L. (2007). Value orientations and environmental beliefs in five countries: Validity of an instrument to measure egoistic, altruistic and biospheric value orientations. *Journal of Cross-Cultural Psychology*, 38(3), 318–332.

De Steur, H., Temmerman, H., Gellynck, X., and Canavari, M. (2020). Drivers, adoption, and evaluation of sustainability practices in Italian wine SMEs. *Business Strategy and the Environment*, 29(2), 744–762.

Dey, P. K., Petridis, N. E., Petridis, K., Malesios, C., Nixon, J. D., and Ghosh, S. K. (2018). Environmental management and corporate social responsibility practices of small and medium-sized enterprises. *Journal of Cleaner Production*, 195, 687–702.

Doranova, A., Mueller, M., Zhechkov, R., Izsak, K., and Roman, L. (2018). Green action plan for SMEs - implement report: Addressing resource efficiency challenges and opportunities in Europe for SMEs. https://www.resourceefficient.eu/sites/easme/files/EREK_report_Implementation_of_SME_Green_Action_Plan.pdf. Accessed: 30/09/2020.

Drake, F., Purvis, M., and Hunt, J. (2004). Meeting the environmental challenge: A case of win-win or lose-win? A study of the UK baking and refrigeration industries. *Business Strategy and the Environment*, 13(3), 172–186.

Dryzek, J. S. Norgaard, Richard B., and Schlosberg, D. (2011). *Climate change and society: Approaches and responses.* Oxford University Press, Oxford.

European Commission. (2009). *Think small first: Considering SME interests in policy making including the application of an "SME Test."* Report of the Expert Group. Enterprise and Industry Directorate General, Brussels. https://ec.euro

pa.eu/docsroom/documents/2664/attachments/1/translations/en/renditions/native. Accessed: 30/09/2020.

European Commission. (2015). Users Guide to the SME Definition. https://op.europa.eu/en/publication-detail/-/publication/79c0ce87-f4dc-11e6–8a35-01aa75ed71a1.

European Commission. (2020a). Small and medium–sized enterprises (SMEs) and the environment. Environment. https://ec.europa.eu/environment/sme/index_en.htm. Accessed: 9/09/2020.

European Commission. (2020b). Small Clean and Competitive. Environmental Compliance Assistance Programmefor SMEs. https://ec.europa.eu/environment/archives/sme/funding/funding_en.htm. Accessed: 29/09/2020.

European Commission Enterprise and Industry (ECEI). (2010). SMEs and the Environment in the European Union. Main Report. PLANET S.A. and Danish Technological Institute, Published by the European Union Commission, DG Enterprise and Industry. http://ec.europa.eu/DocsRoom/documents/13176/attachments/1/translations/en/renditions/native. Accessed: 29/09/2020.

European Investment Bank. (2020). The EIB Circular Economy Guide – Supporting the circular transition. https://www.eib.org/attachments/thematic/circular_economy_guide_en.pdf. Accessed: 29/09/2020.

Everett, J., and Watson, J. (1998). Small business failure and external risk factors. *Small Business Economics*, *11*(4), 371–390.

Eweje, G. (2020). Proactive environmental and social strategies in a small-to-medium-sized company: A case study of a Japanese SME. *Business Strategy and the Environment*, Special Issue Edition, *29*(7), 2927–2938. doi:10.1002/bse.2582.

Factor, A. (2010). Assessment of environmental policy requirements for Australian small-and medium-sized enterprises: A review of the Melbourne region. Final report prepared for Perth Region NRM and the Australian Federal Government, Canberra.

Farrell, J. (2013). Environmental activism and moral schemas: Cultural components of differential participation. *Environment and Behavior*, *45*(3), 399–423.

Fassin, Y., Van Rossem, A., and Buelens, M. (2011). Small-business owner-managers' perceptions of business ethics and CSR-related concepts. *Journal of Business Ethics*, *98*(3), 425–453.

Fawcett, T., and Hampton, S. (2020). Why and how energy efficiency policy should address SMEs. *Energy Policy*, *140*, 111337. doi.org/10.1016/j.enpol.2020.111337.

Fernández-Viñé, M. B., Gómez-Navarro, T., and Capuz-Rizo, S. F. (2013). Assessment of the public administration tools for the improvement of the eco-efficiency of small and medium sized enterprises. *Journal of Cleaner Production*, *47*, 265–273.

Friedman, A. L., and Miles, S. (2001). SMEs and the environment: Two case studies. *Eco-Management and Auditing*, *8*(4), 200–209.

Gadenne, D. L., Kennedy, J., and McKeiver, C. (2009). An empirical study of environmental awareness and practices in SMEs. *Journal of Business Ethics*, *84*(1), 45–63.

Global Reporting Initiative. (2018). *Empowering small business: Recommendations for policy makers to enable corporate reporting for SMEs*. Swiss Confederation, Federal Department of Economic Affairs.

Graafland, J., and Bovenberg, L. (2020). Government regulation, business leaders' motivations and environmental performance of SMEs. *Journal of Environmental Planning and Management*, *63*(8), 1335–1355.

Graafland, J., and Gerlagh, R. (2019). Economic freedom, internal motivation, and corporate environmental responsibility of SMEs. *Environmental and Resource Economics, 74*(3), 1101–1123.

Graafland, J., and Smid, H. (2016). Environmental impacts of SMEs and the effects of formal management tools: Evidence from EU's largest survey. *Corporate Social Responsibility and Environmental Management, 23*(5), 297–307.

Graafland, J., and Smid, H. (2017). Reconsidering the relevance of social license pressure and government regulation for environmental performance of European SMEs. *Journal of Cleaner Production, 141*, 967–977.

Granly, B. M., and Welo, T. (2014). EMS and sustainability: Experiences with ISO 14001 and Eco-Lighthouse in Norwegian metal processing SMEs. *Journal of Cleaner Production, 64*, 194–204.

Grayson, D., and Dodd, T. (2007). Small is sustainable (and beautiful!!): Encouraging European smaller enterprises to be sustainable. A Doughty Centre for Corporate Sustainability Occasional Paper. https://dspace.lib.cranfield.ac.uk/handle/1826/3204. Accessed: 30/09/2020.

Groves, K. S. (2014). Examining leader-follower congruence of social responsibility values in transformational leadership. *Journal of Leadership and Organizational Studies, 21*(3), 227–243.

Groves, K. S. (2020). Testing a moderated mediation model of transformational leadership, values, and organization change. *Journal of Leadership and Organizational Studies, 27*(1), 35–48.

Hamann, R., Smith, J., Tashman, P., and Marshall, R. S. (2017). Why do SMEs go green? An analysis of wine firms in South Africa. *Business and Society, 56*(1), 23–56.

Heavey, C., Simsek, Z., Roche, F., and Kelly, A. (2009). Decision comprehensiveness and corporate entrepreneurship: The moderating role of managerial uncertainty preferences and environmental dynamism. *Journal of Management Studies, 46*(8), 1289–1314.

Henriques, J., and Catarino, J. (2016). Motivating towards energy efficiency in small and medium enterprises. *Journal of Cleaner Production, 139*, 42–50.

Hillary, R. (2000). *Small and medium-sized enterprises and the environment* (1st ed.). Greenleaf, Sheffield.

Howgrave-Graham, A., and van Berkel, R. (2007). Assessment of cleaner production uptake: Method development and trial with small businesses in Western Australia. *Journal of Cleaner Production, 15*, 787–797.

Hughes, S. (2020). *Repowering cities: Governing climate change mitigation in New York City, Los Angeles, and Toronto.* Cornell University Press, Ithaca.

Jenkins, H. (2009). A 'business opportunity' model of corporate social responsibility for small-and medium-sized enterprises. *Business Ethics: A European Review, 18*(1), 21–36.

Jennings, P., and Beaver, G. (1997). The performance and competitive advantage of small firms: A management perspective. *International Small Business Journal, 15*(2), 63–75.

Jia, M., Tong, L., Viswanath, P. V., and Zhang, Z. (2016). Word power: The Impact of negative media coverage on disciplining corporate pollution. *Journal of Business Ethics, 138*(3), 437–458.

Joshi, M., and Anand, V. (2018). Small business owners' external information-seeking behaviors: The role of perceived uncertainty and organizational identity complexity. *Journal of Small Business Strategy, 28*(3), 48–68.

Kiefhaber, E., Pavlovich, K., and Spraul, K. (2020). Sustainability-related identities and the institutional environment: The case of New Zealand owner-managers of small-and medium-sized hospitality businesses. *Journal of Business Ethics, 163*(1), 37–51.

Koirala, S. (2018). SMEs: Key drivers of green and inclusive growth. Environment Directorate, OECD, Issue Paper, GGSD and GGKP6 2018 and Forum Annual Conference Paris 27–29 November. https://www.oecd.org/greengrowth/GGSD_2018_SME%20Issue%20Paper_WEB.pdf. Accessed: 20/07/2020.

Kollmus, A., and A. J. (2002). Mind the gap: Why do people act environmentally and what are the barriers to pro-environmental behavior? *Environmental Education Research, 8*(3), 239–260.

KPMG. (2018). Let's help SMEs to go circular (September). A Project of the European Commission – DG Environment. https://ec.europa.eu/environment/sme/pdf/Trainingmaterials_English.pdf. Access: 26/09/2020.

Kusyk, S. M., and Lozano, J. M. (2007). Corporate responsibility in small and medium-sized enterprises: SME social performance: A four-cell typology of key drivers and barriers on social issues and their implications for stakeholder theory. *Corporate Governance, 7*(4), 502–515.

Lampikoski, T. (2012). Green, innovative, and profitable: A case study of managerial capabilities at Interface Inc. *Technology Innovation Management Review, 2*(11), 4–12.

Langley, A., Mintzberg, H., Pitcher, P., Posada, E., and Saint-Macary, J. (1995). Opening up decision-making: The view from the black stool. *Organization Science, 6*(3), 260–279.

Laroche, H. (1995). From decision to action in organizations: Decision-making as a social representation. *Organization Science, 6*(1), 62–75.

Leavy, B. (2016). Lord John Browne: Beyond CSR - why business needs to engage more radically with society. *Strategy and Leadership, 44*(4), 32–40.

Lee, K. H. (2009). Why and how to adopt green management into business organizations?: The case study of Korean SMEs in manufacturing industry. *Management Decision, 47*(7), 1101–1121.

Lee, K. H. (2011). Integrating carbon footprint into supply chain management: The case of Hyundai Motor Company (HMC) in the automobile industry. *Journal of Cleaner Production, 19*(11), 1216–1223.

Lee, K. H., Herold, D. M., and Yu, A. L. (2016). Small and medium enterprises and corporate social responsibility practice: A Swedish perspective. *Corporate Social Responsibility and Environmental Management, 23*(2), 88–99.

Lee, S. H., and Lee, S. Y. (2018). An analysis of the effects of climate change policy, stakeholder pressure, and corporate carbon management on carbon efficiency on the Korean petrochemical industry. *Sustainability, 10*(12). 4420. doi:10.3390/su10124420.

Levy, M., and Powell, P. (2005). *Strategies for growth in SMEs: The role of information and information systems.* Elsevier Butterworth Heinemann, Oxford.

Lewis, K., and Cassells, S. (2010). Barriers and drivers for environmental practice uptake in SMEs: A New Zealand perspective. *International Journal of Business Studies, 18*(1), 7–21.

Lewis, K. V., Cassells, S., and Roxas, H. (2015). SMEs and the potential for a collaborative path to environmental responsibility. *Business Strategy and the Environment*, 24(8), 750–764.

Lin, C. Y., and Ho, Y. H. (2010). The influences of environmental uncertainty on corporate green behavior: An empirical study with small and medium-size enterprises. *Social Behavior and Personality*, 38(5), 691–696.

Liu, Y., and Bai, Y. (2014). An exploration of firms' awareness and behavior of developing circular economy: An empirical research in China. *Resources, Conservation and Recycling*, 87, 145–152.

Löfving, M., Safsten, K., Winroth, M. (2014). Manufacturing strategy frameworks suitable for SMEs. *Journal of Manufacturing Technology Management*, 25(1), 7–26.

Longenecker, G. J. (1969). *Principles of management and organizational behavior* (2nd ed.). Merill, Colombus.

Lozano, R. (2015). A holistic perspective on corporate sustainability drivers. *Corporate Social Responsibility and Environmental Management*, 22(1), 32–44.

Lubin, D. A., and Esty, D. C. (2010). The big idea: The sustainability imperative. *Harvard Business Review*, 88(5), 43–50.

Lynch-Wood, G., and Williamson, D. (2014). Understanding SME responses to environmental regulation. *Journal of Environmental Planning and Management*, 57(8), 1220–1239.

Lyon, T. P., Delmas, M. A., Maxwell, J. W., Tima Bansal, P., Chiroleu-Assouline, M., Crifo, P., Durand, R., Gond, J. P., King, A., Lenox, M., Toffel, M., Vogel, D., and Wijen, F. (2018). CSR needs CPR: Corporate sustainability and politics. *California Management Review*, 60(4), 5–24.

Madsen, H., and Ulhøi, J. P. (2016). Corporate environmental initiatives in small and medium-sized enterprises and their outcome: A longitudinal study. *Business Strategy and the Environment*, 25(2), 92–101.

Marco-Fondevila, M., Moneva Abadía, J. M., and Scarpellini, S. (2018). CSR and green economy: Determinants and correlation of firms' sustainable development. *Corporate Social Responsibility and Environmental Management*, 25(5), 756–771.

Markle, G. (2019). Understanding pro-environmental behavior in the US: Insights from grid-group cultural theory and cognitive sociology. *Sustainability*, 11(2), 1–14. org/10.3390/su11020532.

Martín-Peña, M. L., Díaz-Garrido, E., and Sánchez-López, J. M. (2010). Relation between management's behavioural intentions toward the environment and environmental actions. *Journal of Environmental Planning and Management*, 53(3), 297–315.

Martín-Peña, M. L., Díaz-Garrido, E., and Sánchez-López, J. M. (2014). Analysis of benefits and difficulties associated with firms' environmental management systems: The case of the Spanish automotive industry. *Journal of Cleaner Production*, 70, 220–230.

McKeiver, C., and Gadenne, D. (2005). Environmental management systems in small and medium businesses. *International Small Business Journal*, 23(5), 513–537.

Miller, K., Neubauer, A., and Varma, A. (2011). *First assessment of the environmental assistance programme for SMEs (ECAP)*. Final report, AEA Technology PLC, London. https://ec.europa.eu/environment/archives/sme/pdf/First%20assessment%20of%20the%20ECAP%20for%20SMEs.pdf. Accessed: 30/09/2020.

Mintzberg, H. (1971). Managerial work: Analysis from observation. *Management Science*, 15(2), 99–109.

Morsing, M., and Perrini, F. (2009). CSR in SMEs: Do SMEs matter for the CSR agenda? *Business Ethics: A European Review*, 18(1), 1–6.

Muller, P., Mattes, A., Klitou, D., Lonkeu, O.-K., Ramada, P., Ruiz, F. A., Devani, S., Farrenkopf, J., Makowska, A., Mankovska, N., Robin, N., and Steigertahl, L. (2018). Annual report on European SMEs 2017/18. SMEs growing beyond borders. *European Union*. https://doi.org/10.1007/s11846-019-00371-2.

Muñoz-Pascual, L., Curado, C., and Galende, J. (2019). How does the use of information technologies affect the adoption of environmental practices in SMEs? A mixed-methods approach. *Review of Managerial Science*, 118–146.

Murillo, D., and Lozano, J. M. (2006). SMEs and CSR: An approach to CSR in their own words. *Journal of Business Ethics*, 67(3), 227–240.

Musavengane, R. (2019). Small hotels and responsible tourism practice: Hoteliers' perspectives. *Journal of Cleaner Production*, 220, 786–799.

Naidoo, M., and Gasparatos, A. (2018). Corporate environmental sustainability in the retail sector: Drivers, strategies and performance measurement. *Journal of Cleaner Production*, 203, 125–142.

Nejati, M., Amran, A., and Ahmad, N. H. (2014). Examining stakeholders' influence on environmental responsibility of micro, small and medium-sized enterprises and its outcomes. *Management Decision*, 52(10), 2021–2043.

Odongo, N. H., and Wang, D. (2018). Corporate responsibility, ethics and accountability. *Social Responsibility Journal*, 14(1), 111–122.

OECD. (2017). Small, medium, strong. Trends in SME performance and business conditions. OECD Publishing, Paris. doi.org/10.1787/9789264275683-en.

Olson, O. T. (2010). On humanization of life. *Cultura International Journal of Philosophy of Culture and Axiology*, 8(2), 148–168.

Papagiannakis, G., and Lioukas, S. (2012). Values, attitudes and perceptions of managers as predictors of corporate environmental responsiveness. *Journal of Environmental Management*, 100, 41–51.

Parker, C. M., Redmond, J., and Simpson, M. (2009). A review of interventions to encourage SMEs to make environmental improvements. *Environment and Planning C: Government and Policy*, 27(2), 279–301.

Patton, D., and Worthington, I. (2003). SMEs and environmental regulations: A study of the UK screen-printing sector. *Environment and Planning C: Government and Policy*, 21(4), 549–566.

Perez-Sanchez, D., Barton, J. R., and Bower, D. (2003). Implementing environmental management in SMEs. *Corporate Social Responsibility and Environmental Management*, 10(2), 67–77.

Petts. J. (2000). Small and medium-sized enterprises and environmental compliance: Attitudes among management and non-management. In R. Hillary (Ed.), *Small and medium-sized enterprises and the environment: business imperatives* (1st ed., 49–60). Greenleaf, Sheffield.

Petts, J., Herd, A., and O'Heocha, M. (1998). Environmental responsiveness, individuals and organizational learning: SME experience. *Journal of Environmental Planning and Management*, 41(6), 711–730.

Radhouane, I., Nekhili, M., Nagati, H., and Paché, G. (2018). The impact of corporate environmental reporting on customer-related performance and market value. *Management Decision*, 56(7), 1630–1659.

Rahbauer, S., Menapace, L., Menrad, K., and Lang, H. (2018). Determinants for the adoption of green electricity by German SMEs - An empirical examination. *Energy Policy, 123*, 533–543.

Raza, J., and Majid, A. (2016). Perceptions and practices of corporate social responsibility among SMEs in Pakistan. *Quality and Quantity, 50*(6), 2625–2650.

Redmond, J., Walker, E., and Wang, C. (2008). Issues for small businesses with waste management. *Journal of Environmental Management, 88*(2), 275–285.

Revell, A., Stokes, D., and Chen, H. (2010). Small businesses and the environment: Turning over a new leaf? *Business Strategy and the Environment, 19*(5), 273–288.

Reverdy, T. (2006). Translation process and organizational change: ISO 14001 implementation. *International Studies of Management and Organization, 36*(2), 9–30.

Reyes-Rodríguez, J. F., Ulhøi, J. P., and Madsen, H. (2016). Corporate environmental sustainability in Danish SMEs: A longitudinal study of motivators, initiatives, and strategic effects. *Corporate Social Responsibility and Environmental Management, 23*(4), 193–212.

Rodwell, J., and Shadur, M. (1997). What's size got to do with it? Implications for contemporary management practices in IT companies. *International Small Business Journal, 15*(2), 51–62.

Rome, A. (2019). Dupont and the limits of corporate environmentalism. *Business History Review, 93*(1), 75–99.

Sáez-Martínez, F. J., Díaz-García, C., and González-Moreno, Á. (2016). Factors promoting environmental responsibility in European SMEs: The effect on performance. *Sustainability, 8*(9), 1–14. doi.org/10.3390/su8090898.

Samuelsson, J., Ljungkvist, T., and Jansson, C. (2016). Formal accounting planning in SMEs. *Journal of Small Business and Enterprise Development, 23*(3), 691–702.

Santos, M. (2011). CSR in SMEs: Strategies, practices, motivations and obstacles. *Social Responsibility Journal, 7*(3), 490–508.

Scerri, A. (2009). Paradoxes of increased individuation and public awareness of environmental issues. *Environmental Politics, 18*(4), 467–485.

Schaefer, A., Williams, S., and Blundel, R. (2020). Individual values and SME environmental engagement. *Business and Society, 59*(4), 642–675.

Schaltegger, S., and Hörisch, J. (2017). In search of the dominant rationale in sustainability management: Legitimacy- or profit-seeking. *Journal of Business Ethics, 145*, 259–276.

Schaper, M. (2002). Small firms and environmental management: Predictors of green purchasing in Western Australian pharmacies. *International Small Business Journal, 20*(3), 235–251.

Schwartz, S. H. (1994). Are there universal aspects in the content and structure of values? *Journal of Social Sciences, 50*(4), 19–45.

Secretariat, O. (2018). Towards the Green Action Task Force Programme of Work for the period 2019–2020. http://www.oecd.org/officialdocuments/publicdisplaydocumentpdf/?cote=ENV/EPOC/EAP(2018)1&docLanguage=En. Accessed: 30/09/2020.

Seidel, M., Seidel, R., Tedford, D., Cross, R., and Wait, L. (2008). A systems modelling approach to support environmentally sustainable business development in manufacturing SMEs. *Proceedings of World Academy of Science: Engineering and Technology, 48*, 899–874.

Sharps, M. J., Hess, A. B., and Ranes, B. (2007). Mindless decision making and environmental issues: Gestalt/feature - intensive processing and contextual reasoning in environmental decisions. *Journal of Psychology: Interdisciplinary and Applied, 141*(5), 525–537.

Simpson, M., Taylor, N., and Barker, K. (2004). Environmental responsibility in SMEs: Does it deliver competitive advantage? *Business Strategy and the Environment, 13*(3), 156–171.

Spence, L. J., and Rutherfoord, R. (2001). Social responsibility profit maximisation and the small firm owner-manager. *Journal of Small Business and Enterprise Development, 8*(2), 126–139.

Steg, L., Bolderdijk, J. W., Keizer, K., and Perlaviciute, G. (2014). An integrated framework for encouraging pro-environmental behaviour: The role of values, situational factors and goals. *Journal of Environmental Psychology, 38*, 104–115.

Stewart, H., and Gapp, R. (2014). Achieving effective sustainable management: A small-medium enterprise case study. *Corporate Social Responsibility and Environmental Management, 21*(1), 52–64.

Studer, S., Welford, R., and Hills, P. (2006). Engaging Hong Kong businesses in environmental change: Drivers and barriers. *Business Strategy and the Environment, 15*(6), 416–431.

Tantalo, C., Caroli, M. G., and Vanevenhoven, J. (2012). Corporate social responsibility and SME's competitiveness. *International Journal of Technology Management, 58*, 129–151.

Tatoglu, E., Frynas, J. G., Bayraktar, E., Demirbag, M., Sahadev, S., Doh, J., and Koh, S. C. L. (2020). Why do emerging market firms engage in unitary environmental management practices? A strategic choice perspective. *British Journal of Management, 31*(1), 80–100.

Taylor, A., Cocklin, C., and Brown, R. (2012). Fostering environmental champions: A process to build their capacity to drive change. *Journal of Environmental Management, 98*(1), 84–97.

The Lancet Plantary Health. (2019). Surging awareness. *The Lancet Planetary Health, 3*(6), 235–236. https://www.thelancet.com/pdfs/journals/lanplh/PIIS2542-5196(19)30096-8.pdf. Accessed: 30/09/2020.

Tilley, F. (1999). The gap between the environmental attitudes and the environmental behaviour of small firms. *Business Strategy and the Environment, 8*(4), 238–248.

TNS Political and Social. (2012). SMEs, resource efficiency and green markets-tables. September 2013, 1–125. https://ec.europa.eu/commfrontoffice/publicopinion/flash/fl_381_sum_en.pdf. Accessed: 29/06/2020.

Tonn, B., English, M., and Travis, C. (2000). A framework for understanding and improving environmental decision making. *Journal of Environmental Planning and Management, 43*(2), 163–183.

Tukker, A. (2006). Environmental product policy. *Journal of Industrial Ecology, 10*(3), 1–4.

Uhlaner, L. M., Berent-Braun, M. M., Jeurissen, R. J. M., and de Wit, G. (2012). Beyond size: Predicting engagement in environmental management practices of Dutch SMEs. *Journal of Business Ethics, 109*(4), 411–429.

Ulhøi, J. P., Madsen, H., and Rikhardsson, P. (1996). Training in environmental management - industry and sustainability. Office for Official Publications for the European Communities, Luxembourg.

US Small Business Administration, (2018). 2018 Small business profile. U.S. Small Business Administration Office of Advocacy. https://www.sba.gov/sites/default/files/advocacy/2018-Small-Business-Profiles-US.pdf. Accessed: 30/09/2020.

Vives, A. (2010). Responsible practices in small and medium-sized enterprises. In G. Aras, and D. Crowther (Eds.), *A handbook of corporate governance and social responsibility* (107 –130). Gower, London.

Walker, B., and Redmond, J. (2015). Changing the environmental behaviour of small business owners: The business case. *Australian Journal of Environmental Education*, 30(2), 254–268.

Wang, J., and Kim, S. (2018). Analysis of the impact of values and perception on climate change skepticism and its implication for public policy. *Climate*, 6, 99. doi.org/10.3390/cli6040099.

Weber-Blaschke, G., Mosandl, R., and Faulstich, M. (2004). History and mandate of sustainability: From local forestry to global policy. In P. A. Wilderer, E. D. Schroeder, and H. Kopp (Eds.), *Global sustainability: The impact of local cultures, a new perspective for science and engineering, economics and politics* (5–19). Wiley-VCH Verlag, Weinheim.

Williamson, D., Lynch-Wood, G., and Ramsay, J. (2006). Drivers of environmental behaviour in manufacturing SMEs and the implications for CSR. *Journal of Business Ethics*, 67(3), 317–330.

Williamson, O. E. (1963). Chapter 9: A model of rational managerial behavior. In R. M. Cyert and J. G. March (Eds.). *A behavioral theory of the firm*. Prentice-Hall, Englewood Cliffs.

Wong, K. K. (2010). Environmental awareness, governance and public participation: Public perception perspectives. *International Journal of Environmental Studies*, 67(2), 169–181.

World Bank. (2020). Small and medium sized enterprises (SMEs) finance: Improving SMEs access to finance and finding innovative solutions to unlock sources of capital. https://www.worldbank.org/en/topic/smefinance. Accessed: 30/09/2020.

Worthington, I., and Patton, D. (2005). Strategic intent in the management of the green environment within SMEs. An analysis of the UK screen-printing sector. *Long Range Planning*, 38(2), 197–212.

Yapici, G., Ögenler, O., Kurt, A. Ö., Koçaş, F., and Şaşmaz, T. (2017). Assessment of environmental attitudes and risk perceptions among university students in Mersin, Turkey. *Journal of Environmental and Public Health*, 2017, 1–8. doi.org/10.1155/2017/5650926.

York, J. G., Vedula, S., and Lenox, M. J. (2018). It's not easy building green: The impact of public policy, private actors, and regional logics on untary standards adoption. *Academy of Management Journal*, 61(4), 1492–1523.

Zsóka, Á. N. (2008). Consistency and "awareness gaps" in the environmental behaviour of Hungarian companies. *Journal of Cleaner Production*, 16(3), 322–329.

3 Mapping the existing methodological SME and sustainability landscape

Aharon Factor and John Parm Ulhøi

3.1 Introduction

Early approaches towards the social responsibilities of small and medium-sized enterprises (SMEs) was criticised by Thompson and Smith (1991) for their lack of methodological rigour and difficulties with researching SMEs. They also recognised the need to expand the scope of future research. In this chapter, we explore how environment research has, ever since, broadened the span of SME research and contributed to methodological development. The environmental dimension of sustainability in SMEs is specifically addressed in this chapter as there have been significant developments in SME and Environment research.

The chapter identifies key methodological approaches that SME and Environment researchers have undertaken and the role of mixed methods in improving the quality of academic enquiry. Although quantitative and qualitative studies make up the main body of SME and Environment research, there exist inherent methodological problems. These concerns were initially brought to the fore by Thompson and Smith (1991). At the time, this topic was only beginning to emerge as a research focus in academia. They reviewed an early set of predominately quantitative studies addressing American SMEs in the 1970s and 1980s. The authors criticise these studies for their use of self-reporting surveys and perceptual measures and they called for the use of more sophisticated statistical techniques and personal interviews that would explore managerial behaviours in depth and enhance theory building.

To a great extent, the methodological quality in SME and Environment research, since the Thompson and Smith (1991) paper, has improved. Nevertheless, SME and Environmental research have similar methodological concerns, as addressed by the authors, such as low response rates, problems in generalising results, conducting regionally focused studies and the use of inexperienced non-random respondents. In response, the authors also call for more creative data collection strategies that are relevant for all types of companies and can improve methodological quality. By integrating qualitative and quantitative studies, mixed method research endeavours to address both the methodological concerns of Thompson and Smith (1991) and also provide Thompson 1991 for more robust data collection designs (Creswell and Plano Clark, 2018). The use of mixed methods also permits researchers to respond to Thompson and Smith's (1991) insight that SME research needs to dig more deeply into owner/manager behaviours rather than use perceptual measures alone. Combining qualitative analysis with quantitative analysis allows for this to happen.

Baylis et al. (1997, 1998) and Petts et al. (1998) recognised these considerations. This enabled both research groups to establish early mixed method approaches to researching environmental behaviours of SMEs. Baylis et al. (1997, 1998), for example, conducted a large-scale survey of SMEs in South Wales. They found that 13% of SMEs had a basic understanding of environmental legislation. Through site visits and interviews, they did unlock the intrinsic motivations of owners/managers. Studies have documented a gap between what managers think and their reported actual environmental performance which they desire (Petts et al., 1998).

The need for multiple methodological approaches to investigate SME environment behaviours and especially their attitudes and perceptions also became the focus of the work of Hillary (2000). While the book reveals insights to key quantitative studies in the field of SMEs and Environment research by several contributing chapter authors (Kemp and Duff, 2000; Gerrans and Hutchinson, 2000; Gerstenfield and Roberts, 2000), qualitative interviews to delve deeply into the key motivators of owners/managers are also described in chapters by Petts (2000), Tilley (2000) and Anglada (2000). Even though these research studies do not provide integrated mixed method approaches as described by the aforementioned pioneering studies by Baylis et al. (1997) and Petts et al. (1998), they do, however, mark an important departure from a predominantly quantitative approach.

The early development of mixed methods by Baylis et al. (1997, 1998) and Petts et al. (1998) began an attempt to bring a more pluralistic methodological approach towards SME and Environment research. In the next section of this chapter, methodological developments in the field are reviewed.

3.2 Methodological review of SME and Environment research

This section discusses literature on SMEs and the environment from a methodological perspective. The aim is to provide a benchmark of mixed method research studies in the field of SMEs and the environment against stand-alone quantitative and qualitative studies. To identify relevant studies, a systematic review of methodological approaches to SME and Environment research has been undertaken for this chapter. This ensures that literature is collected on the basis of rigour and quality (Williams et al., 2017). An 'integrated literature review' has been performed in accordance with the sequenced approach developed by Lopes de Sousa Jabbour et al. (2020, p. 2). The first step in the sequence was to establish the inclusion criteria for the samples of research articles. Only studies that met the following criteria were considered for selection:

a. The selected journal articles were to include a title, abstract or keywords relating to business and environmental management in SMEs.
b. Research methods were to constitute a quantitative, qualitative or mixed method research emphasis.
c. Research was to make theoretical contributions to the fields of business and environment.
d. The articles were to reflect regional variety.
e. The ranking of journals were to be considered.

The next step in the review sequence was to select appropriate databases to search for relevant journal articles. These were:

a. A mix of leading business and science search engines: All Ebsco databases, Greenfile, Emerald, Factiva, JSTOR, Proquest, Science Direct, Scopus and All of Web of Science databases.
b. Google, Google Scholar and Elsevier Mendeley.

This wide range of the leading academic databases allowed for journal searches across Scopus and All of Web Science as well as focused searches through key business search engines such as Business Premier Ebsco and thousands of articles focused on business and environmental issues through Ebsco's GreenFile database.

Once the inclusion criteria had been established, the next step was to conduct a search for the relevant journal articles. The search strategy included terms such as "SME Environmental", "Small and Medium-sized enterprises Environmental", "SME Sustainability", "Small business Environment", "Small business sustainability". The use of sustainability and small business were interjected as search terms since authors often use these terminologies interchangeably with environment and SME conceptualisations. Predominantly, the focus was on business management in SMEs. More specialised studies in subfields such as focused studies on supply chain, marketing, accounting, operations and human relations were included only with a clear management focus.

This first round of search in March 2019 was followed by another search in August 2020 to ensure that an up-to-date and relevant literature set was created. References were managed on Elsevier's Mendeley reference manager. This online web-based tool allowed for managing a wide range of documents and published data. The next stage of sampling was to match each article to the inclusion criteria, from (a) to (e), as mentioned before.

The aim here was to, 'assess the article's potential contribution and level of connection with the main goal of the bibliometric research' (Ferenhof et al., 2014, p. 45). In general, a review of titles, abstracts and article discussions and conclusions provided an insight into the central themes of the papers. In some cases, a complete reading of the articles was needed. This stage of sampling established theoretical relevancy. The final stage was to group the literature by methodological approach. This was established by reading the methodologies of all the journal articles. Quantitative, qualitative and mixed method studies were delineated. Overall, some 280 academic journal articles had been scrutinised for the research methodology that they employed.

Table 3.1 shows the number of journal articles employing quantitative methodologies (the majority being statistical surveys) as well as the number of qualitative and mixed methods. The table shows that between the timeframes of 1990–1999 and 2010–2020, more than half of all published research in the field have used quantitative methodologies. In the 2000–2009 timeframe, however, quantitative representation had dropped by almost half of its representation compared to the other timeframes. At the same time, qualitative representations rose to almost half of all studies in the timeframe and mixed methodologies represented a fifth of all studies. Since 2010, the growth of quantitative studies has surged, regaining their dominant methodological position in the field. Even though qualitative and mixed method studies continue to increase with more studies being published in 2010–2020 timeframe compared to 1990–2009, this is against the backdrop of the fact that 214 of all 280 studies from 1990 to 2020 were published in this timeframe. This means that the field as whole has significantly expanded.

The graph in Figure 3.1 shows that quantitative methodologies not only have regained interest amongst SME and Environment researchers but that the exponential growth rate is faster than qualitative or mixed method

Table 3.1 Analysis of methodologies used between 1990 and 2020 in SME and Environment research studies

Time Frame	Quantitative			Qualitative			Mixed Methods			Time Frame Total
	Studies	% Of Studies	Time Frame	Studies	% Of Studies	Time Frame	Studies	% Of Studies	Time Frame	
1990-1999	7	>5	58	2	>3	17	3	6	25	12 (>5%)
2000-2009	16	11	30	25	32	46	13	25	24	54 (24%)
2010-2020	127	85	59	51	46	24	36	69	17	214 (67%)
Total	150			78			52			280

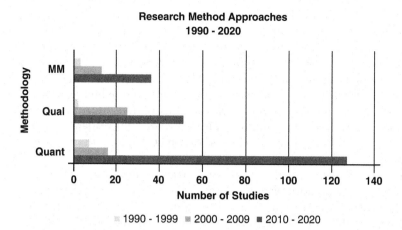

Figure 3.1 Growth rates of quantitative, qualitative and mixed method (MM) studies in SME and Environment research (1990–2020).

approaches. In fact, while Table 3.1 shows that even though qualitative studies had doubled their percentage of studies in the 2010–2020 timeframe compared to the 2000–2009 timeframe, Figure 3.1 shows that the number of qualitative studies still lagged behind the quantitative focus of many researchers in the field. Meanwhile, although mixed methods research has seen a 69% rise in the total number of mixed method studies during 2010–2020, in this period, the actual percentage of studies that used mixed methods was only 17%, compared to 24% in 2000–2009 and 25% in 2010–2020 (see Table 3.1). In other words, there has been an overall drop in mixed methods and a rapid rise in quantitative studies in the field. This dynamic is captured in Figure 3.1.

Some shift away from a predominantly quantitative focus on SME and Environment research is also shown in the results of similar studies by Wiesner et al. (2018) and Johnson and Schaltegger (2016). Table 3.2 shows that qualitative methodologies are more represented as mainly mono-method approaches with inclusion as a component of a smaller set of mixed method studies. Although the review displayed in Table 3.2 does find accord with Stokes' (2000) earlier revelation that quantitative methodologies dominate research approaches into SMEs and the environment, Figure 3.1 does show that qualitative research had come to be more featured in SME and Environment studies.

The work of Johnson and Schaltegger (2016) provides further support to the findings presented in Figure 3.1 regarding this trend. Johnson and Schaltegger's (2016) timeframe from 1991 to 2010, for example, captured the authors' findings that in this timeframe, qualitative work appears to have dominated. The authors' findings do concur with those of Johnson

Table 3.2 Comparative review of SME and Environment research methodologies (1990–2020)

Sources	Time Frame	Scope	Total	Quantitative	Qualitative	Mixed Methods	Notes
Table 3.1	1990–2020	SME and Environment	280	150	78	52	Study for this chapter
Wiesner et al (2018)	1999–2015	Environmental Change Management	33	15	15	2	1 unstated
Johnson and Schaltegger (2016)	1991–2010	Sustainability Management Tools	112	34	43	0	35 conceptual or theoretical

and Schaltegger (2016) which state that from 1991 to 1999, only 9 papers were featured, but 62 papers emerged between 2006 and 2010, showing a strong growing interest in the field.

3.3 Publication trends in SMEs and Environment

In the last section, we explored mixed method trends in the context of the broader publication of SME and Environment research. In this section, we identify the journals in which these are published and the quality of research in terms of journal impact factor. This is represented in Table 3.3 (presented in the Appendices). Four journals in particular have been most prominent in publishing SME and Environment studies, with a balance of quantitative, qualitative and mixed method approaches. These are: Journal of Cleaner Production, Business Strategy and the Environment, Corporate Social Responsibility (CSR) and the Environment and Business Ethics.

While Business Strategy and the Environment was a front runner publishing quantitative studies in the 1990s (e.g., Hutchinson and Chaston, 1994; Merritt, 1998), more recently, the Journal of Cleaner production, especially in the last 10 years, has taken over not only as the front runner in publishing research in the field but of most relevance is the fact that the journal has published 11 mixed method studies. Appendices Table 3.3 also shows that both of these journals are highly rated in the academic community with very high-level impact factors. In addition, CSR and the Environment and Business Ethics are both high-level journals which have published mixed method studies; the literature review, however, could not establish that these journals had published mixed method studies especially addressing SMEs and Environment. Business and Society is also a high-level journal and has published two mixed method studies in the field of SME and Environment.

3.4 Geographical mixed method developments

Another intention of this book is to include and reflect upon the possible geographical spread of mixed method research as well as key studies.

Chapter 2 has shown how the field of SME and Environment research is gaining traction beyond the traditional confines of Europe and has been adopted in Asia, Africa and the Americas. In this section, we outline the mixed method literature by region. We also attempt to show the diversity of mixed-method designs which reflect the precise reasons for the research (Creswell and Plano Clark, 2011) and specifically the manner in which the research questions will be addressed (Bazeley 2009).

In this section, we will also show that although mixed method research data may be collected and analysed simultaneously as exemplified by the Spanish study (described in more detail in Chapter 13) of Cloquell-Ballester et al. (2008), most mixed method studies in the SME and Environment field use a chronological linkage between quantitative and qualitative data collection and analysis, typically known as a sequenced design (Creswell and Plano Clark, 2011).

The regional studies, now discussed, more specifically make use of two types of sequenced designs. One design, in particular, uses a quantitative survey followed by qualitative interviews, while the second design conversely uses qualitative interviews to inform a quantitative sequence design. This forms the main integration approach for mixed methods in the SME and Environment field. Plano Clark and Ivankova (2016) shed further light on the dominancy of one study over the other. They denote studies with a dominant data collection strand with capital letters such as QUAN-Qual or QUAL-Quan. In other words, capitalisation infers a greater use of that methodology in the study. In the following account, we use this denotation approach to exemplify how this approach might be applied to studies in the field. For example, where there is an equal weightage, we have used a QUAN-QUAL approach. We also venture further by showing how some innovative researchers have used variations of this approach to address their research questions.

3.4.1 Regional studies

The use of mixed methods emerged in the UK during the 1990s (e.g., Baylis et al.; Rowe and Hollingsworth, 1996). Comprehensive mixed-method designs were employed using quantitative surveys coupled with site visits, interviews and focus groups. The next decade witnessed the development of mixed methods in SME and Environment investigations in the UK (e.g., Friedman et al., 2000; Peters and Turner, 2004; Simpson et al., 2004) and also began to make an appearance in the rest of Europe (e.g., Biondi et al., 2000; Ammenberg and Hjelm, 2003; López-Gamero et al., 2008) and the United States (Rothenberg and Becker, 2004).

Since 2010, there has been a surge of mixed methods in SME and Environment studies. During this time, only three mixed method research studies focused on UK companies. Sainidis and Robson (2016), for example, used a purposefully designed approach using both quantitative and qualitative data to compensate for the limitations of one methodological approach alone. An important driver for Sainidis and Robson (2016) were calls from the academic community (Boyer and Swink, 2008; Barratt et al., 2011) for greater methodological plurality in researching SME manufacturing companies which have predominantly used quantitative studies. This study followed the QUAN-QUAL sequenced design logic of Plano Clark and Ivankova (2016, p. 122) who describe how a first stage quantitative survey is followed by supporting qualitative research. This approach is used to elaborate, explain or confirm the initial results of Plano Clark and Ivankova (2016, p. 122).

Other authors had different reasons for bringing quantitative and qualitative approaches together. Dey et al. (2019), for example, use qualitative case studies to allow for real-life examples of sustainability practices to strengthen and validate their quantitative findings. They also use a typical QUAN-QUAL mixed method sequence research design as purported by Plano Clark and Ivankova (2016, p. 122). These can be considered to be 'pure' mixed methods (Johnson et al., 2007). In the first stage, they use quantitative survey and this is supported by case study interviews in the second stage. The richer set of data collected using this approach was able to explain why cost rather than process innovations was the driver for leaner production and supply chain efficiencies.

The qualitative dimension was also particularly insightful as to owner/manager's perceptions as to how they could balance economic, environmental and economic considerations. Dey et al. (2018) also used a mixed method study to compare UK and Indian manufacturing SMEs. Using qualitative interviews, followed by a quantitative survey and supportive interviews, the interpretation of their study can be seen as a qual-QUAN-qual design with the statistical approach dominating the study. With regional differences underpinning owner/manager motivations and perceptions, the qualitative dimension to the study was particularly important, even if the study was quantitatively dominant.

In Continental Europe, a Spanish study in recognising the bias that managers bring to EMS implementation, was recognised by Heras and Arana (2010) who used qualitative data to inform a quantitative study. Qualitative data was first captured through stakeholder interviews and case studies to inform the quantitative stage. Adding strength to the study's design, further interviews with key management, operators and consultants were held beyond the quantitative data collection stage. The study could be seen as an equal weighting of data collection at each stage of a Qual-Quan-Qual sequence (Non-capitalisation is used to denote an equal weighting of each strand in this design). The authors concluded that the reason for EMS adoption was the environmental performance of the company rather than due to customer or company image.

Elsewhere in Europe, Ghadge et al. (2017) chose the Greek dairy industry as the focus of an environmental investigation. A quantitative survey was rolled out across different regions of Greece to get a good mix of data. This data was integrated with expert opinions through a multi-criteria decision-making approach to tackle complex environmental problems. Data analysis of the quantitative data was subject to qualitative expert opinion and systems thinking and subjected to a Data Validation Approach of sensitivity analysis and data interpretation. Expert opinions and casual loop findings were used to identify the priority weights. This provided a deeper and added dimension to the data set as expert opinions allowed for the prioritisation of each challenge for implementing sustainable practices.

The growth of mixed method studies beyond the United Kingdom and Europe eventually spread to other regions of the world. In the United States, for example, studies of sustainable entrepreneurship have been undertaken by Gagnon (Gagnon, 2012; Gagnon et al., 2013; Gagnon and Heinrichs, 2016). Both QUAL-QUAN and QUAN-QUAL sequential designs are used in two key studies which are explored in more depth in Chapter 5.

Meanwhile, concern by Chinese SME owners/managers that business competitiveness surveys may have tax, regulatory and competitive implications guided the decision to use a mixed method approach (Tang and Tang, 2012, 2016). The approach by Tang and Tang (2012, 2016), therefore, used a qualitative component in the first instance, before the main quantitative survey. A qual-QUAN design was particularly useful for obtaining a complete insight of the research phenomena, which Teddlie and Tashakkori (2010) describe as characteristically a benefit of using a mixed-method design.

The use of the first 'qual' stage allowed Tang and Tang (2016) to 'verify the face validity of our measures and collect the information beyond the questionnaire.' (p. 153). But it also permitted longitudinal data collection and comprehensive measures to prevent survey bias, so as to improve the study's trustworthiness. The study combined '10 in-depth interviews, a pre-test, and a larger-scale field survey to cross-validate the data.' (p. 153). The findings reveal that government and media have moderating effects on the environmental behaviours of SMEs, with the media identified as having a negative effect on SME environmental performance. The interviews, in particular, are important in verifying the survey findings that customers place cost and delivery time as more important than environmental behaviour. In addition, the interviews showed how SME owners/managers explained ways around environmental compliance. In their second paper (Tang, 2016), they describe how power imbalances between an SME and competitors promotes environmental strengths. This might happen either when the SME becomes a market leader and can afford to invest in environmentally friendly behaviours or identifies as a market laggard and attempts to comply with new market norms.

In the Indian subcontinent, mixed method research in the field was in its ascendancy. In India, Hasan (2016) applies two sequential stages with an initial quantitative survey of 110 SMEs, followed by a more in-depth examination using semi-structured interviews with owner/managers recruited in the first stage. As Hasan (2016, p. 589) explains, 'Two data collection techniques - a self-administered (paper-based) questionnaire survey and semi-structured interviews - were sequentially used.' The inclusion of the qualitative dimension was able to further confirm Petts et al. (1998) UK finding that a gap exists between SME owner/managers attitudes and their behaviours and also to demonstrate this phenomenon beyond the previous UK and European context. The qualitative component points towards an important contradiction. While the quantitative survey shows that Indian SME owners/managers believe that social responsibility goes further than providing donations and has implications for business operations, the interviews reveal that the owners/managers do not understand the concept of philanthropy. In India too, Groot et al. (2019) use a more integrated mixed-method design whereby quantitative data is collected on costs, prices, and technology during the qualitative interviews. This study showed that a broad-ranging stakeholder engagement and technology adoption were sustainability enablers whilst government and market forces acted barriers toward sustainability adoption.

The use of a two-stage quantitative study followed by a qualitative study has also been used in Pakistan. As Raza and Majid (2016) put it: 'The use of these two sources allowed authors in reducing potential bias, increasing the authenticity of the study findings and intensely understanding the background of data analysis methods.' (p. 2631). The study showed that CSR activities were informal with only a few SMEs formalising their operations. The deeper scrutiny in both Indian and Pakistan studies reveals that in a developing country, the social context of philanthropy appears different than the Western concept because giving money is a consequence of religious and culture practices rather than concerted intent to impart CSR practice within business operations.

Meanwhile, in Iran, Hosseininia and Ramezani (2016) used a mixed method approach, employing the use of questionnaires and interviews from a sample size of approximately 130 participants and 12 owner-managers of SMEs in the food industry. Findings from this study showed that certain characteristics of the entrepreneur, including work experience and education, have a significant impact on sustainable entrepreneurship both socially and environmentally. In particular, the authors point out that the mixed methods approach allowed them to get a fuller picture of sustainable entrepreneurship from the study. For example, they state that: 'The results of this study have shown that though considering the future of the earth and environment is ranked second in the qualitative research and fourth according to the quantitative results, in total, this determinant of SE in SMEs of food industry has been given fourth place.' (p. 14).

South America has also seen the rise of mixed methods in SME and environment research, with contributions from Campos (2012, p. 141) describing how they use a 'quali-quantitative' (p. 44) study, as they make use of both quantitative and qualitative methodologies. Predominantly, the study uses a quantitative web-based survey seeking the views about EMS across 1250 industrial and construction SME and larger companies in Southern Brazil. Results from this study showed that there are 10 key criteria for engaging SMEs with EMS which include company policy, understanding legislation concerning environmental aspects, documentation, monitoring and operations. The journal paper presenting this study, however, does not elaborate further on the design of the mixed method approach and how the qualitative aspect is integrated into the study.

Fernández-Viñé et al. (2010, 2013) have developed a comprehensive mixed method approach to understanding environmental issues in Venezuelan SMEs. In their first study, Fernández-Viñé et al. (2010) used a three-part research approach as they found a low level of information on eco-efficiency uptake in Venezuelan SMEs. The first part of the research used a literature review of Venezuelan SME eco-efficiency behaviours, followed by a quantitative survey of 54 Venezuelan SMEs. The final stage employed a qualitative assessment provided by 6 national experts in cleaner production and eco-efficiency, and they provided richer insights.

The practice of bringing in diverse views, that of national experts, demonstrates the added value of using a mixed method research approach (Teddlie and Tashakkori, 2010). The authors developed this approach as they were also informed by Okoli and Pawlowski (2004) in stating that, 'due to the complexity and multi-faceted dimensions of eco-efficiency, qualitative rather than quantitative analysis can be used to explore eco-efficiency development levels in Venezuelan industries' (Fernández-Viñé et al., 2010, p. 738). This particular qualitative approach was further informed by methodologies for engaging expert opinions (Yin, 2003) and resulted in the use of predominately structured interviews. Their results show that Venezuelan SMEs are environmentally reactive only to reducing costs and regulatory compliance. An obvious value of this mixed method study was that it was able to dig deeply into the structural weaknesses in regulatory, market, customer pressure and general stakeholder environments that existed in Venezuela. The authors compared the situation with Europe and Mexico and concluded that not only is the strength of the regulatory environment important but also that public and media pressure only comes to the fore when a nation's environment is degraded or when specific events are reported in the media.

In their second study of Venezuelan SMEs, Fernández-Viñé et al. (2013, p. 266) describe how they use a 'stepwise method'. In a rare practice exhibited in mixed method journal papers, not only do they graphically display their methodology but they link this study to the initial Fernández-Viñé et al. (2010) study. By reviewing both this study and an earlier Venezuelan study, they were able to engage a broader range of technical experts through a Delhi tool regarding barriers, incentives and public administration tools for eco-efficient support. This allowed for development of key criteria of public administration eco-efficiency tools (such as cost, effectiveness and time), and the mathematical modelling of tool effectiveness in SMEs. As in their previous study, from 2010, they found that SMEs do not believe they have significant environmental impacts; rather that protection of the environment is an imposed cost more so than a market opportunity.

In Argentina, a structured, pre-planned mixed method study by Listen-Heyes and Vazquez-Brust (2014) similarly shows that in the context of a developing country, environmental 'reactivism' and weak environmental attitudes are associated with a reliance on economic and regulatory forces to solve environmental problems. Nonetheless, the study shows that the strengthening of these forces can positively change environmental attitudes and can be a powerful intervention in improving SMEs' environmental performance. The study also provides a comprehensive and insightful graphic display of the use of sequential qualitative-quantitative methodology. In the first phase, 50 semi-structured interviews and an analysis of corporate reports and audits have been used. This phase is critical in exploring the beliefs, stories and operating context, and in developing the theoretical framework. It also provides the findings to develop the second phase and demonstrates how sequenced strands (a qualitative strand and then a quantitative strand) can be integrated through a rigorous mixed-method design (Teddlie and Tashakkori, 2010). The second phase was, thus, able to test the framework developed in the first phase. A focus group was initially used to pilot and test the survey instrument which was conducted (n=536) based on Argentinian industrial SMEs. Environmental and senior managers and accountants were surveyed. The survey also helped in achieving the study's third objective, a comparison of environmental beliefs and attitudes of individuals responsible for environmental affairs and the company reports and documentation.

In the Southern hemisphere, several mixed method studies have been undertaken in recent years. In New Zealand, for example, a two-phase mixed method study explored employee perceptions of CSR communication that already held CSR commitments demonstrated through their membership of 'The NZ Business Council for Sustainable Development' and 'Sustainable Business Network' (Brunton et al., 2017). Initially, qualitative interviews with 20 CSR managers were triangulated with website data and revealed insights to the company's CSR initiatives and communication culture. Informed by this first stage, an online quantitative tool was constructed, seeking feedback from the employees. The survey asked questions about the company's CSR activities, with several questions grounded in the findings from the first phase interviews. The results identify that effective CSR communication is a two-way process, requiring a close relationship between company CSR initiatives, heightened environmental awareness and an embedded CSR culture.

Another situation where regulatory enforcement is weak lies in the context of small-scale wineries in South Africa. In their quantitative-qualitative sequential mixed method study, Hamann et al. (2017) explore the environmental proactivity of South African wineries. The study used a quantitative survey of a sample of 500 wine firms with 55 respondents. As the quantitative findings did not appear significantly robust enough, a comparative case study analysis of seven SME wineries was utilised to engage more deeply with the companies, to contextualise the investigation and provide robustness to the study. The qualitative dimension allowed winery owners/managers to reflect on the fact that since they had close control over the company's operations, they were well placed to realise their environmental intentions. Another aspect that the interviews were able to uncover was stated in the study as follows: 'Although South Africa has relatively comprehensive and progressive environmental legislation, the state's enforcement capacity is often limited at the local level, as confirmed also by our interviewees. Wineries' rural location also limits the likely role of NGO activism and residents' complaints.' (p. 46). Importantly too, the study shows that not only is environmental responsibility a driving force for improving environmental performance but also competitiveness.

In Taiwan, Matinaro et al. (2019) use a case study approach to build a sustainable business model. The case study is chosen to investigate real-life contexts (Yin, 1983) and make use of multiple data sources to corroborate, validate and provide consistency in the case study data. The first phase of the case study design uses a literature review and a 'qualitative questionnaire' (p. 1156) which is then analysed using a quantitative GRA method/content analysis. The methodology seeks to strengthen data reliability within the one case study by using multiple analysts to review the results. This allows for data interpretation through multiple theoretical perspectives while examining and interpreting data. The study bears light on the central role that strategy and organisational culture play in developing and implementing a sustainable business model.

Turning to Canada, Westman (2019) wanted to explore the underlying conceptualisation that pervades the SME and sustainability literature that sustainable business practice in SMEs is driven either by profit maximisation or individual values and beliefs. The first phase of the study was developed to understand the antecedents that shape sustainability attitudes and their relative importance in understanding why sustainability issues are important for business. This was examined through a quantitative survey of over 1,600 Canadian SMEs. In the second phase, complementary, semi-structured interviews were used to delve deeper into the actual motivations of business sustainability leaders who had already undertaken sustainability interventions, including those with a sustainable business model. They found that SMEs should be identified as social actors where individual values, internal and external interpersonal relationships and embedment in a social environment form a more holistic view of the manner by which SMEs operate as sustainable businesses.

3.5 Discussion and conclusion

Research inquiry into the environmental behaviours of SMEs has been shown, in this chapter, to have significantly increased since the early 1990s, when a small group of primarily British researchers began to explore the area using mixed-method designs (e.g., Baylis et al., 1998; Petts et al., 1999). At the same time, researchers in Denmark started the Danish Environmental Management Survey initiative which developed a series of more quantitative investigations from 1992 to 2016 (Madsen et al., 1993). This was later expanded to a Nordic Environmental Business Barometer study (Madsen and Ulhøi, 1995). While the quantitative approach had initially also accelerated and dominated research in other countries, since the year 2000, the number of qualitative studies has been on the increase. In recent times, quantitative research has rapidly resumed, ever since the fall in studies from 2000 to 2009. This comes amidst increasingly more sophisticated software and algorithms, and perhaps a more recent focus on the importance of hard data that drives evidence-based policy. Meanwhile, mixed method studies from 1990 to 2020 have constituted an average of around 15% of the total number of studies in the field.

The mapped development in this chapter shows that mixed methods have still to find prominence in the field and that this could be influenced by various factors. Significant quantitative research has been undertaken to determine physical measures pertaining to environmental management as well as perceptual measures of attitudes and motivations for environmental management. In addition, researchers schooled in qualitative research have increasingly informed the field with studies into the underlying characteristics that influence environmental attitudes, motivations and behaviours. It may be this 'schooling effect' that also shapes a strong emphasis by many researchers on using quantitative tools to study sustainability in SMEs.

Different barriers may also be at play. Undertaking mixed method studies, for example, requires either the development of teams of researchers with divergent disciplinary schooling or more extensive training across different quantitative and qualitative methodologies. Another barrier to conducting mixed methods that may influence its low uptake in the field is the high level of research funding and time commitment that is required.

Nonetheless, the existing body of research that mixed method represents may allow researchers to capture a greater sense and understanding of the complexities around sustainability than mono-methods ever could. Its use in sharpening the research questions for quantitative investigations and corroborative capability perhaps allows this smaller body of research to have more reliable and trustworthy output than the broader body of work generated through mono-methods. It is also seen in this chapter that the geographical reach of mixed methods is stretching out, beyond the confines of UK and Europe, to Africa, the Americas and Australasia.

References

Ammenberg, J., and Hjelm, O. (2003). Tracing business and environmental effects of environmental management system - A study of networking small and medium-sized enterprises using a join environmental management system. *Business Strategy and the Environment*, 12(3), 163–174.

Anglada, M. (2000). Small and medium-sized enterprises' perceptions of the environment. In R. Hillary (Ed.), *Small and medium-sized enterprises and the environment: Business imperitives* (1st ed., 61–74). Greenleaf, Sheffield.

Baylis, R.N., Connell, L.M., and Flynn, A. C. (1997). *Pollution and waste regulation survey of manufacturing and processing companies in industrial South Wales: A preliminary analysis, papers in Environmental Planning Research* (No. 14). Cardiff University.

Baylis, R., Connell, L., and Flynn, A. (1998). Company size, environmental regulation and ecological modernization: Further analysis at the level of the firm. *Business Strategy and the Environment*, 7(5), 150–161.

Bazeley, M. (2009). Integrating data analysis in mixed methods. *Journal of Mixed Methods Research*, 3(3), 203–207. Sage, London.

Biondi, V.B., Frey, M., and Iraldo, F. (2000). Environmental management systems and SMEs. *Green Management International*, 29, 55–69.

Boyer, K. K., and Swink, M. L. (2008). Empirical elephants - Why multiple methods are essential to quality research in operations and supply chain management. *Journal of Operations Management*, 26(3), 338–344.

Brunton, M., Eweje, G., and Taskin, N. (2017). Communicating corporate social responsibility to internal stakeholders: Walking the walk or just talking the talk? *Business Strategy and the Environment*, 26(1), 31–48.

Campos, L. M. S. (2012). Environmental management systems (EMS) for small companies: A study in Southern Brazil. *Journal of Cleaner Production*, 32, 141–148.

Cloquell-Ballester, V. A., Monterde-Díaz, R., Cloquell-Ballester, V. A., and Torres-Sibille, A. del C. (2008). Environmental education for small-and medium-sized enterprises: Methodology and e-learning experience in the Valencian region. *Journal of Environmental Management*, 87(3), 507–520.

Creswell, J.W., and Plano Clark, V.L. (2011). *Choosing a mixed methods design*. In *Designing and conducting mixed methods research* (2nd ed., 53–68). Sage, Thousand Oaks.

Creswell, J.W. and Plano Clark, V.L. (2018). *Designing and conducting mixed methods research* (3rd ed.). Sage, Thousand Oaks.

Dey, P. K., Malesios, C., De, D., Chowdhury, S., and Abdelaziz, F. Ben. (2019). Could lean practices and process innovation enhance supply chain sustainability of small and medium-sized enterprises? *Business Strategy and the Environment*, 28(4), 582–598.

Dey, P. K., Petridis, N. E., Petridis, K., Malesios, C., Nixon, J. D., and Ghosh, S. K. (2018). Environmental management and corporate social responsibility practices of small and medium-sized enterprises. *Journal of Cleaner Production*, 195, 687–702.

Ferenhof, H. A., Vignochi, L., Selig, P. M., Lezana, Á. G. R., and Campos, L. M. S. (2014). Environmental management systems in small and medium-sized enterprises: An analysis and systematic review. *Journal of Cleaner Production*, 74, 44–53.

Fernández-Viñé, M. B., Gómez-Navarro, T., and Capuz-Rizo, S. F. (2013). Assessment of the public administration tools for the improvement of the eco-efficiency of small and medium sized enterprises. *Journal of Cleaner Production*, 47, 265–273.

Fernández-Viñé, M. B., Gómez-Navarro, T., and Capuz-Rizo, S. F. (2010). Eco-efficiency in the SMEs of Venezuela. Current status and future perspectives. *Journal of Cleaner Production*, 18(8), 736–746.

Friedman, A. L., Miles, S., and Adams, C. (2000). Small and medium-sized enterprises and the environment: Evaluation of a specific initiative aimed at all small and medium-sized enterprises. *Journal of Small Business and Enterprise Development*, 7(4), 325–342.

Gagnon, M. (2012). Sustainable minded entrepreneurs: Developing and testing a values-based framework. *Journal of Strategic Innovation and Sustainability*, 8(1), 9–25.

Gagnon, M. A., and Heinrichs, P. A. (2016). Food entrepreneur sustainable orientation and firm practices, *International Journal of Food and Agricultural Economics*, 4(4), 11–28.

Gagnon, M., Michael, J., Elser, N., and Gyory, C. (2013). Seeing green in several ways: The interplay of entrepreneurial, sustainable and market orientations on executive scanning and small business performance. *Journal of Marketing Development and Competitiveness*, 7(3), 9–29.

Gerrans, P., and Hutchinson, B. (2000). Sustainable development and small and medium-sized enterprises: a long way to go. In R. Hillary (Ed.), *Small and medium-sized enterprises and the environment: business imperitives* (5th ed., 75–81). Greenleaf, Sheffield.

Gerstenfield, A., and Roberts, H. (2000). Size matters: Barriers and prospects for environmental management in small and medium-sized enterprises. In R. Hillary (Ed.), *Small and medium-sized enterprises and the environment: Business imperitives* (1st ed., 106–118). Greenleaf, Sheffield.

Ghadge, A., Kaklamanou, M., Choudhary, S., and Bourlakis, M. (2017). Implementing environmental practices within the Greek dairy supply chain drivers and barriers for SMEs. *Industrial Management and Data Systems*, 117(9), 1995–2014.

Groot, A. E., Bolt, J. S., Jat, H. S., Jat, M. L., Kumar, M., Agarwal, T., and Blok, V. (2019). Business models of SMEs as a mechanism for scaling climate smart technologies: The case of Punjab, India. *Journal of Cleaner Production*, 210, 1109–1119.

Hamann, R., Smith, J., Tashman, P., and Marshall, R. S. (2017). Why do SMEs go green? An analysis of wine firms in South Africa. *Business and Society*, 56(1), 23–56.

Hasan, M. N. (2016). Measuring and understanding the engagement of Bangladeshi SMEs with sustainable and socially responsible business practices: An ISO 26000 perspective. *Social Responsibility Journal*, 12(3), 584–610.

Heras, I., and Arana, G. (2010). Alternative models for environmental management in SMEs: The case of Ekoscan vs. ISO 14001. *Journal of Cleaner Production*, 18(8), 726–735.

Hillary, R. (2000). *Small and medium-sized enterprises and the environment* (1st ed.). Greenleaf, Sheffield.

Hosseininia, G., and Ramezani, A. (2016). Factors influencing sustainable entrepreneurship in small and medium-sized enterprises in Iran: A case study of food industry. *Sustainability*, 8(10). doi:10.3390/su8101010

Hutchinson, A., and Chaston, I. (1994). Environmental management in Devon and Cornwall's small and medium-sized enterprise sector, *Business Strategy and the Environment*, 3(1), 15–22.

Johnson, M. P., and Schaltegger, S. (2016). Two decades of sustainability management tools for SMEs: How far have we come? *Journal of Small Business Management*, 54(2), 481–505.

Johnson, R. B., Onwuegbuzie, A. J., and Turner, L. A. (2007). Toward a definition of mixed methods research. *Journal of Mixed Methods Research*, 1(2), 112–133.

Kemp, S.A., and Duff, C. (2000). Small firms and the environment: Factors that influence small and medium-sized enterprises' environmental behaviour. In R. Hillary (Ed.), *Small and medium-sized enterprises and the environment: Business imperitives* (1st ed., 24–34). Greenleaf, Sheffield.

Lekhanya, L. M., and Dlamini, L. H. (2017). Customer's perception towards product quality of automotive SMEs operating in Metropolitan areas, and consideration of environmental impact. *Environmental Economics*, 8(1), 36–45.

Liston-Heyes, C., and Vazquez-Brust, D. A. (2016). Environmental protection in environmentally reactive firms: Lessons from corporate Argentina. *Journal of Business Ethics*, 135(2), 361–379.

Lopes de Sousa Jabbour, A. B., Ndubisi, N. O., and Roman Pais Seles, B. M. (2020). Sustainable development in Asian manufacturing SMEs: Progress and directions. *International Journal of Production Economics*, 225. doi.org/10.1016/j.ijpe.2019.107567

López-Gamero, M. D., Claver-Cortés, E., and Molina-Azorín, J. F. (2008). Complementary resources and capabilities for an ethical and environmental management: A qual/quan study. *Journal of Business Ethics*, 82(3), 701–732.

Madsen, H., and Ulhøi, J. P. (1995). Methodological problems in international comparisons based on national surveys. In: Wolff, R., (Ed.), *The Nordic Business Environmental Barometer* (88–95). The Economist's Publishing Company, Oslo.

Madsen, H., Ulhøi, J. P., and Rikhardsson, P. (1993). *Sustainable corporate management in Denmark. Research agenda and planning the initial survey.* DEMS Working Paper 1. The Aarhus School of Business, Aarhus.

Matinaro, V., Liu, Y., Lee, T. R., Jiun S., and Poesche, J. (2019). Extracting key factors for sustainable development of enterprises: Case study of SMEs in Taiwan. *Journal of Cleaner Production*, 209, 1152–1169.

Merritt, J. Q. (1998). EM into SM won't go? Attitudes, awareness and practices in the London Borough of Croydon. *Business Strategy and the Environment*, 7(2), 90–100.

Muñoz-Pascual, L., Curado, C., and Galende, J. (2019). How does the use of information technologies affect the adoption of environmental practices in SMEs? A mixed-methods approach. *Review of Managerial Science*, 118–146.

Okoli, C., and Pawlowski, S. D. (2004). The Delphi method as a research tool: An example, design considerations and applications. *Information and Management*, 42(1), 15–29.

Peters, M., and Turner, R. K. (2004). SME environmental attitudes and participation in local–scale untary intiatives: Some practical applications. *Journal of Environmental Planning and Management*, 47(3), 449–473.

Petts. J. (2000). Small and medium-sized enterprises and environmental compliance: attitudes among management and non-management. In R. Hillary (Ed.), *Small and medium-sized enterprises and the environment: Business imperatives* (1st ed., 49–60). Greenleaf, Sheffield.

Petts, J., Herd, A., and O'Heocha, M. (1998). Environmental responsiveness, individuals and organizational learning: SME experience. *Journal of Environmental Planning and Management*, 41(6), 711–730.

Plano Clark, V.L., and Ivankova, N.V. (2016). *Mixed methods research: A guide to the field*. Sage, Los Angeles.

Raza, J., and Majid, A. (2016). Perceptions and practices of corporate social responsibility among SMEs in Pakistan. *Quality and Quantity*, 50(6), 2625–2650.

Rothenberg, S., and Becker, M. (2004). Technical assistance programs and the diffusion of environmental technologies in the printing industry: The Case of SMEs. *Business and Society*, 43(4), 366–397.

Rowe, J., and Hollingsworth, D. (1996). Improving the environmental performance of small- and medium-sized enterprises: A study in Avon. *Eco-Management and Auditing*, 3, 97–107.

Sainidis, E., and Robson, A. (2016). Environmental turbulence: Impact on UK SMEs' manufacturing priorities. *Management Research Review*, 39(10), 1239–1264.

Simpson, M., Taylor, N., and Barker, K. (2004). Environmental responsibility in SMEs: Does it deliver competitive advantage? *Business Strategy and the Environment*, 13(3), 156–171.

Stokes, A. (2000). Book Reviews: R.Hilary (Ed.) (2000), Small and medium-sized enterprises and the environment: Business imperatives, *International Small Business Journal*, 19(1), 100–102.

Tang, Z., and Tang, J. (2012). Stakeholder-firm power difference, stakeholders' CSR orientation, and SMEs' environmental performance in China. *Journal of Business Venturing*, 27(4), 436–455.

Tang, Z., and Tang, J. (2016). The impact of competitors-firm power divergence on Chinese SMEs' environmental and financial performance. *Journal of Business Ethics*, 136(1), 147–165.

Teddlie, C., and Tashakkori, A. (2010). *Sage Handbook of mixed methods in social and behavioural research* (2nd ed.). Sage, Thousand Oaks.

Thompson, J. K., and Smith, H. L. (1991). Social responsibility and small business: suggestions for research. *Journal of Small Business Management*, 29(1), 30–44.

Tilley, F. (2000). Small firms' environmental ethics: How deep do they go? In R. Hillary (Ed.), *Small and medium-sized enterprises and the environment: Business imperatives* (1st ed., 35–48). Greenleaf, Sheffield.

Ulhøi, J. P., Madsen, H., and Rikhardsson, P. (1996). *Training in environmental management- industry and sustainability*. Office for Official Publications for the European Communities, Luxembourg.

Westman, L., Luederitz, C., Kundurpi, A., Mercado, A. J., Weber, O., and Burch, S. L. (2019). Conceptualizing businesses as social actors: A framework for understanding sustainability actions in small- and medium-sized enterprises. *Business Strategy and the Environment*, 28(2), 388–402.

Wiesner, R., Chadee, D., and Best, P. (2018). Managing change toward environmental sustainability: A conceptual model in small and medium enterprises. *Organization and Environment*, 31(2), 152–177.

Williams, A., Kennedy, S., Philipp, F., and Whiteman, G. (2017). Systems thinking: A review of sustainability management research. *Journal of Cleaner Production*, 148, 866–881.

Yin, R. K. (2003). *Case study research design and methods* (3rd ed.). Sage, New York.

3.6 Appendices

Table 3.3 Journals publishing SME and Environment research

Journal	Clarivate Analytics Web of Science Impact Factor 2019	Scope Cite Score 2020	Quan	Qual	MM
Journal of Cleaner Production	7.246	10.9	22	17	11
Business Strategy and the Environment	5.483	8.4	22	14	8
CSR and Environmental Management	4.542	5.9	11	5	0
Journal of Business Ethics	4.141	7.0	4	13	3
Journal of Environmental Management	5.647	7.6	4	0	2
Long Range Planning	4.041	8.6	0	0	1
Management Decision	2.723	3.9	2	1	0
Small Business Economics	4.803	7.3	2	1	0
International Small Business Journal	3.756	8.9	2	0	0
Business and Society	4.074	9.4	0	1	2
Quant Qual	1.154	NA	0	0	1
Sustainability	2.576	3.2	18	0	2
Business Research Quarterly	2.525	6.2	1	0	0
Business Ethics Quarterly	2.625	4.9	1	0	0
Journal of General Management	0.400	1.3	0	0	1
Journal of Environmental Planning and Management	2.093	3.7	0	1	2
Greener Management International*	0.49	0	1	1	2
Organization and Environment	3.33	9.1	1	0	0
Journal of Small Business Management	3.461	5.9	1	0	0

*Greener Management International has been discontinued.

Key: Quan = Qualitative, Qual = Quantitative and MM = Mixed Methods

Part B
Mixed methods in sustainability SME research
A global outlook

4 Mixed methods research and environmental management

A reflective perspective of a research group and some lessons from experience

José F. Molina-Azorin, Maria D. Lopez-Gamero, Juan Jose Tari, Jorge Pereira-Moliner, and Eva M. Pertusa-Ortega

4.1 Introduction

We are a Spanish research group at the University of Alicante, Spain. Our main research interests in the field of management are strategy, environmental and quality management. From a methodological perspective, we have used several key types of research methods, conducting quantitative, qualitative and mixed methods studies to bring a greater understanding and perspective to these fields of management.

The purpose of this chapter is to describe our mixed methods way of thinking as applied to the field of environmental management. We reflect upon our experiences using mixed methods research in several articles and research projects that we have conducted. In particular, we discuss what justified our methodological choice of implementing mixed methods in our studies and highlight the potential advantages and challenges of mixed methods research. Before we delve into these issues, in the next section, we describe our experience in the field of strategic management, where we took our first steps in combining quantitative and qualitative methods.

4.2 Discovering the usefulness of combining quantitative and qualitative methods

A member of our research team (JFMA) conducted his doctoral dissertation several years ago (from 1996 to 2000). This research was developed in the field of strategic management, and it focused on the relationship between strategic groups and firm profitability in the construction industry. This study analysed whether membership of a firm in a specific strategic group (group of companies with similar competitive strategies) influences its profitability. The research was designed and planned as a quantitative study. The plan was to prepare a questionnaire with closed questions as the main data collection technique, and then to apply planned techniques of statistical analysis to test hypotheses (cluster analysis to determine the strategic groups and next, ANOVA, to test whether there were differences in performance among these groups).

Early in the research process, however, he realised that he needed to carry out some previous steps before conducting the quantitative research. Specifically, primary data would provide the underpinning level of knowledge and understanding pertaining to the research phenomenon (mainly, how companies compete in this specific industry). To this end, a first qualitative phase would be helpful in providing this foundation. He, thus, undertook several interviews with managers and representatives of professional associations in this industry. These interviews helped him to understand the industry context more comprehensively and allowed him to determine the main competitive variables in this industry that were used in the questionnaire for the quantitative phase. Together with these interviews, he also conducted a case study, examining in depth, a construction company through interviews with their managers and analysis of documents.

A key point that we would like to emphasise is that he was conducting a combination of qualitative and quantitative methods without really knowing at that time that there was a specific label and methodological literature for this combination and integration known as mixed methods. Moreover, he was also conducting a prevalence study about the type of articles published on a specific management theory (the resource-based theory). From the outset, the purpose was to determine and compare the number of three groups of studies: conceptual/theoretical, quantitative and qualitative articles. Together with these three types of studies, however, he also found a fourth group that was not planned: articles that combined quantitative and qualitative methods (e.g., Sharma and Vredenburg, 1998). This was challenging as these articles could not be put in the traditional quantitative or in the qualitative box. In consequence, he created a new group, entitled 'combined quantitative and qualitative methods'.

The first combined application of quantitative and qualitative methods was, therefore, not pre-planned. It was not a deliberate research strategy. In both cases (in the doctoral dissertation and in the review literature on the resource-based theory), the combination of quantitative and qualitative methods was considered as an emergent, opportunistic approach.

This acquired knowledge around combining qualitative and quantitative methods, interested him and he began a literature search on this combination. In the University of Alicante library, he found an interesting Spanish book, by Bericat (1998) titled "*La integración de los métodos cuantitativo y cualitativo en la investigación social*" ("The integration of quantitative and qualitative methods in social research"). Reading the references list of this book, he found important and seminal references that examine a combination of quantitative and qualitative methods, such as Brannen (1992), Bryman (1988), Creswell (1994), Greene et al. (1989), Jick (1979), Morgan (1998), Morse (1991) and Sieber (1973). Together with these works, Daft (1983) was also one of his first readings about the combination of quantitative and qualitative research and the view of scholarly research as a craft. Only Jick (1979) and Daft (1983) are scholars from the field of management. Most authors work in other fields (mainly education, health sciences and sociology). These first readings proved to be very important to JFMA, as they increased his interest in the integration of quantitative and qualitative methods.

4.3 Research questions and methodological choices in environmental management research

Some few years later, in our research group, we started to undertake environmental management research. JFMA examined the relationship between environmental management and strategic management, describing how environmental issues can be included in the strategic management process and how environmental management influences firm competitiveness.

Later, two doctoral dissertations (from 2001 to 2005 by MDLG and JPM) addressed this fast-developing field of environmental management. While the doctoral dissertation by MDLG focused exclusively on environmental management in different industries, JPM's dissertation addressed key issues that determined competitiveness in the hotel industry. Not only did this include an examination of environmental management practices but also other important factors such as quality management and human resource management. The methods used in these two dissertations differed and it is, therefore, interesting to examine our choices regarding research questions and methods.

4.4 The research methods we know may determine the research questions we ask

JPM conducted his doctoral dissertation studying key determinants of competitiveness in the hotel industry. The plan was to carry out a quantitative study to examine the influence of key antecedents of competitive advantage in this industry. As in the case of the PhD research on the construction industry, however, he realised that first he needed to identify these key determinants. The best approach, therefore, was to conduct a first qualitative phase based on data collected from interviews with managers and other important stakeholders in the hotel industry. These interviews also helped to increase knowledge of the industry context and to develop theory and hypotheses that was then tested in the second quantitative phase.

A key point that we would like to emphasise is the relationship between research questions and methods. The traditional view is that the research question determines the specific methods (Tashakkori and Teddlie, 1998). Then, scholars are expected to select the best tools available in their methodological toolbox to answer the stated questions. We tend to believe, however, that there is a reciprocal relationship between questions and methods. So, while the research questions indeed influence the methods we use, the methods we master may also influence the research questions we ask (Mertens et al., 2016).

This idea was pretty clear when we began to explore environmental management problems. In the research about strategy in the construction industry, a predetermined statistical analysis was planned. This first quantitative part utilised a cluster analysis to determine the strategic groups (groups of firms with similar competitive strategies) proceeded by an ANOVA analysis to examine whether there are differences in performance among these competitive groups. As we mastered these statistical techniques, we then asked: Are there differences in performance between hotels with different levels of environmental proactivity? This research question was determined because we again wanted to use cluster analysis (to identify environmental groups of companies with similar levels of environmental proactivity) and ANOVA (allowing for analysing whether there are performance differences between these environmental groups). From a methodological point of view, therefore, an important realisation that happened when we conducted our research on environmental management is that the methods we knew, and applied, in competitive strategy and strategic groups tended to determine the research questions we ended up asking in relation to environmental management.

The point here is that scholars are at risk of (implicitly) sticking with and relying on the methods they initially learned and actually used during their doctoral programmes and/or previous training. When researchers develop expertise in using some methods where they feel comfortable, it is hard to break from that (Mertens et al., 2016), which also seemed to be the case in our research group. If methods influence the research questions, then an important consequence is that, by extending our methodological skills, it is possible to improve (broaden/widen) the question-asking process. A key learning, therefore, is that by extending and sharpening our methodological skills, we can increase the rigour of our conceptual thinking, see new ways to answer research questions, and even identify questions that would not have occurred to us otherwise (Edwards, 2008).

In this regard, exposure to and experience with mixed methods can indeed play a key role. As indicated by Mertens et al. (2016, p. 7), 'because mixed methods research combines and integrates quantitative and qualitative methods, the researcher is motivated to develop a broader set of research skills. Training in mixed methods can overcome the tendency to rely on known methods and play an important role in widening and extending our repertoire of methods if the training emphasises the importance of combining, comparing, and mixing different methodologies.' This aspect of widening our toolkit of methods has been a key idea for us not only for trying to provide well-focused answers to research questions but also for identifying interesting and relevant research questions.

4.5 A deliberate and planned combination of quantitative and qualitative methods in environmental management

In the doctoral dissertation by MDLG that addresses the main antecedents and consequences of environmental management in several industries, she conducted research based on a deliberate combination of qualitative and quantitative methods. In 2001, the topic of environmental management was still not mature in the management field, and a combination of qualitative and quantitative methods through a sequential design, with a first qualitative phase, was considered as appropriate for knowing the context, developing theory and determining adequate questions and hypotheses for testing in the second quantitative phase. The first qualitative phase was carried out through several case studies of companies, collecting data from interviews with managers and employees, observation and documents.

Through this research, we were trying to widen our methodological toolkit as MDLG employed new methods that the members of our research group had not previously used: case study research with several firms in the qualitative phase and structural equation modelling in the quantitative phase. In the following sections, we share some further methodological experiences from this dissertation.

4.6 Discovering mixed methods research literature

We then began to apply the term 'mixed methods research' to our work. In the first instance, Molina-Azorin (2007) authored our first publication, explicitly applying mixed methods research to better understand the resource-based theory of the firm; a prominent theory in strategic management.

Two important works we found via an electronic search engine were the "Sage Handbook of mixed methods in social and behavioural research" by Tashakkori and Teddlie (2003) and an important journal article by Johnson and Onwuegbuzie (2004). We also noted a specifically-focused mixed methods conference, held annually in the UK. Striving to acquire more insight into mixed methods we, thus, attended some of these conferences in 2007, 2008 (in Cambridge), 2009 (in Harrogate) and in 2011 and 2012 (in Leeds). Subsequently, we also attended some of the conferences held by the Mixed Methods International Research Association (MMIRA).

We would like to underline, however, that awareness of specific literature on mixed methods (the main mixed methods purposes, designs, and other issues about this methodological approach) aids in planning, designing and conducting a more comprehensive and improved approach to our research studies in environmental management. Our research, however, also reveals the necessity of taking into account the opportunistic nature of mixed methods. This takes us to one of the main lessons learned: a research study (even a mixed methods study) may not only have a predetermined/planned research design, but also that new components may evolve as data is collected and analysed. In addition, we consider that researchers must be creative and must not be limited by the existing mixed methods designs. The key point here is to create and use designs that effectively answer the research questions we want to study.

4.7 The explicit application of mixed methods research in environmental management

Although scholars have mixed quantitative and qualitative methods for many years, current conceptualisations of mixed methods research did not emerge until the 1980s (Bryman, 1988; Greene et al., 1989). Of course, many scholars have conducted studies with integration of quantitative and qualitative methods, without using the label of 'mixed methods research' (Maxwell, 2016). The contemporary and formalised literature on mixed methods research has developed rapidly in these last few years, emerging as a research methodology with a recognised name and distinct identity (Denscombe, 2008).

The attention, however, devoted to mixed methods in our business and management field in general, as well as in environmental management and sustainability research in particular, has been surprisingly low. For example, although there are articles that use a mixed methods approach, the expression "mixed methods" is not usually used in the title of these mixed methods studies (even in articles published in the last few years), and the literature base of mixed methods is rarely included in the reference sections of mixed methods articles. Digging deeper into this methodological situation in the environmental management literature, and 26 mixed methods articles identified in the journal *Business Strategy and the Environment* (Molina-Azorin and Lopez-Gamero, 2016) were reviewed. For example, only three mixed methods articles included one mixed methods work in the references list. This finding suggests that the advantages, possibilities, purposes, designs and potential of mixed methods research are yet to be acknowledged and realised by environmental management scholars, pointing towards an obvious potential to be further exploited. Next, we indicate our experience with using mixed methods research in our articles, research projects and methodological reviews.

Regarding our mixed methods articles, we would like to highlight two studies derived from the doctoral dissertation by MDLG. Firstly, Lopez-Gamero et al. (2008) examined how firm resources and capabilities influence managers' attitudes toward the natural environment as a competitive opportunity. We found that firm internal resources have a strong influence on business managers' ethical attitudes and on the managers' perception of the natural environment as a competitive opportunity. Moreover, the higher the degree to which the managers identify with the natural environment as a competitive opportunity, the higher is the likelihood of developing a proactive environmental management. Regarding firm size, larger-sized firms tend to integrate environmental practices into their organisation earlier than smaller ones. Larger firms were more capable, and expedient, at being able to respond to stakeholder influences, essentially due to greater resources and need for legitimacy.

From a methodological point of view, this study used a sequential exploratory mixed methods design, with development as the main mixed methods purpose (Greene et al., 1989). Through development, the findings of a method (in this case, the first qualitative part) help implement the other method (in our case, the second quantitative phase). The aims of the qualitative phase were: to reconceptualise and extend theory (identifying the main variables and their relationships through specific propositions), to improve the instrument to be used in the quantitative phase (questionnaire) and to help explain and interpret the findings of the quantitative phase. This qualitative part was realised through case studies of several firms from different industries. Three data sources were used: interviews with managers, direct observation (visit to the facilities) and access to internal and external documents. In the quantitative phase, data to test the propositions were collected using a mail survey, and the analysis was conducted using structural equation modelling.

Secondly, a similar mixed methods design was used by Lopez-Gamero et al. (2009) whereby a first phase involved comparative case studies of eight Spanish firms, and the propositions emerging from this first qualitative phase were then tested through a structural equation model. The main aims of this second article were to study how environmental regulations differ across industries and how it can influence managerial perceptions of the role played by the natural environment as a competitive opportunity.

In more recent research projects, we have also published other mixed methods articles in the field of environmental management. For example, in Molina-Azorin et al. (2015) the team of researchers, i.e., Molina-Azorin, Tari, Pereira-Moliner, Lopez-Gamero and Pertusa-Ortega, also used a sequential exploratory mixed methods design in the hotel industry to examine the effects of environmental management and quality management on the competitiveness of this industry. In the first qualitative phase, interviews were conducted with hotel managers and representatives of hotel associations and other institutions. It was considered appropriate to develop an initial qualitative phase due to the inconclusive and contradictory results found in the literature analysing the relationships between environmental management and competitive advantage, and also to the need to contextualise this analysis in the hotel industry. Through this exploratory qualitative stage, several propositions are established which are then tested in the quantitative phase through structural equation modelling with Partial Least Squares (PLS). The main findings indicate that environmental management and quality management permit the improvement of competitive advantages of costs and differentiation. Moreover, hotels implementing quality programmes find fewer obstacles in implementing environmental management.

We have also conducted mixed methods research projects funded by public institutions (mainly by the Spanish government). These research projects are usually connected, and there is a mixed methods logic and way of thinking, both within each research project and across research projects. Figure 4.1 represents this logic.

In these projects, we use sequential mixed methods designs and we consider that all quantitative and qualitative parts are equally important for our research purposes. Next, we describe two research projects that use a mixed methods approach.

In the first research project, we analysed the relationship between environmental management, competitive strategy and quality management, studying the impact of environmental and quality management on competitive advantage in the hotel industry. In order to examine this main research question, we designed a mixed methods study with three sequential phases, using a QUAL → QUAN → QUAL design. Moreover, this three-phase design includes both exploratory and explanatory parts for several reasons.

It was considered useful to develop an initial qualitative stage due to the inconclusive literature results that analysed the relationships between environmental management and competitive advantage, and the contextual setting of the hotel industry. The purpose of this exploratory qualitative stage was to establish some propositions in this industry context which were then tested in the quantitative stage. Moreover, this qualitative phase also helped develop the questionnaire used in the quantitative phase. The main technique for qualitative data collection was semi-structured in-depth interviews on various issues related to the competitive implications of environmental management. On the basis of these qualitative interviews and previous literature, several propositions were formulated. The main mixed methods purpose of this first qualitative part was development. The consequence was that the results from the first qualitative part – that set the propositions, the development of the questionnaire, and a better knowledge of the industry context – helped develop and carry out the next quantitative part. Therefore, several propositions were tested in this quantitative phase. The findings

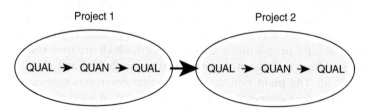

Figure 4.1 Our use of mixed methods research within and across projects.

showed that environmental management impacted cost and differentiation advantages through environmental performance.

The added value and rationale of the third, last qualitative phase in this first research project was to analyse, elaborate and clarify the quantitative results from the point of view of practitioners. We, therefore, conducted new interviews with hotel managers and other stakeholders in the hotel industry with the main mixed methods purpose of complementarity (Greene et al., 1989), an approach used to clarify the quantitative results. These interviews allowed practitioners to elaborate on interesting and relevant insights about the relationships found in the quantitative findings, highlighting the competitive importance of quality and environmental management in the hotel industry. They corroborated the quantitative findings, and therefore achieved another mixed methods purpose, which is to provide more robust and reliable data through triangulation (Greene et al., 1989). Moreover, they also emphasised that competitive strategy, environmental management and quality management must go hand-in-hand in the hotel industry. Furthermore, they also helped to understand how quality management can influence environmental management (through specific processes and similarities).

In addition, an important concept that most managers pointed out during the last qualitative phase of the first research project, was the key role of individuals (managers and employees) in the implementation of environmental management. This concept was found to be highly significant and a thought-provoking finding in the field of environmental management. Furthermore, our knowledge of the academic literature highlighting the importance of human resources management and organisational behaviour to environmental management, was rather limited.

The second research project, currently in progress, has also been designed as a mixed methods study, also with a QUAL → QUAN → QUAL design. We want to analyse the role of employees in the adoption and implementation of environmental management. We considered that it was appropriate to carry out another first qualitative phase before the quantitative part. As in the first research project, the purpose of this exploratory qualitative part is to develop propositions. This qualitative phase also helped us to develop the questionnaire to be used in the quantitative phase. In the next quantitative phase, we are conducting the statistical analysis. And finally, as in the first research project, we will carry out a last explanatory qualitative part to elaborate and clarify quantitative findings from the point of view of practitioners.

We have also conducted methodological reviews about the use of mixed methods. In the field of environmental management, Molina-Azorin and Lopez-Gamero (2016) examined the prevalence, purposes and designs of mixed methods research published from 2004 to 2013, in the journal *Business Strategy and the Environment*. A total of 340 articles were read and 26 mixed methods studies were identified (7.6%). The most common mixed methods purpose were development (the qualitative part helped to improve the understanding of the characteristics of a specific context, facilitating the development of theory and hypotheses, that were next tested in the quantitative part) and expansion (scholars use different methods to assess different facets of a phenomenon) (Greene et al., 1989). Regarding the implementation of data collection, sequential designs were used in most articles (20 articles).

Molina-Azorin and Font (2016) examined the use of mixed methods research in the field of sustainable tourism, examining mixed methods studies published in the *Journal of Sustainable Tourism* from 2005 to 2014. A total of 468 articles were read. The number of mixed methods studies identified was 56 (12%). Again, expansion and development were the main mixed methods purposes. In 30 mixed methods studies, researchers use a sequential implementation (in 20 studies the first phase was the qualitative part). In this methodological review, the authors also conducted interviews with authors of mixed methods studies in order to obtain their opinions and insights about several aspects of mixed methods research (why they choose mixed methods for their studies, the main advantages and added value for sustainable tourism research, the main barriers and challenges, and the role of co-authors in the study).

4.8 Mixed methods, practical relevance and grand challenges for a better society

From our experience, an important opportunity for mixed methods research in management is its potential to examine and solve the grand challenges that face society (George et al., 2016). Grand challenges are ambitious objectives that harness science, technology and innovation to solve important problems. They include issues arising from environmental degradation and climate change, poverty, health, social and economic inequality, and geopolitical instability, among many others issues and may call for new theories, concepts and methods. Here, we believe, is an important role as socially responsible researchers to contribute to social change. For example, as we study the implementation of environmental management in companies, we consider not only the positive competitive effects that environmental management may have on firm profitability, but also the positive impact on the natural environment. Mixed methods research can help address these problems as it allows scholars from diverse groups to have a common language to guide their inquiry, and include participants, stakeholders and policy makers, in these contexts, to be part of the process of problem and solution identification.

These aspects are related to an important problem in the management field, namely, the science-practice divide (Bansal et al., 2012). This problem may be solved through the use of mixed methods. Researchers try to balance the academic rigour of their studies and their practical relevance. From an academic point of view, rigour (in theory development and research design) is usually specified as the main indicator of the quality of a study. Yet, scholars must also consider the practical relevance of their work, both for management practice and for solving societal problems (Tsui, 2013). The purpose of trying to solve grand challenges, therefore, plays a key role within this practical relevance of research approach, especially in the field of environmental management and sustainability.

The use of mixed methods research may facilitate, enhance, consider and broaden the interpretation of the results obtained in order to emphasise the practical implications of a study. With regard to this practical impact, mixed methods can be used to understand the extent to which a study's results are significant in practice by including practitioners' own discourses, with an awareness of inclusion of intended beneficiaries of interventions. In sum, the analysis of grand challenges requires methodological diversity, which may allow mixed methods to play a key role as it promotes the application of a diversity of methods, combining quantitative and qualitative approaches and using information from several and different stakeholders (Molina-Azorin and Fetters, 2019).

4.9 Main obstacles and barriers

There are several obstacles and barriers to conducting mixed methods studies. In this regard, mixed methods studies require extensive time, resources, and effort to carry out the quantitative and qualitative phases, especially the time demands in implementing the quantitative and qualitative parts of the study. Mixed methods research, for example, implies that researchers master a broader set of skills that span both the quantitative and the qualitative (Creswell and Plano Clark, 2018). The need for such skills has definite implications for how researchers need to be trained and has implications for the way academic institutions form education policy for researchers. We recommend the teaching of mixed methods within higher research degree programmes and the building of mixed methods research capacity through mixed methods doctoral workshops (Molina-Azorin and Cameron, 2015).

In addition, there are challenges in publishing mixed methods studies that generally arise from existing constraints. Another challenge of mixed methods studies relates to staying within the page limits. While such limits pose a challenge to all researchers, they are particularly problematic for mixed methods research due to the quantity of information that must be conveyed for a study combining two different methods. Moreover, there is a risk of diluting or diffusing one of the methods (the less important one or the one less accepted by academia) by trying to do too much within the page limit. In summary, by limiting space, journals may discourage the publication of mixed methods research.

4.10 Mixed methods teams

Working as a research team may blend a diverse range of skill sets more able to tackle complexities associated with mixed methods research. In particular, an important issue pertains to working in research teams when undertaking mixed methods studies.

Creswell (2015), for example, points out that there is a growing presence of mixed methods teams that consist of individuals with different methodological orientations (quantitative versus qualitative skills) together with team members who have skills in mixed methods. These mixed methods team members may be a bridge between the quantitative and qualitative members, facilitating the conversation about differences in thinking when they appear. Mixed methods teams may have members with a range of expertise, hold respect for diverse methodological orientations, and have a good leader who bridges across the areas of expertise and methodological orientations.

The team leader ideally must have experience in quantitative, qualitative and mixed methods research. This leader must also pay attention to team composition, give equal treatment to diverse methodologies, help to shape dialogue and values, and involve all team members in decisions. We consider that mixed methods research teams may ask better and more appropriate research questions in the context of sustainability.

4.11 Conclusion

In this chapter, we have indicated our experience with mixed methods. This methodological approach is our way of thinking (Daft, 1983; Greene, 2007) in the environmental management field. There are several positive aspects that we have learned through the use of mixed methods research. Although the research question and context may dictate the choice of the appropriate research methods, and then different methods (quantitative, qualitative and mixed methods) may be chosen depending on the appropriateness of the situational context and research questions, we also consider that the methods we know may determine the questions we ask. Research questions, therefore, inform and are informed by methods. We also consider it is important to plan our research designs, but it is also important to allow slack in the research design as research also has an opportunistic and flexible character. Another important idea is that together with improving research of a specific substantive topic (in our case, environmental management and sustainability issues), we consider it interesting to improve research skills that widen our methodological toolkit. In our case, mixed methods research encourages us to increase our repertoire of methods.

Mixed methods research, however, is not the panacea for all research problems in environmental management research. Moreover, there are several barriers to carrying out mixed methods studies. Mixed methods studies are a challenge because they are perceived as requiring more work and financial input, and they take more time.

As indicated above, mixed methods research is a way of thinking. In our opinion, the advancement of environmental management requires an understanding and application of a variety of research methods, and mixed methods research may play an important role in this use of diverse methods. Mixed methods research shows great promise for addressing environmental topics, but only if scholars understand the design options that accompany this methodological choice. The knowledge of the literature base of mixed methods research and the analysis of empirical papers that use a mixed methods approach can help environmental management scholars to design and conduct these types of studies. A good way of learning how to conduct a mixed methods study is to begin with an analysis of existing empirical mixed methods works, and to examine the features that characterise them as mixed methods research.

References

Bansal, P., Bertels, S., Ewart, T., MacConnachie, P., and O'Brien, J. (2012). Bridging the research-practice gap. *Academy of Management Perspectives*, 26(1), 73–92.

Bericat, E. (1998). *La integración de los métodos cuantitativo y cualitativo en la investigación social*. Ariel, Barcelona.

Brannen, J. (1992). *Mixing methods: Qualitative and quantitative research*. Routledge, London.

Bryman, A. (1988). *Quantity and quality in social science research*. Routledge, London.

Creswell, J.W. (1994). *Research design: Qualitative and quantitative approaches*. Sage, Thousand Oaks.

Creswell, J.W. (2015). *A concise introduction to mixed methods research*. Sage, Thousand Oaks.

Creswell, J.W., and Plano Clark, V. L. (2018). *Designing and conducting mixed methods research* (3rd ed.). Sage, Thousand Oaks.

Daft, R.L. (1983). Learning the craft of organizational research. *Academy of Management Review*, 8(4), 539–546.

Denscombe, M. (2008). Communities of practice. A research paradigm for the mixed methods approach. *Journal of Mixed Methods Research*, 2(3), 270–283.

Edwards, J.R. (2008). To prosper, organizational psychology should … overcome methodological barriers to progress. *Journal of Organizational Behavior*, 29(4), 469–491.

George, G., Howard-Grenville, J., Joshi, A., and Tihanyi, L. (2016). Understanding and tackling societal grand challenges through management research. *Academy of Management Journal*, 59(6), 1880–1895.

Greene, J.C. (2007). *Mixed methods in social inquiry*. San Francisco, Jossey-Bass.

Greene, J., Caracelli, V., and Graham, W. (1989). Toward a conceptual framework for mixed-method evaluation designs. *Educational Evaluation and Policy Analysis*, 11(3), 255–274.

Jick, T. (1979). Mixing qualitative and quantitative methods: triangulation in action. *Administrative Science Quarterly*, 24(4), 602–611.

Johnson, B. and Onwuegbuzie, A. (2004). Mixed methods research: A research paradigm whose time has come. *Educational Researcher*, 33(7), 14–26.

Lopez-Gamero, M.D., Claver-Cortes, E., and Molina-Azorin, J.F. (2008). Complementary resources and capabilities for an ethical and environmental management: A qual/quan study. *Journal of Business Ethics*, 82(3), 701–732.

Lopez-Gamero, M.D., Claver-Cortes, E., and Molina-Azorin, J.F. (2009). Evaluating environmental regulation in Spain using process control and preventive techniques. *European Journal of Operational Research*, 195(2), 497–518.

Maxwell, J. (2016). Expanding the history and range of mixed methods research. *Journal of Mixed Methods Research*, 10(1), 12–27.

Mertens, D.M., Bazeley, P., Bowleg, L., Fielding, N., Maxwell, J., Molina-Azorin, J.F., and Niglas, K. (2016). The future of mixed methods: A five year projection to 2020 (Mixed Methods International Research Association). https://mmira.wildapricot.org/resources/Documents/MMIRA%20task%20force%20report%20Jan2016%20final.pdf

Molina-Azorin, J.F. (2007). Mixed methods in strategy research: applications and implications in the resource-based view. In D. Ketchen and D. Bergh (Eds.) *Research methodology in strategy and management*. Elsevier, Oxford.

Molina-Azorin, J.F., and Cameron, R. (2015). History and emergent practices of multimethod and mixed methods in business research. In S. Hesse-Biber and R.B. Johnson (Eds.), *The Oxford handbook of multimethod and mixed methods research inquiry*. Oxford University Press, New York.

Molina-Azorin, J.F., and Fetters, M. D. (2019). Building a better world through mixed methods research. *Journal of Mixed Methods Research*, 13(3), 275–281.

Molina-Azorin, J.F., and Font, X. (2016). Mixed methods in sustainable tourism research: an analysis of prevalence, designs and application in JOST (2005-2014). *Journal of Sustainable Tourism*, 24(4), 549–573.

Molina-Azorin, J.F., and Lopez-Gamero, M.D. (2016). Mixed methods studies in environmental management research: prevalence, purposes and designs. *Business Strategy and the Environment*, 25(2), 134–148.

Molina-Azorin, J.F., Tari, J., Pereira-Moliner, J., Lopez-Gamero, M.D., and Pertusa-Ortega, E. (2015). The effects of quality and environmental management on competitive advantage: A mixed methods study. *Tourism Management*, 50(1), 41–54.

Morgan, D. (1998). Practical strategies for combining qualitative and quantitative methods: applications to health research. *Qualitative Health Research*, 8(3), 362–376.

Morse, J. (1991). Approaches to qualitative-quantitative methodological triangulation. *Nursing Research*, 40(1), 120–123.

Sharma, S., and Vredenburg, H. (1998). Proactive corporate environmental strategy and the development of competitively valuable organizational capabilities. *Strategic Management Journal*, 19(8), 729–753.

Sieber, S.D. (1973). The integration of fieldwork and survey methods. *American Journal of Sociology*, 78(6), 1335–1359.

Tashakkori, A., and Teddlie, C. (1998). *Mixed methodology. Combining qualitative and quantitative approaches*. Sage, Thousand Oaks.

Tashakkori, A., and Teddlie, C. (2003). *Handbook of mixed methods in social and behavioral research*. Sage, Thousand, Oaks.

Tsui, A.S. (2013). The spirit of science and socially responsible scholarship. *Management and Organization Review*, 9(3), 375–394.

5 Qualitative to quantitative and back

Reflecting on mixed methods approach for examining sustainability and small business

Mark Gagnon

5.1 Introduction

Investigating transformative change that addresses sustainability via small business and entrepreneurship is extremely complex (Belz and Binder, 2017). The process of economic organisation for providing goods and/or services for profit while attending to societal and environmental needs often requires new approaches to commerce. New business models are commonly brought forth in trial capacity, and adjustments occur, as firms interact with a series of shifting contextual forces. A firm's stakeholders, entrepreneurs and agents engage in a process to mitigate contextual forces, hopefully for the benefit of their organisation, society and the environment. The shifting nature of human and social interaction within and between organisations enhances the complexity of researching these phenomena.

The nexus of these fields is relatively new, with the majority of research activity occurring in the last decade (Muñoz and Cohen, 2018). Moreover, each of these subjects is challenging to define and investigate. Mixed methods research provides flexibility in scope (Denscombe, 2008) and depth, to identify, test and validate, salient and non-salient themes, concepts and frameworks. On its own, qualitative research addresses the explorative, thematic, conceptual and relational aspects of small business, entrepreneurship and sustainability, whereas quantitative methods allow for validation and testing of qualitative discovery. However, as one progresses utilising both methodological approaches, significant shifts occur in these traditional paradigmatic boundaries where qualitative data validates and tests and quantitative data offers exploratory, thematic, conceptual and relational understanding. The interplay of both methodical approaches within the same study provides exceptional epistemological insight (Denscombe, 2008). The author's intent is to share this discovery by way of research in this field and in reflections offered in this chapter.

The chapter commences with a review of a 2012 research study on sustainability and entrepreneurship. The first study utilised a qualitative interview approach at first, which was then followed by quantitative research. Readers are taken along the author's journey as the chapter progresses into the review of a second study in 2016. The second study utilises mixed methods by commencing first with quantitative inquiry, and then qualitative follow-on research. Summative, concluding insights are provided at the end of the chapter that should hopefully guide future mixed methods research into the complex phenomena of entrepreneurship, small business and sustainability.

5.2 Qualitative first: Mixed methods research reflections

The United States Department of Agriculture (USDA) funded research called for examining common characteristics of successful entrepreneurs in agriculture. The inquiry was guided to identify best practices and perhaps generate common themes for dissemination and to promote agricultural entrepreneur outreach through Penn State Extension. The initial team was comprised of three faculty members; one with expertise in management and sustainable bio-products, one who is an agricultural economist and extension leader, and a third who has expertise in strategy and organisational behaviour as they relate to bio-products.

After a few pilot interviews, it was discovered that entrepreneurs in food and agriculture were articulating sustainability as part of their company mission and/ or as a driver of their business. A decision was, thus, made by the research team to refine research questions to better capture the company founder's relationships with sustainability. The refined questions were: How can we understand and describe sustainability-minded entrepreneurs? What are the core values of sustainability-minded entrepreneurs? And how do we identify individuals who may become entrepreneurs who implement sustainability in their businesses?

The research team thought it would be best to start with a qualitative approach since the goal was to capture a wide range of themes that contributed to entrepreneur success (Nowell et al., 2017). We had the luxury of utilizing a convenience sample (Etikan et al., 2016) of entrepreneurs that we obtained through introductions with our Extension Team at Penn State. The extension team works across the Commonwealth of Pennsylvania with farmers and agricultural businesses and entrepreneurs by providing knowledge and training on best practices. Particular interest was generated for founding entrepreneurs who were for-profit and espoused to employ sustainable practices in their businesses. Extension agents provided us a list of interview candidates and facilitated introductions. Our inclination was to avoid non-profit ventures and focus on for-profit firms since they have potential for greater economic impact and job creation (Badal, 2010). These topics remain pressing for Pennsylvania, and universities, more recently, have heeded the call to contribute to economic development (Abreu et al., 2016). In this manner, we were able to align the ecological, social and economic imperatives of sustainability in small business.

Twenty-nine entrepreneurs were interviewed who publicly reported practicing sustainability in their businesses. Often sustainability related statements were listed on company websites and communication materials. An initial list of companies was developed by the research team and through colleagues in the College of Agricultural Sciences. Many of these entrepreneurs had interacted with Penn State through extension or were alumni. During the interview process, other entrepreneurs who were often referred to, were known by participants for implementing sustainable practices. Non-randomised snowball sampling (Goodman, 1961) was also used to increase the sample of entrepreneurs.

All interviews were recorded and transcribed for textual analysis. The analysis required reviewing, iteration, and all interview transcripts for content themes (Weber, 1985) required justification and clarification of common themes that emerged across the entire sample. The conversations were particularly enlightening as entrepreneurs are generally quite direct in telling their stories that describe failure and success. Fortunately, a team of students took on the task of transcribing recorded interviews, which reduced the workload of the research team. The interview transcripts were reviewed in-depth with over nine iterations. During the qualitative process of data immersion and abstraction, each entrepreneur story became more familiar and a deeper understanding of what they sought to accomplish became more evident.

For example, the obstacles entrepreneurs endured to successfully grow their businesses were persistent, significant, and often affected their well-being. Stories of little sleep, exhaustion and persistent health issues arose. These stories also indicated deep-level, experiential learning (Kolbe, 2014), when entrepreneurs reflected on prior challenges. Furthermore, personal life experiences provide rich and nuanced content that gets imprinted upon individuals and represents more impactful learning versus being exposed to new knowledge or stories from others. Indeed, new knowledge is retained better if experienced, followed by being contained in the context of a story, and least retained by being imparted in simple thematic form (Dewey, 1938; Richardson, 1994; Daudelin, 1996). The author can relate to these stories (being a former entrepreneur) and finds them useful as lessons for future entrepreneurs.

The lessons learned from these stories provided excellent content for in-residence entrepreneurship teaching. Stories are exceptional vehicles to impart tacit knowledge for learning (Bhardwaj and Monin, 2006). After processing the stories of 29 entrepreneurs, the author realised the limitations of his experience and perspective. The interactive and context-laden process of qualitative research opens avenues of rich discovery, including revealing tacit knowledge. Moreover, these entrepreneurs were at various points along the entrepreneurial journey, from just starting to approaching ten years in business. There was clear evidence of a mindset shift that occurred as time had passed. Entrepreneurs just starting their company were noticeably different than those who had progressed through certain time points.

Entrepreneurs, at the very beginning of starting their business, possess a contagious excitement and joy. Perhaps it is a naïve joy, given all the challenges that lie ahead for growing a viable business. Indeed, transition occurs when one witnesses entrepreneurs along the venture time spectrum. Entrepreneurs who were in their fourth or fifth year of business were often in the depths of struggling to move their businesses forward, towards positive cash flow and sustained growth. These entrepreneurs often ran on pure endurance. Entrepreneurs in their eighth or ninth year of business often demonstrated a noticeable contrast. These individuals were being rewarded by their efforts and some were in the process of considering an exit event (Wennberg and DeTienne, 2014). Indeed, the process is comparable to a marathon.

Over the last ten years, as an entrepreneurship academic, the author has benefitted greatly from perspective attained through his research and interaction with over 300 entrepreneurs and business owners. Their stories resonate and are utilised to help future entrepreneurs improve and understand both the positive and negative aspects of venturing forth. These qualitative interactions have transformed the author's thinking about entrepreneurship, small business and the very process of what is required to succeed.

Grounded theory (Strauss and Corbin, 1998; Creswell and Creswell, 2017) was first used for this research. A framework with distinct themes started to emerge after several iterations of reviewing interview data. Once a values framework started to emerge, literature on values and business through the lens of The Upper Echelons Strategic Perspective was reviewed. The Upper Echelons Theory asserts that executives do impact firm practices and performance (Finkelstein and Hambrick, 1996; Hambrick, 2007; Finkelstein et al., 2009). The extensive body of research shows the impact of executive decisions on firm practices and performance since the seminal Hambrick and Mason (1984) paper. The sample of entrepreneurs interviewed in the 2012 work reported the shared values of morality, holism, frugality and continuous improvement.

Morality is an individual's code of values that frame right versus wrong courses of action with respect to dealing with others (Gagnon, 2012). In the field of entrepreneurship, morality is typically manifest in decision-based contexts. Other scholars have equivocated morals with ethics (Trevino, 1986; Jones and Ryan, 1997; Bryant, 2009). Holism is one's ability to see relatedness versus categories, placing greater weight on context, being comfortable with contradiction, reliance on change and not being quick to assign cause or judgement to phenomena (Nisbett et al., 2001; Choi et al., 2007; Monga and John, 2008). Frugality is defined as enduring short-term sacrifices and avoiding resource depletion to achieve a long-term goal (DeYoung, 1996; Lastovicka et al., 1999). Continuous improvement is an inherent focus on doing better in all aspects of one's life. Dweck's (2008) work on growth versus fixed mindsets illustrates that when individuals frame their skills and abilities as modifiable versus given (fixed), they are able to effect personal change. Her work highlights the value of having an improvement-oriented mindset and her work has helped advance entrepreneurship pedagogy.

Visually mapping the above values on Schwartz's (1992) two-dimensional values structure provided insight as shown in Figure 5.1. The first two values of morality and holistic thinking are grouped in the self-transcendence quadrant, while frugality and continuous improvement worked at opposite ends of the openness to change and conservation spectrums. The qualitative phase in this project set up a series of research propositions that could be empirically operationalised.

While completing the qualitative phase of research, the opportunity was recognised to conduct empirical research with students enrolled in a series of ten core entrepreneurship courses. Figure 5.2 demonstrates the mixed

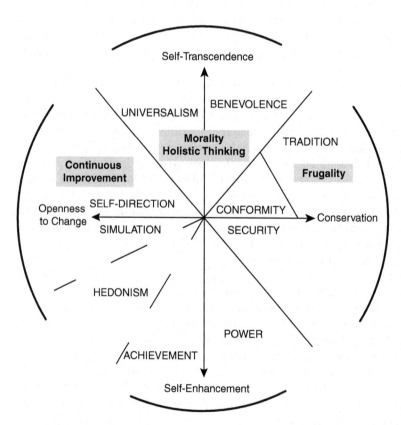

Figure 5.1 Schwartz's values structure with study values (Gagnon, 2012, p. 3).[1]

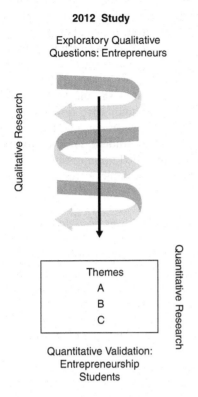

2012 Study

Exploratory Qualitative
Questions: Entrepreneurs

Qualitative Research

Quantitative Research

Themes
A
B
C

Quantitative Validation:
Entrepreneurship
Students

Figure 5.2 Mixed methods approach for the 2012 research.

methods approach. Fortunately, the author was an instructor for two of these courses and had a very supportive network of colleagues. Psychological measurement scales were utilised to measure the individual values listed above for sustainability. Measurement scales were obtained from an industrial organizational psychology item pool (Goldberg et al., 2006) and sustainable orientation (SO) was obtained from Kuckertz and Wagner (2010).

Another goal of this research was to gauge individual attachment to sustainability. Some adjustments were made to extant scales in order to improve question wording with the goal of improving the capture of latent value constructs. The student sample had face validity since it involved individuals in practice with the referent concepts of entrepreneurship, business and sustainability (Nevo, 1985), and ties to entrepreneurial behaviour were present. This was evident since students were enrolled in entrepreneurship classes and some had reported new entrepreneurial behaviour. In addition, the use of Millennial entrepreneurship students was suitable to empirically test the values listed, venturing behaviour, and especially sustainability. The

Millennial generation is known to espouse sustainability values (Hanson-Rasmussen and Lauver, 2018). In summary, the quantitative sample was actively combined with core concepts derived from the qualitative phase of this work. The Entrepreneurship Faculty provided access to students in their classes to administer a short 20-minute pen-and-paper survey. Three hundred and five complete surveys were collected.

Limitations exist for using undergraduates as a sample to empirically evaluate the framework that emerged from the qualitative research. Many students are not engaged in the entrepreneurial process or might be starting a business. In addition, reviewers are wary of student samples for psychology research since they have been heavily relied upon in the past (Bello et al., 2009). However, the opportunity was available to test the recently posited framework, acknowledging that the research sample might be limited.

In this second phase, data collection and analysis was successful and shortly afterwards, proposed relationships were tested. The quantitative student survey was administered and data was coded within two weeks. The data showed correlational support for the relationships of the set of generalizable personal values with sustainability variables. Structural equation modelling (Maruyama, 1997) was utilised to simultaneously evaluate the relationships of morality, holism, frugality and continuous improvement with three individual modes of attachment to sustainability. AMOS Structural Equation Software was used in concert with SPSS Statistical Software (SPSS, 2012). Model findings were limited, indicating that additional theorizing and inquiry was needed. The value of continuous improvement did not empirically fit the set of values that might constitute a sustainable mindset. In addition, the operationalization of frugality and holism were problematic as they demonstrated limited associations with sustainability.

Quantitative analysis failed to reveal robust relationships with the emergent qualitative framework. Questions emerged from the conflicting findings that pertained to what was really going on and about the structures that lay beneath the data that shaped the proposed framework. There was also the need to remove oneself from the data to find perspective (Bazeley, 2013). Allowing four weeks away from the data was, therefore, helpful for a refreshed perspective. After staying away, new analysis further informed the author's thinking about continuous improvement as a value that was associated with entrepreneurialism rather than sustainability. This might be true for frugality as well. Long-term orientation, a specific dimension of holism was also theorised to be perhaps better related to SO since a fair amount of sustainability narratives are focused on protecting our future (Corral-Verdugo and Pinheiro, 2006). This was prior to the release of the seventeen sustainability development goals (United Nations General Assembly, 2015) which likely had also expanded the scope of sustainability. Morality had the strongest relationships with individual sustainability attachment. If mixed methods had not been taken as an approach with this work, these additional insights would likely not be obtained.

Revealing the tensions between both qualitative and quantitative analysis within this study was quite rewarding. Qualitative methods often provide unstructured or semi-structured data with an abundance of interpretative latitude. These methods yield abundant data, potential depth and re-warding context; however, real challenges can exist with defensible inter-pretation and structuring. Conversely, quantitative methods provide immediate structure for the data with reduced discretion of interpretation. Quantitative methods can also limit experiential and contextual discovery. A benefit of this methodological approach is that it lends itself to a de-fensible framework for the researcher.

The qualitative research in 2012 allowed for a rich exploration of en-trepreneur attachment to sustainability and the development of related themes. The work was extremely time consuming; however, the reward of insight was provided. The risks of not discovering a defensible framework and narrative were significant and multiple plausible paths occurred. For example, a professor may wave her hand at a colleague while walking on campus. The interpretation of the act of waving her hand could be that she was either requesting that her colleague stop to talk, or she was being amicable or perhaps being uncivil. Thus, more information and context will be required for us to unpack the meaning in her gesture. Similar enriching and deconstructive approaches are required with research. However, the work was successful since rich, experiential insight was provided by en-trepreneurs and the role of varying contexts on business formation and growth were identifiable. These insights were exceptional for in-residence education and course module development. In addition, the abstracted framework from these insights provided interesting content for future theory building.

The use of quantitative methods in the 2012 study allowed for testing hypothesised relationships that were discovered in the qualitative work. A challenge with deploying quantitative methods in this research was that a fair number of the relationships were not significant. The benefit of uti-lizing mixed methods approach afforded the opportunity to look deeper into the data for instances of statistical significance, and non-significance. Moreover, qualitative findings and stories are often improved when me-trics are applied (Damodaran, 2017). A similar analogy resonates when one describes a hike. An individual could state that he/she hiked up half of the mountains in the Pemigewassett loop. However, when adding metrics, the same statement demonstrates the gravity of the challenge. Over the course of 16 hours, 25.6 miles of trail were hiked and six mountains were ascended and descended, each exceeding 4300 feet in elevation. Coupling qualitative and quantitative insights provides opportunity to construct a more impactful narrative.

5.3 Quantitative first: Mixed methods research reflections

Shortly after the 2012 paper, an opportunity was presented to conduct additional research on food entrepreneurs with Ms Pamela Heinrichs. Pamela was a recent economics graduate who was preparing to attend graduate school at another university. She was available to conduct research for several months and assist the project. A different approach was selected for the 2016 paper entitled Food Entrepreneur Sustainable Orientation and Firm Practices. This work commenced with quantitative data collection. The intention was to collect quantitative profile data from a convenience sample of food entrepreneurs.

The second study contained a set of more specific research questions that were informed by the 2012 study. The research questions were: 1) Do entrepreneurial beliefs about sustainability relate to new firm sustainable practices? 2) Are there relationships between the decision-influencing factors of morality, long-term orientation and holistic cognition with SO and mindset? And 3) Do relationships exist between SO, sustainable mindset and firm performance?

Excellent access was afforded to food entrepreneurs through attending two food shows for the 2016 study. Twice a year in San Francisco and New York, the Specialty Food Association holds, The Fancy Food Tradeshow (Specialty Food Association, 2019). These shows focus on food startups and growing food businesses. Entrepreneurs were approached in person at these shows before data collection. Attending the tradeshows facilitated rapport building (Bello and Lohtia, 1993) with entrepreneurs. Each show provided an opportunity to try entrepreneurs' products and listen to part of their stories; depending on how busy the show was or if a buyer was near. Opportunities also existed to stop by multiple times and engage study prospects for 15–30 minutes. The approach worked well since entrepreneurs were personally invited to participate in the study. Asking them to complete a quantitative profile survey appeared to be a natural step before a qualitative telephone interview occurred. Figure 5.3 shows the mixed methods approach for the 2016 study. The profile survey was available online via a web-link and in print, if respondents wished to complete the survey during the show. Most entrepreneurs completed the web version.

Variables with corresponding measurement scales that had worked well in the 2012 study were utilised. In addition, the decision was made to modify the research framework based on prior discovery. Self-reported sustainability practices and new venture performance were of particular interest since linkages to firm performance is the foundation of strategic management. Proxy performance measures such as years in business, revenues and number of employees were collected. These measures augmented assessment scales from the interview narratives.

The web-based profile surveys were populated with data rather quickly compared to respondents that elected to complete a paper copy that was provided to them at the tradeshow. Utilizing correspondence to schedule interviews with study participants provided an opportunity to remind them

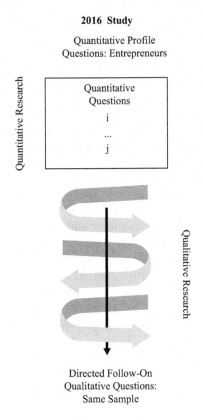

2016 Study

Quantitative Profile
Questions: Entrepreneurs

Quantitative Research

Quantitative
Questions

i

...

j

Qualitative Research

Directed Follow-On
Qualitative Questions:
Same Sample

Figure 5.3 Mixed methods approach for the 2016 research.

to complete the profile questionnaire. The decision was made not to analyse the profile data until all phone interviews were complete. Had the profile data been analysed before the interviews, these findings and interpretations would result in bias as far as the follow-up interviews were concerned (Roulston and Shelton, 2015). The researchers took extra precautions to maintain process integrity since prior quantitative results must not confound qualitative discovery.

Thirty interviews over the course of three months were obtained. In addition, profile survey data was collected with 45 profile surveys completed. A larger list of prospects was maintained, so the target of 30 completed interviews could be achieved in case individuals declined to be interviewed. A team of advanced undergraduate students transcribed the recorded phone interviews using a common word processing program. Additional care was taken to train students to write responses verbatim which was a challenge since spoken conversation does not translate well into written prose. However, the wealth of expression in raw interview data drives discovery and illustrates new ideas often better than well-crafted prose (Poland, 1995).

Verbatim textual data provided by respondents illuminate concepts in raw, provocative, more meaningful ways that capture our attention and often connect us emotionally (Gilbert, 2001). For example, the benefit of direct transcription from verbatim textual data is evidenced through contrary comments by one of the entrepreneurs. She memorably said, 'sustainability, it better be green first, that is I'd better make money being sustainable or otherwise forget it. I have a business to run.' Her direct statement highlighted a core premise of sustainable business; that is, a company will not exist if it is not profitable. Her views are aligned with Friedman (1970, 2007) whose provocative work stated that business profit maximization is a societal requirement. This example contextualises the pragmatic tensions that occur with implementing sustainability in business.

Once the interviews were complete and transcription was underway, Ms Heinrichs worked on cleaning and organising the profile data in SPSS. The scales utilised demonstrated acceptable scale reliabilities and data quality. Cronbach's Alpha along with descriptive statistics were used, including visual item distributions. Rating scales were developed to quantitatively assess sustainable practices, mindset and performance by a number of thematic instances mentioned for each interview. The authors modelled topic and theme counts from prior work (Dey, 1993; Namey et al., 2008) with the addition of applying a five-point Likert-type rubric to instance counts. The scales are listed in Table 5.1.

Table 5.1 Rating scales for textual data evaluation[2]

Sustainable mindset (5-point scale)
1 = no reported sustainable practices and no expressed desire to support sustainability
2 = slight attention to sustainability with one or fewer practices reported
3 = modest attention to sustainability with less than three practices reported some desire to do more about sustainability
4 = entrepreneurs who are engaged in 3 but no more than 5 substantial practices and are actively incorporating sustainability in their business beyond just environmental
5 = entrepreneurs are engaged in 5 or more practices including and beyond environmental practices and their business core is grounded in sustainability

Sustainable practices (count)
We counted the number of discrete practices that entrepreneurs reported during their interviews.

Performance (5-point scale)
1 = poor performance, in risk of closing business
2 = marginal performance, more needs to be accomplished to make the business viable
3 = acceptable performance, appear to be accomplishing goals
4 = good performance, notable goal accomplishment and financial vitality
5 = exceptional financial performance, growth is occurring and goals are being exceeded

The author first reviewed and evaluated the interview data using the scales listed in Table 5.1. Ms Heinrichs and another graduate student were asked to conduct a similar review and evaluation. Having two additional analysts review 30 interview transcripts consumed a fair amount of time. Initial analysis was complete after three months. Ms Heinrichs carefully managed our data set during this time as we added measures from our qualitative data assessment.

Inter-rater reliability and agreement of interpretation was critical for this research. The author and two raters generally interpreted and assessed sustainability and performance qualitative interview data in a similar manner. The interclass correlation coefficient (ICC) was used to determine inter-rater reliability (McGraw and Wong, 1996; Hallgren, 2012). The ICCs for sustainability and performance Cohen's Kappa measure scores exceeded 0.80 for these items. The results indicated that the three coders interpreted sustainable mindset evidence across the interviews in a reasonably similar manner (Landis and Koch, 1977).

Moderate digression occurred for collective interpretation of entrepreneur values of morality, holism and long-term orientation. A different scale was used to assess these values which likely created the problem. A three-point scale was administered that ranged from "did not use," to "somewhat," to "extensively used" values in respondent decision-making. The results may have been better by counting discreet instances of entrepreneurs discussing each value. In addition, these concepts are difficult to evaluate. Perhaps better agreement would have occurred if the three coders had reviewed the voice recordings from the interviews. Fortunately, sufficient inter-rater reliability (ICC ranges 0.49–0.62) were calculated. In summary, all measures occupied acceptable ranges with the lowest being 0.49 and the highest being 0.85 (Cicchetti, 1994).

The correlational model yielded partial results with only the value of long-term orientation demonstrating significant relationships with sustainability measures. Several sustainability measures demonstrated significant linkages with each other as was expected. These findings were encouraging, given the small sample of 30 respondents. The sustainability performance relationships demonstrated mixed results as well. Correspondingly, due to sample size, statistical power was limited along with degrees of freedom for analysis. A larger sample would likely have improved relationship determination among the variables since moderate to slight correlations were witnessed. Schönbrodt and Perugini (2013) indicate that correlational relationships stabilise at sample sizes of 250 respondents.

Realising the limitations with our data, a decision was made to quantitatively split measures into high and low quadrants (exemplar cases) for our key measures of value, sustainability and performance. Interview transcripts were examined for reflective statements for those participants who occupied more extreme positions with these measures. Yin (1989) highlights the informative role of exemplars on how their extreme views of the phenomenon can inform new areas of discovery.

The quotes from these exemplar entrepreneurs were quite informative as they added additional depth and context to high/low anchor responses. In this instance, qualitative findings provided substance for the empirical sets that were determined. The idea for running the post-hoc analysis was informed by prior strategy research of Miles and Snow (1978) where exemplars were utilised to make a statement about distinct firm strategic positions.

There were several aspects that were reassuring with this study. First, conducting the quantitative profile survey in the earlier stages of the project allowed some insurance for discovery. The author was confident that differences would exist in the sample. A handful of empirical dimensions and deeper insight would be gained with the follow-up qualitative data. Utilising a personalised approach and quantitative format survey worked well. These methods were strengthened by meeting participants in person since respondents were able to personally interact with the researchers.

5.4 Discussion and conclusion

Several themes emerged after reflecting on both these studies and the use of mixed methods. Starting with qualitative and then moving on to quantitative, the 2012 study was helpful for exploring and then testing research questions. Using qualitative inquiry first allowed for casting a bigger net to capture themes and underlying structures with the research sample. Taking a qualitative approach also allowed for the discovery of anomalies and outliers within the data. Often there is a tendency to focus on identifying shared themes with data sets. Important, Outlier discoveries might be overlooked with this approach. Often these unique cases and perspectives inform shared structures.

Outliers provide rich perspective on common phenomena (Yin, 1989). Evaluating individuals with differing perspectives from the group illuminate the role of variance and how these differences inform our perspectives of small business and entrepreneurship. Several entrepreneurs in both studies were notably distinct from the others, whether it was their background story or if they were serial entrepreneurs. Serial entrepreneurs are very different from novice entrepreneurs and often rely on skills developed over time and that improves their odds for venture success (Westhead et al., 2005; Gompers et al., 2006). One entrepreneur who was interviewed obtained his venture idea while he was serving time in prison. After his release, he started and developed a well capitalized, successful business. His story was one of redemption and hope for stigmatised populations. Entrepreneurship is often seen as one of few viable paths for economic well-being for former inmates (Cooney, 2012).

Qualitative inquiry with empirical validation in the first study allowed for the development of measures and testing prior to observation. The measures used were problematic, yet provided direction and informed thinking about what had been observed from the interview data. Developing and then testing research propositions in the same study helps rapidly advance inquiry, which is very rewarding. Having an acceptable sample of students allowed for testing propositions shortly after the qualitative phase. The trade-off of using a student sample limited our generalisability and restrained academic conference and peer-reviewed journal options. Student samples are generally frowned upon in management research due to the lack of justifying theoretical relevance, excessive convenience and their overuse in the past (Sears, 1986; Wintre et al., 2001; Bello et al., 2009). A research study must have strong justification for its research design to utilise students and the first study was sufficient because students were practicing entrepreneurship and generationally espoused strong values supporting sustainability.

The 2012 study established a baseline of measures to test during the 2016 study. Prior scales were utilised and improved upon, allowing for the second study to start with quantitative data collection. Both studies benefitted from a very supportive group of research participants. Meeting participants in person at the food tradeshow proved particularly useful for this group of informants. Following up with a profile survey while scheduling interview times enhanced the data collection process. Participant engagement felt more natural than working a multi-staged process to boost response rate (e.g., Dillman et al., 2014). Research participants became vested in the process as a result of personalised engagement. Participants were provided with a report sharing summative findings that was well received. Several participants in both studies found the summary reports to be helpful. Returning value back to participants is important since they were very generous with their time.

Living with the tension of unanalysed data while collecting interview data for the project's second phase provided anticipatory energy. A renewed vigour to complete 30 interviews occurred as progress was being made with 20 completed. Possessing quantitative profile data at the beginning was particularly useful for partitioning cases by quantitative break points. Cases were sorted into high and low mean quartiles for Kuckertz and Wagners' (2009) SO measurement scale. Once these extreme scoring cases were identified, textual interview data about sustainability from phase two was reviewed. The narratives demonstrated excellent face validity as those who scored in the highest mean quartile of SO shared narratives that were embedded with sustainable practices and thinking, whereas respondents who were placed in the lowest SO mean quartile reported narratives that did not report or were in opposition to sustainable practices. The following themes for mixed methods research have been developed during the review of these studies.

- Prior knowledge informs methodological selection
- Research questions influence the selection of methodologies
- Research subject population and sample selection and characteristics will shape the choice of methods and approach.

Starting with qualitative or quantitative inquiry depends on one's prior knowledge that informs research questions. In 2010, during the commencement of the research that generated the 2012 paper, discovery and dissemination about sustainability, entrepreneurship and small business was limited. At this time, definitions about these phenomena were being developed and debated (Dean and McMullen, 2007; Shepherd and Patzelt, 2011; Muñoz and Cohen, 2018). Mixed methods starting with qualitative, in this instance, appeared to be the most sensible approach. The goal was to gather information on exploratory themes and then use a narrow set of quantitative measures to test these themes. Overall, this approach was moderately successful as compelling themes were generated from qualitative inquiry and measures to pursue these themes in greater depth. Naturally, with this process and approach limitations, error and bias did exist. Discovery occurred, nevertheless, that helped establish direction for future inquiry.

In cases where prior knowledge is developed, quantitative inquiry can be employed to open new avenues of understanding that can then be augmented with qualitative follow-up work as in the 2016 study. The field of sustainable entrepreneurship and small business was growing rapidly, and research dissemination was accelerating including receptiveness from some of the leading academic journals (Muñoz and Cohen, 2018). In addition, the findings from the 2012 study provided a framework to build upon.

The degree of specificity of research questions helped methodological choice with both studies that were reviewed. The 2012 study was guided with generalisable, exploratory questions. Thus, starting with qualitative interviews appeared to be the most logical approach. The 2016 study benefitted from having a greater body of prior research to draw upon and this allowed for more refined research questions. In this instance, starting with quantitative research first and then adding depth from qualitative interviews made the most sense.

Both studies involved entrepreneurs in food and agriculture, with the 2016 study being exclusively for food entrepreneurs. The population of entrepreneurs in both fields were fairly similar in the way they tended to be direct and generally approachable, if one could make the case that the research being conducted was of value for them. Demonstrating the importance of the research improves the likelihood of response (Heberlein and Baumgartner, 1978). Both samples required some type of warm introduction, whether it was a referral from a known peer and/or meeting with respondents in person before data collection. Being a well-known land grant university greatly assisted with respondent engagement. In many instances, respondents had benefitted from prior university engagement via extension, short courses and/or programmatic activities. Prior value creation by the university allowed for greater respondent access. Once access was obtained, it was best to first engage qualitatively by engaging respondents in a conversation rather than engage with quantitative scales and/or measures. Once these first actions had been established, there was a need to develop further rapport with entrepreneurs to advance inquiry on both qualitative and quantitative fronts.

Mixed methods research is beneficial due to the depth of understanding that it affords and the ability to tell a rich story with the data. Both the richness and context of qualitative understanding in conjunction with the precision and abstract power of quantitative measures facilitates well-rounded discovery. Mixed methods also address the trade-offs that exist with qualitative and quantitative approaches. Telling a story with the data is easier when research findings complement methodologies. Divergence between qualitative and quantitative findings can be challenging and these moments can be used to step back from the analysis and question any held assumptions. Often, these moments provide a deeper level of discovery and indicate the value of researching complex topics.

So why mixed methods to investigate small business, entrepreneurship and sustainability? The editors' premise for assembling this book resonated with the author's work. That is, singular methods may not adequately capture a complex phenomenon like sustainability and small business. The same may be true for entrepreneurship, which is just as complex as investigating sustainability. The complex fields of entrepreneurship and sustainability are challenging to understand, and mixed methods research helps unpack complexity. The author's understanding is somewhat informed, yet limited at best, even with a decade of practice and academic work in this area.

Fortunately, the call for inquiry into sustainability, small business and entrepreneurship remains robust as real challenges exist. Ecological constraints driven by human population growth continue to be one of society's greatest challenges. The field of agricultural sciences is once again experiencing transformative changes on a scale that has not been seen since the 1950s. Research, new technology and business activity in food, agriculture and bio-renewables (AgTech) is experiencing considerable growth (Dutia, 2014). New and emerging business models having sustainability as a core component provide munificent ground for research and application. Moreover, there is considerable excitement about the interdisciplinary nature of research with AgTech that is already providing significant discovery. The use of mixed methods is an essential component of this work and will provide insight for addressing the grand challenges we face.

Notes

1 Permissions granted for reprint with express permission of the copyright holder: North American Business Press.

2 Table 5.1 is included with express permission of the copyright holder: International Journal of Food and Agricultural Economics. The Table is an abstraction of materials from Gagnon and Heinrichs (2016).

References

Abreu, M., Demirel, P., Grinevich, V., and Karatas-Özkan, M. (2016). Entrepreneurial practices in research-intensive and teaching-led universities. *Small Business Economics*, 47(3), 695–717.

Badal, S. (2010). *Entrepreneurship and job creation: Leveraging the relationship. Gallup white paper*. Gallup. Washington, D.C.

Bazeley, P. (2013). *Qualitative data analysis: Practical strategies*. Sage, Thousand Oaks.

Bello, D., Leung, K., Radebaugh, L., Tung, R. L., and Van Witteloostuijn, A. (2009). From the editors: Student samples in international business research. *Journal of International Business Studies*, 40(3), 361–364.

Bello, D. C., and Lohtia, R. (1993). Improving trade show effectiveness by analyzing attendees. *Industrial Marketing Management*, 22(4), 311–318.

Belz, F. M., and Binder, J. K. (2017). Sustainable entrepreneurship: A convergent process model. *Business Strategy and the Environment*, 26(1), 1–17.

Bhardwaj, M., and Monin, J. (2006). Tacit to explicit: An interplay shaping organization knowledge. *Journal of Knowledge Management*, 10(3), 72–85.

Bryant, P. (2009). Self-regulation and moral awareness among entrepreneurs. *Journal of Business Venturing*, 24, 505–518.

Choi, I. Koo, M., and Choi, J. A. (2007). Individual differences in analytic versus holistic thinking. *Personality and Social Psychology Bulletin*, 33(5), 691–705.

Cicchetti, D. V. (1994). Guidelines, criteria, and rules of thumb for evaluating normed and standardized assessment instruments in psychology. *Psychological Assessment*, 6(4), 284–290.

Cooney, T. M. (2012). Reducing recidivism through entrepreneurship programmes in prisons. *The International Journal of Entrepreneurship and Innovation*, 13(2), 125–133.

Corral-Verdugo, V., and Pinheiro, J. Q. (2006). Sustainability, future orientation and water conservation. *Revue Européenne de Psychologie Appliquée/European Review of Applied Psychology*, 56(3), 191–198.

Creswell, J. W., and Creswell, J. D. (2017). *Research design: qualitative, quantitative, and mixed methods approaches*. Sage, Thousand Oaks.

Damodaran, A. (2017). *Narrative and numbers: the value of stories in business*. Columbia University Press, New York.

Daudelin, M. W. (1996). Learning from experience through reflection. *Organizational Dynamics*, 24(3), 36–48.

Dean, T. J., and McMullen, J. S. (2007). Toward a theory of sustainable entrepreneurship: Reducing environmental degradation through entrepreneurial action. *Journal of Business Venturing*, 22(1), 50–76.

Denscombe, M. (2008). Communities of practice: A research paradigm for the mixed methods approach. *Journal of Mixed Methods Research*, 2(3), 270–283.

Dewey, J. (1938). *John Dewey experience and education*. McMillan, New York.

Dey, I. (1993). *Qualitative data analysis: a user-friendly guide for social scientists*. Routledge, London.

DeYoung, R. (1996). Some psychological aspects of reduced consumption behavior: The role of intrinsic satisfaction and competence motivation. *Environment and Behavior, 28*(3), 358–409.

Dillman, D. A., Smyth, J. D., and Christian, L. M. (2014). *Internet, phone, mail, and mixed-mode surveys: The tailored design method.* Wiley, New Jersey.

Dutia, S. G. (2014). Agtech: Challenges and opportunities for sustainable growth. *Innovations: Technology, Governance, Globalization, 9*(1–2), 161–193.

Dweck, C. S. (2008). *Mindset: The new psychology of success.* Random House Digital, New York.

Etikan, I., Musa, S. A., and Alkassim, R. S. (2016). Comparison of convenience sampling and purposive sampling. *American Journal of Theoretical and Applied Statistics, 5*(1), 1–4.

Finkelstein, S., and Hambrick, D. (1996). *Strategic leadership.* West Educational Publishing, St. Paul, Minneapolis.

Finkelstein, S., Hambrick, D. C., and Cannella, A. A. (2009). *Strategic leadership: Theory and research on executives, top management teams, and boards.* Oxford University Press, Oxford.

Friedman, M. (2007). The social responsibility of business is to increase its profits. In *Corporate ethics and corporate governance* (173–178). Springer, Verlag Berlin, Heidelberg.

Gagnon, M. A. (2012). Sustainable minded entrepreneurs: Developing and testing a values-based framework. *Journal of Strategic Innovation and Sustainability, 8*(1), 9–25.

Gagnon, M. A., and Heinrichs, P. A. (2016). Food entrepreneur sustainable orientation and firm practices. *International Journal of Food and Agricultural Economics, 4*(4), 11–28.

Gilbert, K. R. (2001) *The emotional nature of qualitative research.* CRC, London.

Goldberg, L. R., Johnson, J. A., Eber, H. W., Hogan, R., Ashton, M. C., Cloninger, C. R., and Gough, H. G. (2006). The international personality item pool and the future of public–domain personality measures. *Journal of Research in Personality, 40*(1), 84–96.

Gompers, P., Kovner, A., Lerner, J., and Scharfstein, D. (2006). *Skill vs. luck in entrepreneurship and venture capital: Evidence from serial entrepreneurs (No. w12592).* National Bureau of Economic Research. Cambridge, MA.

Goodman, L. A. (1961). Snowball sampling. *The Annals of Mathematical Statistics, 32*(1), 148–170.

Hallgren, K. A. (2012). Computing inter-rater reliability for observational data: An overview and tutorial. *Tutor Quantitative Methods Psychology, 8*(1), 23–34.

Hambrick, D. C. (2007). Upper echelons theory: An update. *Academy of Management Review, 32*(2), 334–343.

Hanson-Rasmussen, N. J., and Lauver, K. J. (2018). Environmental responsibility: Millennial values and cultural dimensions. *Journal of Global Responsibility, 9*(1), 6–20.

Heberlein, T. A., and Baumgartner, R. (1978). Factors affecting response rates to mailed questionnaires: A quantitative analysis of the published literature. *American Sociological Review, 43*(4), 447–462.

Hinkin, T. R. (1998). A brief tutorial on the development of measures for use in survey questionnaires. *Organizational Research Methods, 1*(1), 104–121.

Jones, T. M., and Ryan, L. V. (1997). The link between ethical judgment and action in organizations: A moral approbation approach. *Organization Science*, 8(6), 663–680.

Kolbe, D. A. (2014). *Experiential learning: Experience as the source of learning and development*. FT Press, New Jersey.

Kuckertz, A., and Wagner, M. (2010). The influence of sustainability orientation on entrepreneurial intentions–Investigating the role of business experience. *Journal of Business* Venturing, 25(5), 524–539.

Landis J. R., and Koch G. G. (1977). The measurement of observer agreement for categorical data. *Biometrics*, 33(1), 159–174.

Lastovicka, J. L., Bettencourt, L. A., Hughner, R. S., and Kuntze, R. J. (1999). Lifestyle of the tight and frugal: Theory and measurement. *Journal of Consumer Research*, 26, 85–98.

Maruyama, G. M. (1997). *Basics of structural equation modeling*. Sage, Thousand Oaks.

McGraw K. O., and Wong S. P. (1996). Forming inferences about some intraclass correlation coefficients. *Psychological Methods*, 1(1), 30–46.

Miles, R. E., and Snow, C. C. (1978). *Organizational strategy, structure and process*. McGraw Hill, New York.

Monga, A. B., and John, D. R. (2008). When does negative brand publicity hurt? The moderating influence of analytic versus holistic thinking. *Journal of Consumer Psychology*, 18(4), 320–332.

Muñoz, P., and Cohen, B. (2018). Sustainable entrepreneurship research: Taking stock and looking ahead. *Business Strategy and the Environment*, 27(3), 300–322.

Namey, E., Guest, G., Thairu, L., and Johnson, L. (2008). Data reduction techniques for large qualitative data sets. In G. Guest and K. MacQueen (Eds.) *Handbook for team-based qualitative research* (137–161).

Nevo, B. (1985). Face validity revisited. *Journal of Educational Measurement*, 22(4), 287–293.

Nisbett, R. E. Peng, K. Choi, I., and Norenzayan, A. (2001). Culture and systems of thought: Holistic versus analytic cognition. *Psychological Review*, 108(2), 291–310.

Nowell, L. S., Norris, J. M., White, D. E., and Moules, N. J. (2017). Thematic analysis: Striving to meet the trustworthiness criteria. *International Journal of Qualitative Methods*, 5, 80–92.

Poland, B. D. (1995). Transcription quality as an aspect of rigor in qualitative research. *Qualitative Inquiry*, 1(3), 290–310.

Price Waterhouse Coopers. (2008). Millennials at work: Perspectives from a new generation. https://www.pwc.de/de/prozessoptimierung/assets/millennials–at–work–2011.pdf. Accessed: 30/09/2020.

Richardson, J. G. (1994). Learning best through experience. *Journal of Extension*, 32(2). https://www.joe.org/joe/1994august/a6.php. Accessed: 15/02/2021.

Roulston, K., and Shelton, S. A. (2015). Reconceptualizing bias in teaching qualitative research methods. *Qualitative Inquiry*, 21(4), 332–342.

Schönbrodt, F. D., and Perugini, M. (2013). At what sample size do correlations stabilize? *Journal of Research in Personality*, 47(5), 609–612.

Schwartz, S. H. (1992). Universals in the content and structure of values: Theoretical advances and empirical tests in 20 countries. *Advances in Experimental Social Psychology, 25*, 1–65.

Sears, D. O. (1986). College sophomores in the laboratory: Influences of a narrow data base on social psychology's view of human nature. *Journal of Personality and Social Psychology, 51*(3), 515–530.

Shepherd, D. A., and Patzelt, H. (2011). The new field of sustainable entrepreneurship: Studying entrepreneurial action linking "what is to be sustained" with "what is to be developed". *Entrepreneurship Theory and Practice, 35*(1), 137–163.

Shulman, L. S. (1986). Those who understand: Knowledge growth in teaching. *Educational Researcher, 15*(2), 4–14.

Specialty Food Association. (2019). Summer Fancy Food Show (June 1, 2019). https://www.specialtyfood.com/shows–events/. Accessed: 30/09/2020.

SPSS, 2012. *SPSS base applications guide.* SPSS Inc., Chicago.

Strauss, A., and Corbin, J. (1998). *Basics of qualitative research: Techniques and procedures for developing grounded theory.* Sage, Thousand Oaks.

Trevino, L. K. (1986). Ethical decision making in organizations: A person-situation interactionist model. *Academy of Management Review, 11*(3), 601–617.

UN General Assembly (UNGA). (2015). Transforming our world: The 2030 Agenda for Sustainable Development Resolution. A/RES/70/1, 25, 1–35.

Weber, R. P. (1985). *Basic content analysis.* Sage, Beverly Hills.

Wennberg, K., and DeTienne, D. R. (2014). What do we really mean when we talk about 'exit'? A critical review of research on entrepreneurial exit. *International Small Business Journal, 32*(1), 4–16.

Westhead, P., Ucbasaran, D., and Wright, M. (2005). Experience and cognition: Do novice, serial and portfolio entrepreneurs differ? *International Small Business Journal, 23*(1), 72–98.

Wintre, M. G., North, C., and Sugar, L. A. (2001). Psychologists' response to criticisms about research based on undergraduate participants: A developmental perspective. *Canadian Psychology/Psychologie Canadienne, 42*(3), 216–225.

Yin, R. K. (1989). *Case study research: Design and methods* (Rev. ed.). Sage, Newbury Park.

6 Mixed-methods

A pragmatic approach to researching SMEs and sustainability

Alessandro Bressan

6.1 Introduction

The author's interest, passion and involvement in social responsibility and environmental sustainability began almost 20 years ago. At that time, the issue of sustainability in small and medium-sized enterprises (SMEs) as a topic for research was emerging and there was a need for further research from both academics and practitioners. The author has worked with Italian and European institutions to evoke environmentally and socially responsible cultures among different organisations, paying special attention to the needs of SMEs. For example, he was an active member of the International Standard Organisation (ISO) Committee to develop the ISO 26000 International Guidelines on Corporate Social Responsibility.

This chapter discusses how the author then engaged with a PhD study in Sydney (Australia), making use of an innovative mixed method research design to comprehensively investigate sustainability in SMEs. In particular, this breadth and depth of the research design also provided for a detailed examination of the opportunities and challenges that arose from integrating these practices within SME business models. This situation provided for a richer understanding of the complexities of sustainability than what mono-methods such as a survey or interviews alone could provide. The relevance of the research is particularly important in contributing to a more sustainable world as SMEs are considered central to most economies (OECD, 2019) as well as being faced with a complex environment of limited resources where decision-making is residual with the owner/manager (Jenkins, 2004; Besser and Miller, 2013).

With the need to consider the SME owners/managers and the way they make decisions, it was considered important to be close to the practitioners in the research setting, and provide for a broader view on the pragmatic issues faced by SMEs. Even more so, a methodological approach which integrates qualitative and quantitative data could contribute to unveil, and further understand the dynamics of sustainability within SMEs. From a theoretical perspective, a mixed methods research (MMR) approach also permits researchers to advance and generate new knowledge as to how

SMEs behave towards and/or approach sustainability (Molina-Azorín and López-Gamero, 2016).

MMR acknowledges the strengths of each method and can provide a rich and comprehensive analysis of phenomena and research results (Teddlie and Tashakkori, 2003). The integration of methods within the field of SMEs and sustainability, however, is still fragmented and more research is needed to understand how MMR could add additional value to advancing knowledge in the sustainability field.

This chapter discusses how an integrative approach brings together the research paradigm, SME features and sustainability elements in an integrative manner. This mixing of a quantitative and a qualitative approach was deemed essential when designing the mixed method study for the PhD. In particular, a set of motivations drove the research process to:

1. Provide a more complex, in-depth and different understanding, analysis and interpretation of the research questions.
2. Increase clarity of definitions and analysis of innovative problems.
3. Contribute to theory building and elaboration.

The structure of the chapter is, therefore, designed to elaborate further on these three sets of motivations. Firstly, the chapter provides a brief introduction of the rationale of using a mixed method approach when researching the field of SMEs and sustainability. Then, it illustrates the main perspectives and identified purposes of MMR and concludes by reflecting on the inherent challenges and potential solutions associated/involved with MMR in the context of green business.

6.2 Mixed methods research and sustainability

Organisations today are dealing with the increase in global competition as well as the need to balance a variety of grand challenges (e.g., climate change, clean energy, poverty), which have proved to be critical for any organisation, not only from a moral and responsible viewpoint but also from a managerial and organisational perspective (Ferraro et al., 2015). For example, how businesses strategize their way to avoid and/or reduce environmental impact associated with their operations has implications on the community and the broader society. In this context, firms, including SMEs (Jansson et al., 2017; Malesios et al., 2018) need to demonstrate their ability to develop and engage with stakeholders for organisational success and long-term survival (Freeman et al., 2010).

Sustainability related issues are numerous, and the multiplicity of interests as well as the dynamic factors involved in the process of development and implementation of sustainability related practices requires a holistic approach to understanding the sustainability phenomena (Klewitz and Hansen, 2014). The United Nations (UN), in its most recent commitment to the global sustainable development agenda (United Nations, 2015, p. 3) adopted a set of 17 Sustainable Development Goals (SDGs) to tackle wicked problems with an intent to 'stimulate action over the next 15 years in areas of critical importance for humanity and the planet'. Most importantly, the framework and approach of the SDGs recognise that government action alone may be limited. Realising the aspirations of the 17 SDGs will, therefore, require participation and commitments from various actors, and involve both public and private sector organisations as drivers and enablers of sustainable development of the economy and society (United Nations, 2015). The complexity associated with a great variety of stakeholders, all with their own sustainability interpretations, agendas and concerns, conspire to form strategic challenges for organisations. Furthermore, the 2020 outbreak of the COVID 19 global pandemic has further exacerbated complexity and challenges for organisations (Bapuji et al., 2020; Eggers, 2020).

The main consideration from the author's viewpoint was to design a research approach that could capture this complexity. The aim, therefore, was to use a methodological approach for the PhD which integrates qualitative and quantitative data, which could contribute to unveil, and further understand the dynamics of sustainability within SMEs. This was quite a novelty in the field of SME and sustainability when designing the study in 2011. Indeed, even though the relationship between SMEs and sustainability is being increasingly discussed by scholars (as presented in Chapter 3), methodologically, this has been quite challenging, as the use of a mono-method approach using either qualitative or quantitative methods has been predominant (Molina-Azorín and López-Gamero, 2016). Yet, in the broader fields of CSR and sustainability, the use of mixed methods is limited (Taneja et al., 2011; Molina-Azorín and Font, 2016). This data confirms that the use of alternative and more creative methodological approaches, such as MMR is still limited, especially in the context of research exploring social responsibility and environmental sustainability (Soundararajan et al., 2018).

In response, the PhD study aimed for an innovative research approach which considered both qualitative and quantitative techniques which better enabled the PhD research to contribute to enhancing and understanding the relationships between SMEs and sustainability. Conducing MMR, however, is more demanding when compared to singular approaches and it requires that researchers have the knowledge and capabilities to be able to combine quantitative and qualitative methods and use the strengths of research (Teddlie and Tashakkori, 2003). This, amongst other concerns, implies a stronger emphasis on methodological preparation of the researcher, which in turn needs to be reflected in the researcher's training. Indeed, as in other research designs, MMR must also be effectively designed and conducted. Molina-Azorín and Font (2016), on this point, suggest that more concern and commitment to training may be considered to enabling MMR in the field of sustainability. Similarly, the need for extra resources such as the time it takes to develop and implement both methods, the cost involved in the process of collecting both qualitative and quantitate data and the energy in developing, implementing and conducting MMR (Creswell and Plano Clark, 2017) are relevant aspects to take into consideration. Furthermore, challenges may also emerge in the research publication process (Bryman, 2007). Indeed, despite MMR being positively perceived and appreciated by many editors, the number of research components and the task to assign fully qualified reviewers may limit the chance to publish.

All these issues have a direct impact when researchers evaluate the possibility of integrating both qualitative and quantitative methods in her/his study. Indeed, MMR can be a resource-intensive approach and may not be considered as the first option for the researcher, especially when there is institutional pressure to publish and/or the resources may be constrained. Potentially, researchers would not add another layer of complexity in a process that is already highly competitive and complicated and thus, choosing a mono-method over an MMR approach can result in a more convenient, immediate and known choice. Research design, however, is a choice, where researchers need to know what the available options are and how to evaluate those options while, at the same time, being somewhat familiar with a variety of methods. Thus, it should be essential to think of the methods that researchers use, as tools which can provide a set of strengths that can be used to accomplish a range of goals (Morgan, 1998). Furthermore, the complexity involved in researching sustainability also renders it critical for researchers to go beyond methodological approaches of one's discipline.

6.3 A mixed-method PhD research study

This section discusses the underlying concepts that were considered when the author designed the mixed methods approach for his PhD research. Figure 6.1 (see p. 108) provides a visual illustration of the sequential mixed methods implemented by the author in his PhD study. The qualitative phases helped in understanding the perceptions of SME owners and managers towards environmental and social issues, and they also provided a means to focus on the interests and values of the owners/managers who participated in the study.

The field work of this research was conducted in the Western Sydney region (New South Wales, Australia). Western Sydney has a population of more than 2 million people and is located about 20 km West, North West and South West of Sydney. Western Sydney is considered to be Sydney's major future growth area with a significant population and employment

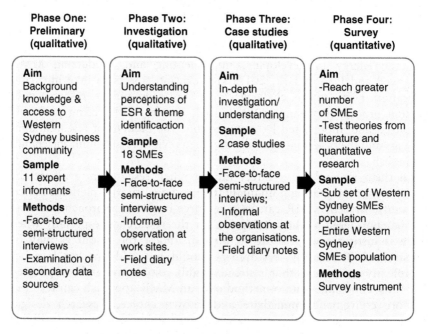

Phase One: Preliminary (qualitative)	Phase Two: Investigation (qualitative)	Phase Three: Case studies (qualitative)	Phase Four: Survey (quantitative)
Aim Background knowledge & access to Western Sydney business community **Sample** 11 expert informants **Methods** -Face-to-face semi-structured interviews -Examination of secondary data sources	**Aim** Understanding perceptions of ESR & theme identificaction **Sample** 18 SMEs **Methods** -Face-to-face semi-structured interviews -Informal observation at work sites. -Field diary notes	**Aim** In-depth investigation/ understanding **Sample** 2 case studies **Methods** -Face-to-face semi-structured interviews; -Informal observations at the organisations. -Field diary notes	**Aim** -Reach greater number of SMEs -Test theories from literature and quantitative research **Sample** -Sub set of Western Sydney SMEs population -Entire Western Sydney SMEs population **Methods** Survey instrument

Figure 6.1 Plan of the sequential mixed methods (Bressan, 2014).[1]

growth projected over the next 25 years (Parramatta City Council, 2013; PricewaterhouseCoopers, 2016).

One area of sustainability that has been richly researched is the area of environmental management and SMEs. As such, much of the environmental management field has developed from quantitative research and has developed a mature field (e.g., Molina-Azorín and López-Gamero, 2016). Nonetheless, the sustainability and SMEs field of research has missed opportunities to be informed by studies which look at the problem from a qualitative perspective, leaving the research field in an intermediate stage. Hence, providing for a chance to theoretically enrich the field. This has left the field still in theoretical progression. Molina-Azorin et al. (2017) suggest that for theories in a middle stage (intermediate maturation stages), an integration of qualitative-quantitative methods may fit well.

As the more mature aspect of sustainability and SME research has been in the area of environmental management, a qualitative first stage was implemented to delve more deeply into what was known, which was followed by a series of more investigative qualitative stages. The qualitative element can provide preliminary insight to relationships and thus promote insight and rigour when the integration is applied correctly (Molina-Azorin et al., 2017). Thus, by cross-framing, researchers can, on the one hand, inductively understand a phenomenon (theory building), and on the other hand, deductively confirm/test it (theory testing). Furthermore, MMR can support the researchers to reach a greater number of respondents, thus overcoming the limitations of the experiential worldview of one person, that is the qualitative researcher (Creswell and Plano Clark, 2017). Adding to it, the use of both methodologies together can strengthen the validity of studies and overcome potential bias and skewed results which can emerge when qualitative and quantitative approaches are taken on their own (Onwuegbuzie et al., 2009). This is particularly important in attempting to understand complex phenomena such as sustainability, and an integrative approach using quantitative and qualitative methodologies in the same study can better facilitate this understanding.

Along with the increasing interest in MMR, scholars such Creswell and Tashakkori (2007) and Teddlie and Tashakkori (2011) have proposed four main perspectives when examining MMR, namely: methods, methodology, paradigm and practice perspectives. The *method perspective* focuses on the process and outcomes of implementing both qualitative and quantitative methods, types of data and collection of data. The *methodology perspective* views MMR as a distinct methodology that integrates aspects of the process of research such as worldview, questions, methods, and inferences or conclusions. The *paradigm perspective* provides a philosophical foundation for MMR and it was especially important when the researcher designed his study. Indeed, it supported in the identification of issues and the deeper reasons to combine different worldviews. In the *practice perspective*, MMR research is viewed as a means, or set, of procedures to use as scholars conduct their research designs, whether these designs are survey research, ethnography, or others. Practically too, MMR contributes to a level of sophistication for researcher's pioneering new research techniques (Creswell and Creswell, 2017).

The paradigm perspective provides the rationale at the base of an MMR choice, and more concretely, it contributes to support how qualitative and quantitative methods could be combined to enhance the understanding of social phenomena (Johnson and Onwuegbuzie, 2004; Tashakkori and Teddlie, 2010; Creswell, 2013) due to the practicality in choosing the best approach 'that works' (Patton, 2002, p. 117). For example, the author's first practical consideration was in relation to the real challenge in collecting data (qualitative and quantitative) from SME owners/managers who are busy with their day-to-day activities and do not have the time or interest to respond.

The use of only qualitative methods may be problematic in terms of the time and cost consumed to reach enough businesses to have a good representation of the entire population. Thus, the author envisaged that the use of both qualitative and quantitative methods could be helpful in addressing the challenges of accessing SMEs (Creswell, 2013). Also Johnson and Onwuegbuzie (2004, p. 14) discuss the possibility of integrating paradigms and different worldviews in the same study, arguing that despite the paradigmatic differences between the two approaches, a non-purist approach which identifies similarities such as empirical observations, examination of human beings phenomena, exists and thus, combining 'both quantitative and qualitative research are important and useful'.

The mixing of philosophical assumptions (paradigms and worldviews) into the same study also presents important research implications. This may affect the mixed method research process, including prioritisation of methods and the contextual significance of integration (Plano Clark and Ivankova, 2016). In addition, the critique of mixed methods by Timans et al. (2019) demonstrates that researchers should be aware of the limitations and challenges of mixing philosophical assumptions. They suggest that mixed methods researchers need to identify the 'black box' that ontologically present different views of the world. Though, Creswell and Plano Clark (2017) describe that resolving the issue of reconciling paradigms still remains, the paradigm debate has somewhat more recently abated as pragmatism emerged as a philosophical grounding for mixed methods.

Reflecting this sense of pragmatism, and in a more holistic way, paradigms can be seen as 'systems of beliefs and practices that influence how researchers select both the questions they study and methods that they use to study them' (Morgan, 2007, p. 49). The paradigmatic emphasis thus supports the decision-making process of issues such as research design over practical considerations (Morgan, 2014). Identifying the paradigm associated with a research approach is, therefore, important because it provides a guide for the researcher in the investigation process, as well as aligning their own beliefs and values. Moreover, when researchers share their beliefs, it provides the readers with an understanding of the philosophical background of the research and thus, the potential impact of the research.

MMR also considers the workable approaches to problem-solving, rejecting an incompatibility thesis between qualitative-quantitative research domains (Johnson et al., 2007; Morgan, 2014). By integrating both approaches, researchers can mutually use the strengths of both approaches and more ably compensate for any weakness in one particular method. For example, in the context of the author's research, the personal interaction with owners and managers of the firms was useful to gain a first understanding of the valuable business context in preparation for a subsequent quantitative survey. More specifically, semi-structured face-to-face interviews can be used primarily to delve deeper into an understanding of the investigated phenomena and to encourage the participants to reflect more freely, and deeply, on their personal experience (Leech and Onwuegbuzie, 2011). Also, the qualitative phase, especially when conducted via semi-structured interviews, could be useful as an addition to complement and enhance depth to other methods (Newcomer et al., 2015).

As noted by Timans et al. (2019), however, researchers who adopt mixed methods are required to compromise their epistemological position in order to allow the integration of elements of a positivistic approach associated with quantitative methods with those of a constructivist approach associated with qualitative methods. Nevertheless, a researcher's pragmatic worldview may facilitate the implementation of a more flexible epistemological framework that supports the implementation of an MMR. Timans et al. (2019) view is worthy of consideration by pragmatists in the challenges they face in developing robust MMR strategies and research designs.

In designing the PhD, it was also important to consider whether to use convergent or sequenced approaches. This began by understanding the research questions which were developed to extend knowledge.

1. What are the specific environmental and social issues that SMEs address?
2. How do owners/managers conceptualise environmental and social responsibility?
3. What are the perceptions of owners/managers in relation to drivers of, and barriers to environmental and social responsibility?
4. Why do owners/managers become involved with environmental and social responsible practices?

Since the qualitative phases seek to explore, 'what, how or why' as well as perceptions and personal experience, one of the core objectives of this research, the qualitative phases carried more weight compared to the quantitative phase in this particular research (Creswell, 2013). Consequently, a sequential approach where the qualitative component played a relevant/dominant role was undertaken. The quantitative survey was designed to reach a larger number of SMEs and to test the theories that arose out of the literature review and the qualitative findings.

The researcher experienced that the data from the quantitative component contributed to achieve the scope and aims of the research. For example, the quantitative component confirmed that participants in the study were familiar with the concept of sustainability and they were showing commitment and responsibility to give back to their stakeholders. The social commitment and sense of responsibility for their employees and close community emerge in both qualitative and quantitative findings as more prominent compared to the concerns about environmental issues. These were important results for the scope of the PhD research.

A low response rate, however, seems to be a general problem with survey (Fan and Yan, 2010), especially when engaging with SMEs (Gunasekaran et al., 2011) due to the lack of time and potentially, the scepticism about the research topic on the part of owners/managers. However, these limitations can be overcome when the qualitative component is prominent in the research. In the next section, the author provides his view and rationale in the adoption of MMR when investigating SMEs and sustainability.

6.4 Mixed-methods approach – 'an obvious' choice when investigating sustainability within SMEs

SMEs are known for their unique features such as being highly social entities (Morsing and Spence, 2019) and the strong interrelation between management and ownership (Spence and Rutherfoord, 2003; Schaefer et al., 2020). Thus, scholars researching within the field of SMEs may require a more 'creative and nuanced understanding' when designing their research approach which aims to contribute to the advancement of knowledge and theories in the specificity of SMEs. Then MMR can play a relevant role. For this purpose, it provides the research with the complete 'tool-kit' which may stimulate the researcher to search for more in-depth interpretations of his/her research questions.

The author's specialisation and interest towards MMR began during his doctoral research. During this period, he came to the realisation that, different data gathering techniques could offer significant potential for exploring new and relevant dimensions of sustainability within SMEs. The purpose of his PhD research was to extend knowledge towards SMEs and sustainability, especially what motivated SME owners/managers to become involved in socially and environmentally responsible practices. For example, the position of the owner/manager being central in all decisions and functioning of the organisation is completely different when compared to larger organisations.

Using MMR research unlocks key information both around the owner/manager's decision-making process and her/his influence over physical and human organisational resources. MMR supported the author, in capturing insights about owner/manager's perceptions of sustainability through participants' actions, decisions, values and social behaviours; while also addressing the limitations of taking an approach based only on one method. For example, reaching a greater number of participants and minimising the use of human and financial resources. Furthermore, the MMR approach contributed to the discovery of interesting, relevant and innovative research questions, which supported the author in the advancement of the knowledge and understanding of intertwined and innovative topics such as social and environmental issues within SMEs.

Integrating both qualitative and quantitative methods when studying sustainability within SMEs can contribute to enhancing knowledge in this field of research. Indeed, while the qualitative component explores perceptions and the personal experience of participants, the quantitative component can support the researcher to achieve a greater number of respondents by using a pre-coded quantitative survey, thus overcoming the limitations of the experiential worldview of one person: the qualitative researcher (Creswell, 2013). For instance, Factor et al. (2010) noted that in the specific area of environmental responsibility, MMR was usually applied where it was necessary to draw on multiple data sources to understand complex concepts. Similarly, Seuring (2011), in studying sustainability in the context of supply change management, points out, for example, that the benefit of mixing qualitative and quantitative methods offers potential to gain insights and it also facilitates the conceptualisation of the research in the field of study. In this regard, sustainability is a complex concept and research into the field can benefit from the coherent integration of qualitative and quantitative approaches.

MMR offers the potential, therefore, to explore new and relevant research dimensions and allows researchers to think and discover interesting, essential and innovative research questions (Mason, 2006, 2017; Scheyvens, 2014). All in all, the implementation of MMR enables the broadening, and further development, of methodological scope, as well as strengthening methodological skills; especially in the context of sustainability and SMEs where researchers may face challenges in accessing data. In particular, Greene et al. (1989) identify five purposes for MMR, namely: triangulation, complementarity, development, initiation and expansion.

The *triangulation* design is known as the most common approach in mixing methods (Creswell and Plano Clark, 2017). Triangulation is used when a researcher wants to directly compare and contrast quantitative statistical results with qualitative finding or to validate or expand quantitative results with qualitative data. Researchers can take benefit from triangulation by seeking convergence, corroboration and correspondence of results from different methods with the result of yielding an enriched, elaborated understanding of the investigated phenomenon (Denzin, 1970; Jick, 1979). The aim of this design is to best understand the research problem by obtaining different but 'complementary data on the same topic' (Morse, 1991, p. 122).

Complementarity further allows for more robust analysis and for taking advantage of the strengths of both approaches. The quantitative and qualitative methods can be used sequentially, whereby the first method helps inform the *development* of the second one. This is the case when one type of data provides a supportive, secondary role in a study based primarily on the other type (Creswell and Plano Clark, 2017). At the base of this approach, a single data set is not sufficient. For example, different questions need to be answered, and each type of question also requires different types of data. Researchers use this design approach when they need to include qualitative or quantitative data to answer a research question within a largely quantitative or qualitative study. This is the approach taken by the author in his doctoral research where the qualitative method is dominant.

Furthermore, Greene et al. (1989) explain how an MMR can be purposively selected for *the initiation*, which involves the discovery of paradox and fresh perspectives rather than constituting a planned intent. The rationale for this approach is to increase the depth of enquiry, research results and interpretation by analysing through the lenses of different methods and paradigms. In this sense, MMR can provide the researcher with an approach that can better inform the researcher and offer a more solid understanding and explanation of the topic. Finally, the purpose of Greene's (1989) *expansion* relates to the opportunity of using a diverse set of research tools to increase the scope of inquiry across a broader range of research phenomena. The extension of research techniques allows different approaches to collecting, analysing and applying both qualitative and quantitative data and it is likely to strengthen research on topics such as sustainability and SMEs which requires more complete and robust data sets to produce a more detailed understanding of the issues under investigation.

6.5 Conclusion

The author, during his PhD study, specifically used a sequential combination of qualitative and quantitative methods where each phase was built on the findings of the previous phase (Creswell, 2013; Creswell and Plano Clark, 2017). The study was structured into four phases: three qualitative phases followed by a quantitative phase (as indicated above). He came to the realisation that qualitative methods would be better able to capture the perceptions of SME owners/managers on social and environmental responsibility and explore the intangible aspects and benefits of social capital such as goodwill, reciprocity and trust.

Before undertaking this Australian research study, the author worked on various research-based and consulting projects, advising small firms on the implementation of practices related to environmental and social sustainability. Being in direct contact with practitioners allowed the author to better understand SMEs' dynamics, and features, and their pragmatic approach to problem-solving, including tackling environmental and social issues. Indeed, within SMEs, the founder/owner of the business plays a primary role, and their passion and care for the business are relevant drivers to achieve firm success. These traits have been shown to be key determinants on how firms deal with social and environmental issues/practices in their day-to-day operations.

From a research point of view, it is important to take into consideration these aspects. MMR provides researchers with the flexibility to design the research approach, in light of the dynamics and idiosyncrasies of SMEs in order to capture the trends and details of the investigated situations. For example, researchers have the choice of giving more emphasis/weight to either the qualitative or the quantitative component, depending on the features of the field as well as the type of data collection method that is best suited to address the study's goals and purpose; and, perhaps, their own disciplinary training, and potential to work in teams with other researchers.

Furthermore, SMEs often play a key role in their local community, such as employing local people or investing in local businesses. Through various forms of civic, social and economic engagement, SME owners/managers (and their employees) interact with a variety of individuals and groups (stakeholders), creating a network of formal and informal relationships within – and sometimes beyond – the surrounding community (Cooke and Wills, 1999; Lähdesmäki et al., 2017). The possibilities of combining methodological approaches provided the author with several advantages, including flexible and adaptive tools for studying the peculiarities of SMEs and sustainability within an embedded community. For example, a combination of qualitative and quantitative strategies allowed the author to gather data from a variety of internal and external stakeholders which, for practical considerations such as finance, time and knowledge resources, could not have been possible with the application of a single method alone.

Likewise, the author envisaged that the use of both qualitative and quantitative methods could help address other challenges when doing research with SMEs such us data access and limited budgets. For example, while engaging with SMEs during his research, he found that getting 'close' to the participants helped him to acquire a deeper understanding of participants' perceptions of the phenomena investigated (Shaw, 1999; Leitch et al., 2010). Similarly, acting as an informal participant-observer gave him a deeper understanding of the participants' actions, decisions, values and social behaviours that he could not have captured with quantitative methods alone. Conversely, the difficulty in accessing SME owners/managers for research purposes, particularly through a quantitative survey delivered online, could be compensated with a qualitative component (Fan and Yan, 2010). Thus, the possibility of using elements from both qualitative and quantitative approaches can enable the researchers to find the best answers to their research questions (Johnson and Onwuegbuzie, 2004).

Research in the context of sustainability might be challenging, and the layers of complexity might increase when the field work is conducted within SMEs. Thus, neither quantitative nor qualitative methods may be enough/sufficient on their own, to capture the all trends and details of situations. Quantitative and qualitative methods should complement each other, allowing for more robust analysis and for taking advantage of the strengths of both methods, providing robustness, validity and context to the research undertaken (Creswell and Plano Clark, 2017).

In conclusion, MMR offers insights into the topic investigated and addresses the limitations of taking an approach based only on one method, with great potential to contribute towards addressing issues and advancing research in the context of SMEs and sustainability. Conducting research with and within SMEs is not easy, and researchers face challenges. It is notoriously difficult to gain access and to have time to engage with owners and managers (e.g., Hasle et al., 2012). In this chapter, however, the author has discussed and included his reflections on the adoption and implementation of MMR while investigating SMEs and sustainability during his PhD study. He found that the use of MMR is essential to advance further knowledge and understanding in the field of sustainability and SMEs. Furthermore, the author found that despite all the challenges in undertaking MMR, the advantages are evident, especially from the perspective of the researcher's experience. Finally, in times of COVID-19, when doing field work and research is becoming more complex and challenging due to social distancing, and there is a lack of interaction with participants besides other limitations created by this health pandemic, the MMR approach can offer a valid alternative to overcome these constraints.

Note

1 Figure 6.1 as presented in Bressan (2014) PhD thesis awarded by Western Sydney University, which according to the author this figure has not previously been published.

References

Bapuji, H., de Bakker, F. G. A., Brown, J. A., Higgins, C., Rehbein, K., and Spicer, A. (2020). Business and society research in times of the corona crisis. *Business and Society, 59*(6), 1067–1078.

Besser, T. L., and Miller, N. J. (2013). Social capital, local businesses, and amenities in US rural prairie communities. *Journal of Rural Studies, 32,* 186–195.

Bressan, A. (2014). Environmental and social responsibility within SMEs: Managerial perspectives from Western Sydney, Australia. PhD Thesis, University of Western Sydney.

Bryman, A. (2007). Barriers to integrating quantitative and qualitative research. *Journal of Mixed Methods Research, 1*(1), 8–22.

Cooke, P., and Wills, D. (1999). Small firms, social capital and the enhancement of business performance through innovation programmes. *Small Business Economics, 13*(3), 219–234.

Creswell, J. W. (2013). *Research design: Qualitative, quantitative, and mixed methods approaches.* Sage, Thousand Oaks.

Creswell, J. W., and Creswell, J. D. (2017). *Research design: Qualitative, quantitative, and mixed methods approaches.* Sage, Thousand Oaks.

Creswell, J. W., and Plano Clark, V. L. (2017). *Designing and conducting mixed methods research.* Sage, Los Angeles.

Creswell, J. W., and Tashakkori, A. (2007). Editorial: Differing perspectives on mixed methods research. *Journal of Mixed Method Research, 1*(4), 303–308.

Denzin, N. K. (1970). *The research act: A theoretical introduction to sociological methods.* Aldine Publishing Company, Chicago.

Eggers, F. (2020). Masters of disasters? Challenges and opportunities for SMEs in times of crisis. *Journal of Business Research, 116,* 199–208.

Factor, A., Francis, G., and Theiler, S. (2010). A mixed-method investigation of environmental practice in Australian Small-Scale manufacturing. 9th European Conference on Research Methodology for Business and Management Studies IE Business School, Madrid, Spain 24-25 June 2010.

Fan, W., and Yan, Z. (2010). Factors affecting response rates of the web survey: A systematic review. *Computers in Human Behavior, 26*(2), 132–139.

Ferraro, F., Etzion, D., and Gehman, J. (2015). Tackling grand challenges pragmatically: Robust action revisited. *Organization Studies, 36*(3), 363–390.

Freeman, E., Harrison, J., Wicks, A., Parmar, B., and De Colle, S. (2010). *Stakeholder theory: The state of the art.* Cambridge University Press, Cambridge.

Greene, J. C., Caracelli, V. J., and Graham, W. F. (1989). Toward a conceptual framework for mixed-method evaluation designs. *Educational Evaluation and Policy Analysis, 11*(3), 255–274.

Gunasekaran, A., Rai, B., and Griffin, M. (2011). Resilience and competitiveness of small and medium size enterprises: An empirical research. *International Journal of Production Research, 49*(18), 5489–5509.

Hasle, P., Limborg, H. J., Kallehave, T., Klitgaard, C., and Andersen, T. R. (2012). The working environment in small firms: Responses from owner-managers. *International Small Business Journal, 30*(6), 622–639.

Jansson, J., Nilsson, J., Modig, F., and Hed Vall, G. (2017). Commitment to sustainability in small and medium-sized enterprises: The influence of strategic orientations and management values. *Business Strategy and the Environment, 26*(1), 69–83.

Jenkins, H. (2004). A critique of conventional CSR theory: An SME perspective. *Journal of General Management, 29*, 37–57.

Jick, T. D. (1979). Mixing qualitative and quantitative methods: Triangulation in action. *Administrative Science Quarterly, 24*(4), 602–611.

Johnson, B., Onwuegbuzie, A. J., and Turner, L. A. (2007). Toward a definition of mixed methods research. *Journal of Mixed Methods Research, 1*(2), 112–133.

Johnson, R., and Onwuegbuzie, A. (2004). Mixed methods research: A research paradigm whose time has come. *Educational Researcher, 33*(7), 14–26.

Klewitz, J., and Hansen, E. G. (2014). Sustainability-oriented innovation of SMEs: A systematic review. *Journal of Cleaner Production, 65*, 57–75.

Lähdesmäki, M., Siltaoja, M., and Spence, L. J. (2017). Stakeholder salience for small businesses: A social proximity perspective. *Journal of Business Ethics, 158*, 373–385.

Leech, N. L., and Onwuegbuzie, A. J. (2011). Beyond constant comparison qualitative data analysis: Using NVivo. *School Psychology Quarterly, 26*(1), 70.

Leitch, C. M., Hill, F. M., and Harrison, R. T. (2010). The philosophy and practice of interpretivist research in entrepreneurship: Quality, validation, and trust. *Organizational Research Methods, 13*(1), 67–84.

Malesios, C., Skouloudis, A., Dey, P. K., Abdelaziz, F. B., Kantartzis, A., and Evangelinos, K. (2018). Impact of small-and medium-sized enterprises sustainability practices and performance on economic growth from a managerial perspective: Modeling considerations and empirical analysis results. *Business Strategy and the Environment, 27*(7), 960–972.

Mason, J. (2006). Mixing methods in a qualitatively driven way. *Qualitative Research, 6*(1), 9–25.

Mason, J. (2017). *Qualitative researching.* Sage, Thousand Oaks.

Molina-Azorin, J. F., Bergh, D. D., Corley, K. G., and Ketchen Jr., D. J. (2017). Mixed methods in the organizational sciences: Taking stock and moving forward. *Organizational Research Methods, 20*(2), 179–192.

Molina-Azorín, J. F., and Font, X. (2016). Mixed methods in sustainable tourism research: An analysis of prevalence, designs and application in JOST (2005-2014). *Journal of Sustainable Tourism, 24*(4), 549–573.

Molina-Azorín, J. F., and López-Gamero, M. D. (2016). Mixed methods studies in environmental management research: Prevalence, purposes and designs. *Business Strategy and the Environment*, 25(2), 134–148.

Morgan, D. L. (1998). Practical strategies for combining qualitative and quantitative methods: Applications to health research. *Qualitative Health Research*, 8(3), 362–376.

Morgan, D. L. (2007). Paradigms lost and pragmatism regained: Methodological implications of combining qualitative and quantitative methods. *Journal of Mixed Methods Research*, 1(1), 48–76.

Morgan, D. L. (2014). Pragmatism as a paradigm for social research. *Qualitative Inquiry*, 20(8), 1045–1053.

Morse, J. M. (1991). Approaches to qualitative-quantitative methodological triangulation. *Nursing Research*, 40, 120–123.

Morsing, M., and Spence, L. J. (2019). Corporate social responsibility (CSR) communication and small and medium sized enterprises: The governmentality dilemma of explicit and implicit CSR communication. *Human Relations*, 72(12), 1920–1947.

Newcomer, K. E., Hatry, H. P., and Wholey, J. S. (2015). Conducting semi-structured interviews. *Handbook of practical program evaluation.* (4th ed.). Jossey-Bass, San Francisco.

OECD (2019). *OECD SME and Entrepreneurship Outlook 2019.* https://www.oecd.org/industry/oecd-sme-and-entrepreneurship-outlook-2019-34907e9c-en.htm Accessed: 30/08/2020.

Onwuegbuzie, A. J., Johnson, R. B., and Collins, K. M. (2009). Call for mixed analysis: A philosophical framework for combining qualitative and quantitative approaches. *International Journal of Multiple Research Approaches*, 3(2), 114–139.

Parramatta City Council. (2013). Parramatta Future Generation, Parramatta investing in Western Sydney. https://www.greater.sydney/ Accessed: 20/07/2020.

Patton, M. Q., (2002). *Qualitative research and evaluation methods* (3rd ed.). Sage, Thousand Oaks.

Plano Clark, V. L., and Ivankova, N. V. (2016). How to use mixed methods research?: Understanding the basic mixed methods designs. In *Mixed methods research: A guide to the field* (105–134). Sage, Thousand Oaks.

PricewaterhouseCoopers. (2016). *Parramatta 2021 Unlocking the potential of a new economy.* https://www.wsbc.org.au/resources/Pictures/Resource%20Library/City_of_Parramatta_2021.pdf Accessed: 26/07/2020.

Schaefer, A., Williams, S., and Blundel, R. (2020). Individual values and SME environmental engagement. *Business and Society*, 59(4), 642–675.

Scheyvens, R. (2014). *Development fieldwork: A practical guide.* Sage, Thousand Oaks.

Seuring, S. (2011). Supply chain management for sustainable products-insights from research applying mixed methodologies. *Business Strategy and the Environment*, 20(7), 471–484.

Shaw, E. (1999). A guide to the qualitative research process: Evidence from a small firm study. *Qualitative Market Research: An International Journal*, 2(2), 59–70.

Soundararajan, V., Jamali, D., and Spence, L. J. (2018). Small business social responsibility: A critical multilevel review, synthesis and research agenda. *International Journal of Management Reviews*, 20(4), 934–956.

Spence, L., and Rutherfoord, R. (2003). Small business and empirical perspectives in business ethics: Editorial. *Journal of Business Ethics*, 47(1), 1–5.

Taneja, S., Taneja, P., and Gupta, R. (2011). Researches in corporate social responsibility: A review of shifting focus, paradigms, and methodologies. *Journal of Business Ethics*, 101, 343–364.

Tashakkori, A., and Teddlie, C. (2010). *Sage handbook of mixed methods in social and behavioral research*. Sage, Thousand Oaks.

Teddlie, C., and Tashakkori, A. (2003). Major issues and controveries inthe use of mixed methods in the social and behvioral sciences. *Handbook of mixed methods in social and behavioral research* (3–50). Sage, Thousand Oaks.

Teddlie, C., and Tashakkori, A. (2011). Mixed methods research. *The Sage handbook of qualitative research* (4th ed., 285–300). Sage, Thousand Oaks.

Timans, R., Wouters, P., and Heilbron, J. (2019). Mixed methods research: What it is and what it could be. *Theory and Society*, 48(2), 193–216.

United Nations (2015). Transforming our world: The 2030 agenda for sustainable development. *General Assembley 70 session*. Available at https://sustainabledevelopment.un.org/post2015/transformingourworld/publication

7 Reflecting on the use of mixed methods in the subject of sustainable strategies in manufacturing SMEs

Eustathios Sainidis

7.1 Introduction

This chapter provides a discussion and critique on the application of mixed methods in researching the adoption of sustainable business practices within small and medium-sized enterprises (SMEs) in the manufacturing sector. The author has extensive research experience in the subject of manufacturing strategy in SMEs and has worked with both mono-method and multi-methods data collection and analysis approaches. It is the experience and lessons drawn from a mono-method approach and in particular the limitations of quantitative data in exploring the complexity, dynamic nature and uncertainty which drives SMEs' decisions on sustainability which attracted the author of this chapter to the prospects of mixed methods. Indeed, as the chapter will illustrate, a mixed methods approach offers a better understanding of what the data is trying to say and consequently, a deeper insight on how sustainability is taking shape within the arena of manufacturing SMEs.

The study draws lessons from UK-based primary data containing two datasets: quantitative (QUAN) and qualitative (QUAL). The combination of two datasets informs the mixed methods research (MMR) strategy and the ontological and epistemological stance of the study. It is, therefore, useful to start the discussion with defining ontology and epistemology in business and management research and how these two 'worlds' contribute to the enquiry of sustainability strategies in manufacturing SMEs. The study, then, continues with the 'development-type' integration of QUAN and QUAL data (Greene et al., 1989) and the adoption of the associated data evaluation tools of descriptive statistics and template analysis (King, 2004; King and Brooks, 2017). Finally, the chapter concludes with a review of mixed methods validation techniques relevant to the study of sustainability strategies in manufacturing SMEs.

The study presented in this chapter is driven by the epistemological stance of *pragmatism*. Pragmatism is important to sustainability research due to the contemporary nature of the topic and offers greater depth and insight into the phenomenon. The study's research journey is based on the blending of the two QUAN and QUAL datasets. It is the blending and integration of the data which provides evidence of a mixed methods approach. Figure 7.1 (as presented on p. 122) provides a visual presentation of the research roadmap for the study. The details of the roadmap will be discussed in this chapter. The study focuses on the manufacturing SMEs (MSMEs) sector, using a sample of MSMEs located in the United Kingdom. It makes use of a purposive sample of MSMEs by engaging their senior managers in a survey (QUAN) and interview (QUAL). The purpose of the study is to investigate the reasons MSMEs introduce sustainability in their operations, how they go about adopting a sustainability strategy and the impact of such practices on their business performance.

The chapter starts with an overview on the subject of sustainability in the MSME sector to allow the reader a degree of familiarity with the academic focus of the study. A review of the methodological position follows and how the study fits within the epistemology of pragmatism. It then reviews mixed methods as a tool to evaluate sustainability in the MSME arena, the benefits of a mixed methods approach, challenges and limitations.

7.1.1 Sustainability and manufacturing strategy in the SME sector

Research strategies on the subject of manufacturing strategy have considerably developed since Skinner's seminal work in the late 1960s on how manufacturing relates to and supports corporate strategy (Skinner, 1969). The research methodologies used within sustainability in research related to manufacturing SMEs have mainly been quantitative, less so qualitative and a limited number of studies have adopted a mixed methods research (MMR) approach. Researchers have called for a more equal balance between positivist and constructivist studies (Kang and Evans, 2020). Of particular interest to this chapter is the argument that mixed or qualitative research is better suited to studies across subjects. This is evident in the work by Younis et al. (2019) and Molina-Azorin and Lopez-Gamero (2016), and also Barratt et al. (2011) which indicate an 'integrative' approach within sustainability in manufacturing strategy research (SMSR) combined with operations management theories (Voss and Winch, 1996; Salvador et al., 2002; Sousa, 2003).

It is worth summarising the engagement of past and current researchers with various research methods within manufacturing strategy research. Table 7.1 (see p. 123) presents, in chronological order, a selection of influential researchers in the manufacturing strategy field, their research focus and applied research method(s).

Table 7.1 evidences lack of mixed methods within the subject which echoes calls from Boyer and Swink (2008) and Barratt et al. (2011), and more recently, Edwards et al. (2018) for further adoption of mixed methods in manufacturing strategy research.

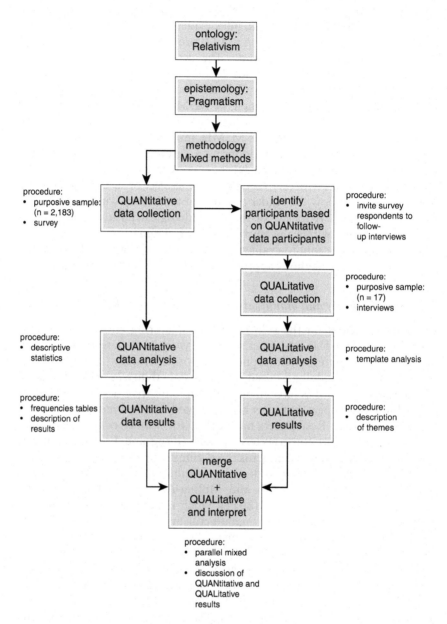

Figure 7.1 Research roadmap of study.

Proponents of mixed methods have pointed to the all-encompassing perspective of methodological concerns which include philosophical considerations, disciplinary worldviews as well as the methods used within the methodological process.

Table 7.1 Research methods applied within the subject of sustainability and manufacturing strategy

Researchers (chronological order)	Manufacturing Research Emphasis	Research method
Ünal E and Shao J (2019)	Sustainability strategies	Quantitative
Zarte et al (2019)	Sustainability decision models	Conceptual, literature review
Venugopal and Saleeshya (2018)	Environmental priorities	Quantitative
Dangelico et al (2017)	Environmental priorities	Conceptual
Longoni and Cagliano (2015)	Environmental and social priorities	Quantitative (survey)
Gimenez et al (2012)	Environmental priorities	Quantitative (survey)
Hallgren et al (2011)	Priorities configurations	Quantitative (survey)
Grössler and Grübner (2006)	Strategy configurations	Quantitative (survey)
Kiridena et al (2009)	Process	Case studies
Kathuria (2000)	Strategy taxonomies	Quantitative (survey)
Bozarth and McDermott (1998)	Strategy configurations	Conceptual, literature based
Ward et al (1996)	Strategy configurations	Conceptual, literature based
Hayes and Pisano(1994)	Process	Case study
Hill (1992)	Process and content	Conceptual, case studies
Anderson et al (1989)	Strategy typology	Conceptual, literature review
Kotha and Orne (1989)	Strategy typology	Case studies
Miller (1986)	Strategy configurations	Conceptual, literature based
Hayes (1985)	Process	Conceptual, descriptive
Hayes and Wheelwright (1984)	Content	Conceptual, descriptive
Stobaugh and Telesio (1983)	Strategy taxonomies	Conceptual, case studies
Skinner (1969, 1974)	Process and content	Conceptual, case studies

7.2 The philosophy of science perspective

Understanding the philosophical underpinnings of alternative research routes will assist in the design and refinement of the research project (Easterby-Smith et al., 2018). Establishing the ontological and philosophical position of the research project at an early stage guides the researcher as to how, when and why data is to be collected and interpreted, and the role of theory in the data interpretation process. *Ontology* defines the researcher's perspective on how truth can be described, its location and how it is observed (Crotty, 1998). Relativism as an ontology argues that many scientific laws may exist, aiming to explain the same phenomena (Ashton et al., 2020).

Pragmatism is associated with the use of mixed methods for data collection purposes (Biesta, 2010; Morgan, 2014). Pragmatism as an epistemology is pluralistic in its view of conducting research, driven by the research question and using 'what works best' rather than theoretical constraints of the two main philosophical positions, positivism and constructionism. Research driven by pragmatism values both objective and subjective knowledge, may be deductive and inductive at different stages within the research journey, and utilises the advantages of quantitative and qualitative data (Creswell and Plano Clark, 2017).

Sustainability is a complex interplay of multiple truths and worldviews. This is particularly true in business and management where multiple business functions need to collectively contribute to the sustainable business model. If the actions of organisations are the outcome of an equilibrium of complex internal organisational factors (resources) and external business environment influences (Barnard, 1971), all of which represent variables that are impossible to control and measure simultaneously, we may conclude that a single law alone does not exist to explain the actions of manufacturing SMEs when they develop a sustainability agenda. As such, relativism as an ontological stance arguably sits closer to sustainable manufacturing research and its overarching objectives.

Research driven by pragmatism values both objective and subjective knowledge and may be deductive and inductive at different stages within the research journey and utilises the advantages of quantitative and qualitative data (Creswell and Plano Clark, 2017). The advantages of a combination of quantitative and qualitative data allows for richer and well-grounded constructs which are essential for the development of sustainable manufacturing research. Hence the adoption of mixed methods in the study illustrated in this chapter.

7.3 Mixed methods

Epistemologically, mixed methods marry the two research paradigms of positivism and constructionism (interpretivism), which are typically seen within the literature as two opposite paradigms. Realism and pragmatism will tell us that what ultimately matters are the data collection and analysis tools that the two paradigms, in combination, can offer to answer the particular research questions (Smith and Heshusius, 1986; Carey, 1993; Kaushik and Walsh, 2019). From a purely operational perspective, the two approaches with their wealth of data collection and analysis tools can offer great benefits to the research enquiry on sustainability in manufacturing within the SMEs sector. As Creswell and Plano Clark (2017) recommend, the use of mixed methods is appropriate when one source of data (e.g., survey-based data) is insufficient to explain its results, and therefore, a second dataset (e.g., interview-based data) will enhance the exploration and explanation of the studied phenomena.

This was particularly evident to the researchers of the study presented here. Their previous experience of a mono-method (QUAN) approach failed to explain a critical perspective of the rationale of manufacturing SMEs engaging in sustainability practices and the impact these business practices have on their financial and market performance. It was, therefore, decided to engage in a mixed methods approach to benefit from a multi-method strategy and also contribute to the lack of mixed methods in sustainable manufacturing research, as is evident from Table 7.1. Howe (1988, 1992) supports this position by urging social scientists to move away from the pointless and never-to-be-resolved debate (Miles and Huberman, 1994) on which data collection and analysis method, and associated philosophy of science, is best suited to explain human beliefs, behaviour or attitudes. Instead, researchers of social phenomena should free themselves from the restrictive boundaries of positivism and interpretivism, and embrace the compatibility of the tools the two epistemologies can offer.

The debate amongst researchers still abounds, nonetheless. For example, some users of mixed methods will even argue that qualitative research can have evidence of positivism within its approach (Reichard and Rallis, 1994; De Block and Vis, 2018). This is evident in the growing trend of qualitative-data based studies adopting thematic analysis (and its derivatives) to quantify their results using statistical tests typically associated with positivistic studies (see King and Brooks, 2017). Alternatively, Bryman (2006) adds to the argument by suggesting that researchers favouring quantitative data will eventually take an open-ended reporting approach during the interpretation of their data, often adopting an imaginative application of statistical techniques and somehow moving away from the mechanistic style of analysis typically associated with positivism. From this perspective, therefore, the boundaries between the two paradigms of positivism and interpretivism tend to be too blurred in practice to exclude mixing data collection and analysis methods from each epistemology.

Discussion within the literature on MMR has also addressed the issues of data analysis concerns. For example, Bryman (2007) and Sale et al. (2002) report on the failure of several studies to fully integrate the findings from their quantitative and qualitative data analysis. Addressing this, within the research on sustainable manufacturing in SMEs, the *development* design is applied, as defined by Greene et al. (1989) to ensure effective 'integration' and 'nesting' of the two datasets QUAN and QUAL (Howell Smith et al.,

2020). Creswell and Plano Clark (2017) refer to a similar mixed methods design with the term *explanatory*.

The explanatory MMR by design was especially useful for this study as explanatory designs sequentially proceed with the quantitative stage. This was of particular value to this study on sustainable manufacturing in SMEs as it allowed for setting off from an initial quantitative survey to inform the sampling of participants for face-to-face interviews, with the same data collection instrument (questionnaire) being used in stages. Once the data had been collected, combining the two methods was conducted in the interpretation stage, with separate analysis stages for each quantitative and qualitative datasets; the aim being to ensure evidence of interaction, influence and debate between the two datasets QUAN and QUAL. This follows the logic of Greene et al. (1989), namely, *higher order expansion design*, which aims to combine both methods to assess the same phenomena.

7.4 Research design

7.4.1 Sampling and selection

Deciding on the type and size of a sample suited for the purpose of an MMR approach involves a combination of well-established quantitative and qualitative techniques (Teddlie and Yu, 2007; Guetterman et al., 2019). With reference to Creswell and Plano Clark's (2011) explanatory design where quantitative data is collected first and informs the sample of the subsequent qualitative phase, the following recommendations by the authors were closely followed within the research project presented here (Creswell and Plano Clark, 2017, p. 181), hence:

- Individuals who participate in the qualitative phase belong to the sample of the quantitative phase.
- The qualitative follow-up phase has a smaller sample size than the quantitative phase.
- During the quantitative data analysis stage, any unclear or unexpected statistical results are to be explored, informed and explained with the aid of qualitative data results.
- The purposive qualitative sample has to bear some degree of association with the demographics of the quantitative phase participants. As such, the purposeful qualitative sample mirrors the characteristics of the random quantitative sample.

Within the research project described in this chapter, the research team (Sainidis and Robson, 2016, 2017) used a suitable survey and interview sample drawn from the population of UK-based manufacturing SMEs. The study made use of purposive samples for both its quantitative and qualitative data collection phase. Furthermore, the greater depth of data interpretation that purposeful sampling offers rather than the generalisability of results from probability random sampling, aligns with the aims and purpose of the research study (Patton, 2002; Palinkas et al., 2015).

In the United Kingdom, close to 28,580 companies are manufacturing SMEs (or 9.8% of the total UK manufacturing population[1]). The study targeted manufacturing SMEs based in the UK by inviting their senior managers to participate in the online survey and follow-up interviews. Online surveys offer a cost advantage over postal surveys and are easy to administer and store the collected data (Nair and Adams, 2009; Evans and Anil, 2018). The literature acknowledges the potential of a low response rate (Dennis, 2003; Dommeyer et al., 2004; Porter, 2004; Kamel and Lloyd, 2016). Four reminder messages were sent to non-responding SMEs. The 104 responses received (4.7% response rate) compares well with previous academic research in the SME sector.

Subsequently, the 104 participating manufacturing SMEs were invited to take part in follow-up interviews, which resulted in an agreement to participate by 17 manufacturing SMEs. Although the literature advises on interview samples of 6-12 units (Collins, 2010), in order to ensure mirroring between the survey and interview samples and to ensure representation of SME (size, turnover, ownership), SIC code, manufacturing (production types) and geographical location, all 17 manufacturing SMEs which accepted the follow-up interview invitation were included in the interview sample.

7.5 Research instrument: questionnaire design

Given the mixed methods methodology used in this study, a single data collection instrument was developed for both survey and interview purposes. The study had a well-defined aim and research objectives with a clear purpose. The design of the questionnaire was influenced by the relevant sustainability and manufacturing strategy literature and similar studies on manufacturing SMEs. Seventeen questions were included in the questionnaire, using either a 5-,6-, or 7-point semantic differential scale. Frohlich (2002), Forza (2002), Dennis (2003) and Bryman and Bell (2007) have all advised piloting the research instrument, in this case, the survey and interview questionnaire, to allow for structural and wording corrections and develop the researcher's experience in conducting interviews. The prototype questionnaire was piloted in two phases before it was used for the UK-wide survey and follow-up interviews.

7.5.1 Quantitative data collection

The survey used a self-administered online (web-based) questionnaire structured around seven sections:

1. Covering statement: to introduce the purpose and benefits of the research and inform participants of the ethical policy governing the research.
2. Definition of the term 'manufacturing strategy': to ensure a common understanding by the participants in the research.
3. Participant's details (company name and management position): to ensure senior management participation and avoid response error.
4. Participating manufacturing SME's demographic details: to allow for sample profiling.
5. Eight questions capturing data on the issue of 'sustainability in manufacturing SMEs': to capture the necessary data in order to address the research question.
6. Feedback on questionnaire experience: to allow for minor adjustments to the data collection instrument during the survey rounds.
7. Participant's contact details to confirm request for brief report on survey results: to act as a response incentive.

The survey administration followed the best practice, taking advice from Frohlich (2002), Forza (2002) and Dennis (2003). Prior to the survey questionnaire being issued, participants were informed of the value of the survey to raise awareness and interest. Non-respondents were reminded over four rounds.

The collection of qualitative data, by means of semi-structured interviews, was informed by Lee (1999) and Golden–Biddle and Locke (1997) and a more editorially-inclined paper by Bansal et al. (2018). The average duration of the interviews was 45 minutes. The research team also took the advice of Arskey and Knight (1999) and Azungah (2018) regarding communication, questioning and conversation techniques, as well as ethical issues during an interview situation.

7.6 Data analysis

The collected data has been subject to a mixed data analysis strategy, as proposed by Tashakkori and Teddlie (1998). The parallel mixed analysis method allows the researcher to utilise the traditional types of quantitative and qualitative analysis techniques within the same study. A survey (quantitative data) is followed by interviews (qualitative data), the quantitative data is subject to descriptive statistics (frequencies), and the qualitative data is subject to thematic analysis.

In the first phase of the parallel design, the quantitative stage used nominal and mostly ordinal scales. Forza (2002) recommends, in the case of surveys with non-representative samples, the use of preliminary data analysis which includes frequency distribution of variables. Relating to the first phase, as Caracelli and Greene (1993), and Tashakkori and Teddlie (1998) suggest, where mixed methods apply, the quantitative data should be subject to descriptive statistics to explore frequencies of variables. Within this research project, descriptive statistics also allow for a reasonably in-depth overview of the manufacturing SME sector and its adoption of sustainable strategies. This is in line with the epistemological stance of this study, to explore and explain the studied phenomenon, without necessarily testing for any particular theory.

All 17 interviews were digitally recorded using Nvivo as a thematic analysis software. Qualitative data collected from the interviews was analysed using template analysis as developed by King (2004). King's template analysis method is a form of thematic analysis, but at the same time, is influenced by the more structured data analysis methods of grounded theory and interpretative phenomenological analysis (IPA), and can be used through a variety of epistemological positions (Waring and Wainwright, 2008; King et al., 2018).

Template analysis builds upon the earlier work of Miles and Huberman (1994). King (2004, 2018) defines the template analysis method as a list of codes representing themes identified within the collected qualitative data. The codes are in most cases defined a priori, typically driven by the relevant literature. However, some codes may develop during the data analysis process, as concepts emerge within the textual data which were not necessarily identified during the literature review process. As such, the template analysis allows for a degree of flexibility and creativity within the researcher's role. The list of codes generated makes the template. During the construction of the template, similar codes are grouped together in clusters (codes) with the final result presenting a hierarchy of codes. This hierarchy identifies what King defines as higher order codes, lower order codes and next level order codes.

Higher order codes include the broader concepts identified within the textual data across all data items (each interview in this case). The breakdown of each higher order code into fine distinctions within and across data extracts (interview quotes in this case) generates lower order codes. When the template is complete, the next stage of the analysis can commence with the interpretation of the coded data, by exploring patterns within the coded data to identify themes. The emerging patterns should then be interpreted by the researcher in order to develop themes. Figure 7.2 (see p. 130) illustrates the template analysis process used within this research project.

The interpretation of the template analysis results took advice from King and Brooks (2017). It was structured around the main themes, utilising powerful data extracts to prove each theme. Themes represent the core of this approach, with data extracts in the form of interview quotes complementing the themes. This approach allows for a clear and concise thematic discussion; however, there is a danger of making the discussion too broad with too much generalisation, failing to pay attention to the experiences of the study participants. The latter is important, given the contemporary nature of sustainability in the SMEs of the manufacturing sector.

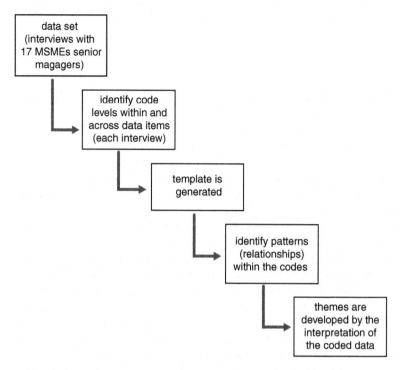

Figure 7.2 Template analysis process used within this study.

The research team aimed to capture the management beliefs and business practices on sustainability and its impact on business performance.

7.7 Discussion: mixing of datasets

Creswell and Plano Clark (2017) list three challenges when applying mixed methods. First, the researcher's level of skills required to collect and analyse quantitative and qualitative data. In particular, they stress that training in quantitative and qualitative data analysis methods or taking advice by experienced researchers in mixed methods is advisable. Second, time and resources required to collect and analyse both sets of data. Online surveys have short lead time and cost advantages over a postal survey. The use of the specialised software packages of SPSS and Nvivo for analysis of the quantitative and qualitative datasets, respectively, contribute in speeding up the process. Third, supporting the validity of mixed methods. Mixed methods research is seen as a 'novice' approach, with researchers questioning its lack of philosophical grounding and rigour (Johnson et al., 2017). However, within the subject of sustainable manufacturing, there is a growing trend towards the publication of MMR, see for example, Journal of Cleaner Production, Risk Management, Journal of Quality in Maintenance Engineering.

Onwuegbuzie and Johnson (2006, p. 52), and more recently Creamer (2018, 2017), add to the debate by pointing to the 'problem of integration' in MMR. This work notes that in the case of parallel mixed analysis, the researcher needs to ensure that the discussion of results derived from the two independent sets of quantitative and qualitative data, shows evidence of true integration and avoids it from becoming two separate research reports. Yin (2006) recommends a 'nesting' sampling technique where the samples used for each method bear a degree of relationship and commonality. The analyses and discussion of results should also show evidence of integration with all datasets addressing and commenting upon the same variables. The experience of the authors agrees with the views of Harrison et al. (2020) and Almandoz (2012) who view QUAN data as offering objective evidence on sustainability in the SMEs in the manufacturing sector but it is the QUAL data which offers rich context to allow for a greater level of interpretation of the overall results. In particular, the authors found the integration and nesting of the QUAN and QUAL datasets to be complementary, and also discovered crossover mechanisms during the interpretation and discussion of the study results.

This study used the same data requirements table for both QUAN and QUAL datasets. The developed data collection instruments were ethically approved by the researchers' university before they were piloted and finalised in their design. Using a common data requirements table for both QUAN and QUAL ensured early integration of the data collection methods (Bryman 2007). The sampling process ensured that the interview participants had already participated in the survey. This allows for a greater response rate to the follow-up interviews as the survey generates interest in the study. A mixed methods scenario allows for better consistency, mirroring and nesting between the QUAN and QUAL datasets. Within sustainability research, a common data collection instrument and survey and interview samples offered a greater insight into the decision-making factors, attitudes and beliefs residual in the owners/managers, critical in understanding sustainability in SMEs.

7.7.1 Study validation

Extant literature on mixed methods offers a range of criteria to assess the validity of a research study. Creswell and Plano Clark (2017) recommend that researchers applying mixed methods should consider the quality of their study and reflect on the criteria used by other researchers. The literature on mixed methods provides some further checklists as to how to validate the data collected and analysed. These checklists question the process of conducting the research when mixed methods are used. Bryman et al. (2008) suggest four criteria to test the rigour of applying mixed methods within a study:

- The use of mixed methods needs to be relevant to the research aim and questions. In this research project, the primary research question as to how UK-based SMEs in the manufacturing sector develop and implement a sustainability agenda requires an exploratory approach in identifying, understanding and explaining the underlying factors of the SMEs' owners/managers in adopting sustainability policies which have strategic, operational, product, market and certainly financial implications. A mixed methods approach offers an in-depth evaluation and discussion of the complexity of sustainability decisions and the role of cross-functional relationships within an SME environment. In addition, mixed methods offer the advantages of both quantitative (identifying) and qualitative (understanding and explaining) research methodologies.
- The researcher should provide evidence of data analysis to offer transparency about the mixed methods procedures. Collins (2010) offers an insight into transparency in mixed methods, with the use of interview debriefing protocol. Sustainability in the SMEs of the manufacturing sector is a contemporary and 'still under development' discipline, and for mixed methods to become an established research methods strategy, it requires an honest and open account of the data presented and how it is discussed.
- The findings need to be integrated or mixed. A parallel mixed method approach (Tashakkori and Teddlie, 1998) was applied in the study presented here. Certainly, the experience of the authors of this chapter has been that many mixed methods-based studies on the topic of sustainability do not, in many cases, provide a transparent and evident account of data nesting. Although mixed methods is a powerful tool in exploratory research, researchers do not always provide strong evidence of how the datasets are integrated.
- A rationale for the application of mixed methods. Mixed methods literature offers a wealth of sources, approaches and justifications for future studies in sustainability and, in particular, SMEs in the manufacturing arena. Researchers should base their choice of research tools on either past examples of MMR or identify gaps and opportunities where MMR can add innovation to the choice of research method.

In addition to the above mixed methods validation process, O'Cathain et al. (2008) have developed a more extensive set of criteria to validate the process of mixed methods within a study, known as Good Reporting of a Mixed Methods Study (GRAMMS):

- The planning quality of the mixed methods study: feasibility and transparency. During the planning stage of this research, the required IT resources (Kompass UK, surveymonkey.com account, access to SPPS and Nvivo) and funding were identified and allocated early to ensure the feasibility of the study. The issue of transparency has already been discussed above, using the Bryman et al. (2008) framework.

- Design quality: suitability of the design, strength and rigour. As discussed above, the use of mixed methods as research design allowed for the exploration of the research phenomena in question and corresponds to research methodology development within the subject of manufacturing strategy in SMEs.
- Data quality: detailed description, rigour and validity of sampling and data analysis.
- Interpretative rigour: relationship of research findings to relevant literature, exploring agreements and inconsistencies with other researchers.
- Inference transferability: conclusions applied to other settings. Although the primary focus of the present study is restricted by its research question, the research findings extend to issues of public policy on UK manufacturing and, in particular, on its SME sector.
- Reporting quality: successful completion and reporting of study. The ultimate outcome of the study carried out is the compilation of publishable research outputs. Participants and policy developers of the study will also benefit by issuing a practitioner-oriented report posted to them.
- Synthesisability: whether the study provides evidence of synthesis.
- Utility: the value of the results.

7.8 Conclusion

Two sets of data were used in our research to explore the phenomenon of sustainability in manufacturing SMEs in the United Kingdom; one quantitative, the other qualitative. MMR offers an innovative, value-added strategy and great opportunity for the collection of rich and powerful data. The datasets collected as part of an MMR approach were integrated and nested which allowed for greater insights into the phenomenon studied and well-informed conclusions. Challenges obviously exist in both process and outcome of a mixed methods approach. The researcher needs to ensure the integration and nesting of data and avoid bias towards one or the other ontological positions of realism or relativism but instead, stay faithful to pragmatism. Finally, the validation of the study is vital to ensure justification of the choice of data collection method, process of analysis and reporting mechanism.

This chapter identified the advantages of using MMR-based research for the exploration of the contemporary topic of sustainability in the particularly dynamic business sector of SMEs in the manufacturing sector. There is good evidence, within the discipline of sustainability in SMEs of the manufacturing sector, of an increased interest and adoption of mixed methods.

The limitations of a mono-method approach are well documented in the literature of SMEs (Reilly and Jones, 2017; Harrison et al., 2020). A recent study by Muñoz-Pascual et al. (2019) also supports the need for a mixed method approach in the discipline of SMEs and the engagement of SMEs with sustainability-oriented business practices. This is particularly true in the uncertain, complex and diverse business environments that SMEs tend to operate in.

Note

1 https://assets.publishing.service.gov.uk/government/uploads/system/uploads/attachment_data/file/836562/BPE__2019_detailed_tables.xls

References

Almandoz, J. (2012). Arriving at the starting line: The impact of community and financial logics on new banking ventures. *Academy of Management Journal*, *55*(6), 1381–1406.

Anderson, J., Cleveland G., and Schroeder R. (1989). Operations strategy: a literature review. *Journal of Operations Management*, *8*(2), 133–158.

Arskey, H., and Knight, P. (1999). *Interviewing for social scientists*. Sage, Thousand Oaks.

Ashton A., Kusch M., McKenna R., and Sodoma K. (2020). *Social epistemology and relativism*. Routledge, Abingdon.

Azungah, T. (2018). Qualitative research: deductive and inductive approaches to data analysis. *Qualitative Research Journal*, *18*(4), 383–400.

Bansal, P., Smith, W., and Vaara, E. (2018). New ways of seeing through qualitative research. *Academy of Management Journal*, *61*(4), 1189–1196.

Barnard, C. (1971). *The role of the executive*. Harvard University Press, Cambridge, M.A.

Barnes, D. (2001). Research methods for the empirical investigation of the process of formation of operations strategy. *International Journal of Operations and Production Management*, *21*(8), 1076–1095.

Barratt, M., Choi, T., and Li, M. (2011). Qualitative case studies in operations management: trends, research outcomes, and future research applications. *Journal of Operations Management*, *29*(4), 329–342.

Bazeley, P. (2010). Computer assisted integration of mixed methods data sources and analyses. In A. Tashakkori and C. Teddlie (Eds.). *Handbook of mixed methods research for the social and behavioral sciences* (2nd ed.). Sage, Thousand Oaks.

Biesta, G. (2010). Pragmatism and the philosophical foundations of mixed methods research. In Tashakkori A. and Teddlie C. (Eds). *Handbook of Mixed Methods Research for the Social and Behavioral Sciences* (2nd ed.). Sage, Thousand Oaks.

Bowman, C., and Ambrosini, V. (1997). Using single respondents in strategy research. *British Journal of Management*, *8*(2), 119–131.

Boyer, K., and Swink, M. (2008). Empirical elephants - why multiple methods are essential to quality research in operations and supply chain management. *Journal of Operations Management*, *26*(3), 337–348.

Bozarth, C., and McDermott, C. (1998). Configurations in manufacturing strategy: a review and directions for future research. *Journal of Operations Management*, 16(4), 427–439.

Bryman, A. (2006). Integrating quantitative and qualitative research: how is it done? *Qualitative Research*, 6(1), 97–113.

Bryman, A. (2007). Barriers to integrating quantitative and qualitative research. *Journal of Mixed Methods Research*, 1(1), 8–22.

Bryman, A., Becker, S., and Sempik, J. (2008). Quality criteria for quantitative, qualitative, and mixed methods research: A view from social policy. *International Journal of Social Research Methodology*, 11 (4), 361–376.

Bryman, A., and Bell, E. (2007). *Business research methods* (2nd ed.). Oxford University Press, Oxford.

Caracelli, V., and Greene, J. (1993). Data analysis strategies for mixed-method evaluation designs. *Educational Evaluation and Policy Analysis*, 15(2), 195–207.

Carey, J. (1993). Linking qualitative and quantitative methods: integrating cultural factors into public health. *Qualitative Health Research*, 3(3), 139–152.

Collins, K. (2010). Advanced practices and emerging trends in the social and behavioral sciences. In A. Tashakkori and C. Teddlie (Eds.), *Handbook of mixed methods research for the social and behavioral sciences*. 2nd ed. Sage. Thousand Oaks.

Crabtree, B., and Miller, W. (1999). Using codes and code manuals: a template organising style of interpretation. In F. Crabtree and L. Miller (Eds.). *Doing qualitative research*. 2nd ed. Sage, Thousand Oaks.

Creamer, E. (2017). *An Introduction to Fully Integrated Mixed Methods Research*. Sage, Thousand Oaks.

Creamer, E. (2018). Striving for methodological integrity in mixed methods research: the difference between mixed methods and mixed-up methods. *Journal of Engineering Education*, 107(4), 526–530.

Creswell, J., and Plano Clark, V. L. (2017). *Designing and conducting mixed methods research*. (3rd ed.). Sage, Thousand Oaks.

Crotty, M. (1998). *The foundations of social research - Meaning and perspective in the research process*. Sage, Thousand Oaks.

Dahlberg, B., Barg, F., Gallo, J., and Wittink, M. (2009). Bridging Psychiatric and anthropological approaches: The case of "nerves" in the United States. *Ethos*, 37(3), 282–313.

Dangelico, R. M., Pujari, D., and Pontrandolfo, P. (2017). Green product innovation in manufacturing firms: A sustainability-oriented dynamic capability perspective. *Business Strategy and the Environment*, 26(4), 490–506.

De Block, D., and Vis, B. (2018). Addressing the challenges related to transforming qualitative into quantitative data in qualitative comparative analysis. *Journal of Mixed Methods Research*, 13(4), 503–535.

Dennis, W. (2003). Raising response rate in mail surveys of small business owners: results of an experiment. *Journal of Small Business Management*, 41(3), 278–295.

Dommeyer, J., Baum, P., Hanna, W., and Chapman, S. (2004). Gathering faculty teaching evaluations by in-class and online surveys: their effects on response rates and evaluations. *Assessment and Evaluation on Higher Education*, 29(5), 611–623.

Easterby-Smith, M., Thorpe, R., Jackson, P., and Jaspersen L. (2018). *Management Research* (6th ed.). Sage, Thousand Oaks.

Edwards, C. D., Reeping, D., Taylor, A., and Bowers, A. (2018). Media review: An introduction to fully integrated mixed methods research. *Journal of Mixed Methods Research*, *13*(3), 201–402.

Evans, J., and Anil, M. (2018). The value of online surveys: A look back and a look ahead. *Internet Research*, *28*(4), 854–887.

Forza, C. (2002). Survey research in operations management: A process-based perspective. *International Journal of Operations and Production Management*, *22*(2), 152–194.

Frohlich, M. (2002). Techniques for improving response rates in OM survey research. *Journal of Operations Management*, *20*(1), 53–62.

Gimenez, C., Sierra, V., and Rodon, J. (2012). Sustainable operations: their impact on the triple bottom line. *International Journal of Production Economics*, *140*(1), 149–159.

Golden-Biddle, K., and Locke, K. (1997). *Composing qualitative research: Crafting theoretical points from qualitative research*. Sage, Thousand Oaks.

Greene, J., Caracelli, V., and Graham, W. (1989). Toward a conceptual framework for mixed-method evaluation designs. *Educational Evaluation and Policy Analysis*, *11*(3), 255–274.

Grössler, A., and Grübner, A. (2006). An empirical model of the relationships between manufacturing capabilities. *International Journal of Operations and Production Management*, *26*(5), 458–485.

Guetterman, T., Babchuk, W., Howell Smith, M., and Stevens, J. (2019). Contemporary approaches to mixed methods-grounded theory research: A field-based analysis. *Journal of Mixed Methods Research*, *13*(2), 179–195.

Hallgren, M., Olhager, J., and Schroeder, R. (2011). A hybrid model of competitive priorities. *International Journal of Operations and Production Management*, *31*(5), 511–526.

Harrison, R., Reilly, T., and Creswell, J. W. (2020). Methodological rigor in mixed methods: An application in management studies. *Journal of Mixed Methods Research*, 14(4), 473–495.

Hayes, H. (1985). Strategic planning-forward in reverse? *Harvard Business Review*, *63*(6), 111–119.

Hayes, H., and Pisano, G. (1994). Beyond world-class: The new manufacturing strategy. *Harvard Business Review*, *72*(1), 77–86.

Hayes, R., and Wheelwright, S. (1984). *Restoring our competitive edge: Competing through manufacturing*. Wiley, New York.

Hill, T. (1992). Incorporating manufacturing perspectives in corporate strategy. In C. A. Voss (Ed.). *Manufacturing strategy: Process and content*. Chapman and Hall, London.

Howe K. (1988). Against the quantitative-qualitative incompatibility thesis (or dogmas die hard). *Educational Researcher*, *17*(8), 10–16.

Howell Smith, M., Babchuk, W., Stevens, J., Garrett Wang, S., and Guetterman, T. (2020). Modeling the use of mixed methods - Grounded theory: developing scales for a new measurement model. *Journal of Mixed Methods Research*, *14*(2), 184–206.

Johnson, B., Russo, F., and Schoonenboom, J. (2017). Causation in mixed methods research: The meeting of philosophy, science and practice. *Journal of Mixed Methods Research*, *13*(2), 143–162.

Kamel, M., and Lloyd, H. (2016). Response rates in business and management research: an overview of current practice and suggestions for future direction. *British Journal of Management*, 27(2), 426–437.

Kang, D., and Evans, J. (2020). Against method: exploding the boundary between qualitative and quantitative studies of science. *Quantitative Science Studies*, 1(3), 930–944.

Kathuria, R. (2000). Competitive priorities and managerial performance: a taxonomy of small manufacturers. *Journal of Operations Management*, 18(6), 627–641.

Kaushik, V., and Walsh, C. (2019). Pragmatism as a research paradigm and its implications for social work research. *Social Sciences*, 8(9). doi 10.3390/socsci8090255

King, N. (2004). Using templates in the thematic analysis of text. In C. Cassell and G. Symon (Eds.). *Essential guide to qualitative methods in organisational research*. Sage, Thousand Oaks.

King, N., and Brooks, J. (2017). *Template analysis for business and management students*. Sage, Thousand Oaks.

King, N., Brooks, J., and Tabari, S. (2018). Template analysis in business and management research. In M. Ciesielska and D. Jemielniak (Eds.). *Qualitative methodologies in organization studies*. Palgrave Macmillan, Cham.

Kiridena, S., Hasan, M., and Kerr, R. (2009). Exploring deeper structures in manufacturing strategy formation processes: a qualitative inquiry. *International Journal of Operations and Production Management*, 29(4), 386–417.

Kotha, S., and Orne, D. (1989). Generic manufacturing strategies: A conceptual synthesis. *Strategic Management Journal*, 10(3), 211–231.

Lee, T. (1999). *Qualitative methods in organisational research*. Sage, Thousand Oaks.

Longoni, A., and Cagliano, R. (2015). Environmental and social sustainability priorities: The integration of operations strategies. *International Journal of Operations and Production Management*, 35(2), 216–245.

Miles, M., and Huberman, M. (1994). *Qualitative data analysis - an expanded sourcebook*. (2nd ed.). Sage, Thousand Oaks.

Miller, D. (1986). Configurations of strategy and structure: towards a synthesis. *Strategic Management Journal*, 7(3), 233–249.

Molina-Azorin, J., and Lopez-Gamero, M. (2016). Mixed methods studies in environmental management research: Prevalence, purposes and designs. *Business Strategy and the Environment*, 25(2), 134–148.

Morgan, D. (2014). *Integrating qualitative and quantitative methods: A pragmatic approach*. Sage, Thousand Oaks.

MRS. http://www.mrs.org.uk/ Accessed: 30/09/2020.

Muñoz-Pascual, L., Curado, C., and Galende, J. (2019). The triple bottom line on sustainable product innovation performance in SMEs: A mixed methods approach. *Sustainability*, 11. doi.org/10.1007/s11846-019-00371-2

Nair, S. C., and Adams, P. (2009). Survey platform: a factor influencing online survey delivery and response rate. *Quality in Higher Education*, 15(3), 291–296.

O'Cathain, A., Murphy, E., and Nicholl, J. (2008). The quality of mixed methods studies in health science service research. *Journal of Health Services Research and Policy*, 13(2), 92–98.

Onwuegbuzie, A., and Johnson, B. (2006). The validity issue in mixed research. *Research in the Schools, 13*(1), 48–63.

Palinkas, L., Horwitz, S., Green, C., Wisdom, J., Duan, N., and Hoagwood, K. (2015). Purposeful sampling for qualitative data collection and analysis in mixed method implementation research. *Adminstration Policy Mental Health, 42*(5), 533–544.

Patton, M. Q. (2002). *Qualitative research and evaluation methods.* 3rd ed. Sage, Thousand Oaks.

Porter, R. (2004). *Overcoming Survey Research Problems.* Jossey-Bass, San Francisco.

Reichard, C., and Rallis, S. (1994). Qualitative and quantitative inquiries are not incompatible: a call for a new partnership. *New Directions for Program Evaluation, 61*(1), 85–91.

Reilly, T., and Jones, R. (2017). Mixed methodology in family business research: Past accomplishments and perspectives for the future. *Journal of Family Business Strategy, 8*(3), 185–195.

Robson, C. (1993). *Real world research: A resource for social scientists and practitioner researchers.* Blakewell, Hobroken.

Sainidis, E., and Robson, A. (2016). Environmental turbulence: impact on UK SMEs' manufacturing priorities. *Management Research Review, 39*(10), 1239–1264.

Sainidis, E., and Robson, A. (2017). SMEs and environmental practices: a study of the UK-based manufacturing SMEs sector. Institute of Small Business and Entrepreneurship Conference, Belfast, 8-9 Nov 2017.

Sale, J., Lohfeld, L., and Brazil, K. (2002). Revisiting the quantitative-qualitative debate: implications for mixed-methods research. *Quality and Quantity, 36*(1), 45–53.

Salvador, F., Forza, C., and Rungtusanatham, M. (2002). Modularity, product variety, production volume, and component sourcing: theorizing beyond generic prescriptions. *Journal of Operations Management, 20*(5), 549–575.

Scudder, G. D., and Hill, C. A. (1998). A review and classification of empirical research in operations management. *Journal of Operations Management, 16*(1), 91–101.

Skinner, W. (1969). Manufacturing - the missing link in corporate strategy. *Harvard Business Review, 47*(3), 136–145.

Skinner, W. (1974). The focused factory. *Harvard Business Review, 52*(3), 113–121.

Smith, J., and Heshusius, L. (1986). Closing down the conversation: The end of quantitative-qualitative debate among educational inquirers. *Educational Researcher, 15*(1), 4–12.

Sousa, R. (2003). Linking quality to manufacturing strategy: An empirical investigation of customer focus practices. *Journal of Operations Management, 21*(1), 1–18.

Stobaugh, R., and Telesio, P. (1983). Match manufacturing policies and product strategy. *Harvard Business Review, 61*(2), 113–120.

Tashakkori, A., and Teddlie, C. (1998). *Mixed methodology - combining qualitative and quantitative approaches.* Sage, Thousand Oaks.

Teddlie, C., and Yu, F. (2007). Mixed methods sampling - a typology with examples. *Journal of mixed Methods Research, 1*(1), 77–100.

Ünal, E., and Shao, J. (2019). A taxonomy of circular economy implementation strategies for manufacturing firms: Analysis of 391 cradle-to-cradle products. *Journal of Cleaner Production.* 212, 754–765.

Venugopal, V., and Saleeshya, P. G. (2018). Manufacturing system sustainability through lean and agile initiatives. *International Journal of Sustainable Engineering*, 12(3), 159–173.

Voss, C., and Winch, G. (1996). Including engineering in operations strategy. *Production and Operations Management*, 5(1), 78–90.

Ward, P., Bickford, J., and Leong, K. (1996). Configurations of manufacturing strategy, business strategy, environment and structure. *Journal of Management*, 22(4), 597–626.

Waring, T., and Wainwright, D. (2008). Issues and challenges in the use of template analysis: two comparative case studies from the field. *The Electronic Journal of Business Research Methods*, 6(1), 85–94.

Yin, R. K. (1994). *Case study research* (2nd ed.). Sage, Thousand Oaks.

Yin, R. K. (2006). Mixed methods research: Are the methods genuinely integrated or merely parallel? *Research in the Schools*, 13(1), 41–47.

Younis, H., Sundarakani, B., and O'Mahony, B. (2019). Green supply chain management and corporate performance: developing a roadmap for future research using a mixed methods approach. *IIMB Management Review.* doi.org/10.1016/j.iimb.2019.10.011

Zarte, M., Pechmann, A., and Nunes, I. (2019). Decision support systems for sustainable manufacturing surrounding the product and production life cycle - A literature review. *Journal of Cleaner Production, 219*, 336–349.

8   A longitudinal mixed-method study of Australian SME environmental behaviour

Aharon Factor

8.1 Introduction

Australian researchers addressing the sustainability behaviours of small and medium-sized enterprises (SMEs) have generally relied upon the singular use of either a survey or participatory interviews. While this has provided a useful foundation for future studies, Australia is now facing increasingly critical environmental and social problems which need greater exploration and scrutiny than stand-alone methodologies can provide. This chapter provides insights into a longitudinal mixed-method design that has been deployed to capture the growing sustainability complexities associated with Australian SMEs in particular.

Sustainability complexities in Australia are manifested by multiple factors. Australia is warming faster than the global world average which in 2020 led to between 12 and 14 million acres as well as around half a million animals being lost to wildfires (Buchholz, 2020). At the same time, drought has led to water shortages and the outbreak of disease (Kenyon, 2020). Meanwhile, Australia is also regarded as one of the world's most important biodiversity communities which is also facing one of the highest species extinctions in the world (Australian Government, 2014; OECD, 2019). For example, the Great Barrier Reef faces increased bleaching due to climate change while Eastern Australia is recognised by the World Wildlife Fund as a global deforestation hotspot (Verweij, 2013).

Sustaining Australia against this backdrop might appear challenging, considering that its largest economic driver is a commodity-led finance community (Australian Government The Treasury, 2016) and Australia is, by far, the largest coal exporter in the world (Workman, 2020). There is also an urgent need to close the gap between indigenous and non-indigenous standards of living (Askew et al., 2020), fundamentally a goal of the UN SDGs that no one should be left behind (United Nations, 2017). Nonetheless, a shift is occurring in Australia with commitment amongst the business leaders, academic and institutional stakeholders, to build a more sustainable future in line with global initiatives such as the UN SDGs (ASIC, 2019). How far this changing landscape is influencing change in the

Australian SME sector has been the focus of a purposively-designed mixed method study in Melbourne.

8.2 The Melbourne mixed-method study

8.2.1 Background developments

The study discussed in this chapter builds on a previous initiative by the Australian Federal Government, enacted through a regional government entity, The Swan Catchment Council[1]. They had worked with a team at Edith Cowan University in Western Australia. The intention was to address two key propositions that awareness does not necessarily translate into action and that waste generation in one industrial location could be extrapolated to show the impact that SMEs have as a whole on the environment. As an exploratory investigation, the methodological approach was to use a quantitative survey to collect categorical information from SME owners/managers (Redmond et al., 2008). The study also collected some written qualitative data to explain further any barriers to the adoption of waste management practices. The propositions shaped three key 'what' questions around environmental attitudes, barriers to engaging with waste management practices and approximation of weekly waste, and informed the design of a research instrument. After stakeholder input and pilot testing of the survey instrument, a 30-item survey instrument was constructed. This was delivered in Perth between 2005 and 2006 (Redmond et al., 2008).

The survey was later re-administered to other sites in the Greater Perth Metropolitan area and further refined. Checks to confirm face and content validity (Cavana et al., 2001) were made prior to the delivery of the survey. In 2007, the survey was delivered by the Swan Catchment Council (Walker et al., 2007) to SMEs through one-to-one face delivery and data collected through a hand-held Personal Digital Assistant (PDA). Overall, the Swan Catchment Council had collected data from approximately 4500 SME sites. This led to significant waste management interventions and communication strategies. This project demonstrated that close relationships between academic and non-academic actors can have positive impacts on sustainability actions within the community.

Construction of the survey tool was intended to collect mainly categorical variables such as "Yes" and "No" answers concerning a respondent's use of energy, water and wastes. The survey tool also included limited rating scales and some opportunity for short hand-written qualitative responses. This meant that the survey tool provided for insight rather than casual linkages and explanation. The researcher's background which was grounded in qualitative research informed the need for a more rigorous methodological approach. As such, a qualitative investigation was built into the research design.

The Perth-based study, however, was a descriptive account of SME owner/managers' environmental perspectives and how they managed their energy, water and wastes. The categorical information was collected as mainly "Yes" or "No" answers, representing limited opportunity for meaningful statistical analysis. Meanwhile, the qualitative written insights did not provide opportunity for discussion to elucidate more depth. To address sustainability in SMEs, however, a more rigorous and deeper examination behind the "Yes or No" answers provided by the descriptive statistical analysis was deemed necessary. In particular, sustainability in SMEs is dictated internally by owners/managers' personal cognitions and externally by an increasingly complex set of sustainability issues. This need to deepen understanding around SMEs and environmental issues as well as develop greater confidence in the data formed the main aims of the Melbourne study. The focus on achieving one's goals through method is described by Kvale (1989) and the selection of a method, therefore, begins with defining the purpose of the study and the phenomena the researcher wishes to investigate (Patton, 1990).

Initially, the purpose of the Melbourne study was to conduct a trial of the Perth-based survey instrument in a new location so as to compare and contrast findings amidst concerns of cultural bias, having only conducted the research in the one local setting. The Australian Federal Government sought to develop such developments across Australia. The Swan Catchment Council, therefore, sought to deploy their survey instrument in other Australian states. With this aim, the author was contacted with the possibility of engaging Melbourne-based SMEs with the survey instrument. Even though the 30-item instrument had been further developed to a 49-item instrument and included a small number of short answer, qualitative hand-written items, the author recognised that the stand-alone exploratory quantitative approach did not bring enough depth, scrutiny or academic rigour. Critical scholars in the field of environmental management had long urged for a deeper reflection. Furthermore, Welford (1998) advocates a postmodern perspective of corporate environmental management and sustainable development, emphasising the need for a critical research agenda. The researcher, as explained, also wanted to develop critical questions so as to gain deeper insights as to how Australia is able to combat key issues facing Australia today, such as climate change, drought, carbon emissions, landfill impacts and land availability.

In responding to these issues, understanding the complexities associated with the SME owner/manager's decision-making is also needed. This presents a complex set of internal and external variables. The significant number of unknown variables complicates these issues and provides an unfamiliar research terrain (Denzin, 1994). It also demands further exploration to ascertain, for example, as Patton (1990) asks: "What did people really mean when they marked that answer on the questionnaire? What elaborations can respondents provide to clarify responses? How do the various dimensions of analysis fit together as a whole from the perspective of respondents?" This approach is not only particularly important in supporting descriptive statistics that alone cannot explain causal links between variables nor provide sufficient confidence and validity of findings but also in strengthening the validity of responses to surveys where there are likely to be language or cultural biases. Addressing these concerns, Monárrez et al., 2018, p. 170) use an 'open approach' to add further context to the quantitative data and to ask respondents the reasons for answering their survey questions.

The integration of a qualitative dimension to the original Perth-based quantitative tool offered the researcher the opportunity to design a purposeful mixed method approach. This new design could, therefore, account for the limitations of the Perth-based survey instrument as a stand-alone descriptive tool, and allow for a more meaningful, deeper investigation into the complexities associated with the environmental behaviours of SME owners/managers. This also builds on the works of Greene and Caracelli (1997) and Collins et al. (2006) whose research rationale seeks to mix quantitative and qualitative tools to provide robustness, validity and context to the research undertaking. Furthermore, the sparse literature on SME and environment behaviour lends well to the development of a research approach that goes beyond problem quantification, delving deeper through qualitative exploration. While this new design recognised that while mono-methods may be no lesser a research tool, it was these advantages of a purposeful mixed-method design that was better able to address the study's problems and questions (Molina-Azorín and López-Gamero, 2016).

Initially, the primary aim was to answer the following questions: What is the usage of energy and water? How do small, light industries in Melbourne make use of energy and water? To what extent are the waste streams of the Melbourne light industry significant? Why do managers recycle or not recycle waste materials? How are managerial behaviour, attitudes and perceptions influential on environmental performance in this sector?

8.3 Mixing the methods

Central to the mixed-method design is the way different data sets are connected. This can occur through various means, including question specification, participant selection and instrument development. These concerns are central to the model of Collins et al. (2006) that emphasises four rationales that influence the research process: i) Partial enrichment (e.g., mixing quantitative and qualitative research to optimise the sample of participants ensuring that each participant selected is appropriate for inclusion); ii) Instrument fidelity (e.g., assessing the appropriateness and/or utility of existing instruments and creating new instruments); iii) Treatment integrity (e.g., assessing fidelity of intervention); and iv) Significance enhancer (e.g., facilitating thickness and richness of data, augmenting interpretation and usefulness of findings).

Collins et al.'s (2006) work informed the mixed-method design in the following ways. Firstly, it informed the development of the research questions beyond the initial Perth mono-method that used a categorical approach to questions. By using a purposeful design, an overall set of questions could be developed that sought to attain answers from both quantitative and qualitative methodologies. Furthermore, question specification occurred through the mixing of the two methods in the same study. In the first quantitative study, explanatory questions categorised the levels of energy and water, the types and quantities of waste streams and the level of managerial environmental behaviours, attitudes and perceptions in similar fashion as the Perth study. The influence of the aforementioned authors aided in recognising that the integration of a qualitative phase could help develop instrument fidelity as it would make the study more appropriate by digging deeper into the complexities surrounding environmental issues in SMEs.

From the outset, the funding body in discussion with the author recognised the importance of instrument fidelity, treatment integrity and significance enhancer but their considerations were towards testing the utility of the existing instrument within a different Australian geographical location and testing the consistency of replication and augmentation of the Perth findings with a new data collection phase in Melbourne. The training of the researcher as a qualitative researcher, however, recognised that to address environmental issues in SMEs more appropriately, a redesigned instrument that included a qualitative component would better address the Significance Enhancer rationale and facilitate greater thickness and enrichment of the study's data. In particular, by asking questions that drilled down into how and why participants ticked boxes on the survey instrument allowed the researcher to dig more deeply into the barriers to the implementation of environmental initiatives and may be more fruitful than the survey alone in providing 'information-rich' qualitative data (Walley and Stubbs, 1999; Tilley, 2000). The interview participants were selected through a cluster analysis of the quantitative survey, to ensure a purposeful integration between the quantitative and qualitative data sets. The aim was to select participants as they best fit the interview criteria (on the premise of their survey responses) and company characteristics. Cluster analysis was subsequently undertaken to develop a scale ranging from reactive to proactive SSMB environmental behaviour. Factors used in the cluster analysis were:

- Level of environmental concern from low to high (based upon their rating of environmental issues, environmental decision-making, and internal operations).

- Tendency to either, employ more people and own their premises or to employ fewer people and lease their premises.
- Establishment size from smaller to larger.
- Level of knowledge of how to reduce energy and water use.
- Implementation of energy and water reduction practices.
- Types of waste materials produced.
- Degree of knowledge and practice of recycling and landfilling of waste materials.

Within each of these categories, where possible, a variety of responses to water, energy, business type and environmental concern clusters were selected. Further details concerning the cluster analysis can be found in Appendix 1. The author recognised that cluster analysis data from the survey instrument could be used to select participants for a deeper, qualitative investigation through semi-structured and open-ended interviews. In the letter of invitation to participate, prospective interviewees were asked if they would be available for further possible interviews beyond the first stage. This set up the possibility of a longitudinal qualitative research within the mixed-method design.

The semi-structured interviews were designed to augment and corroborate the quantitative findings. By verifying, or refuting, the quantitative findings, they also provide a test of Treatment Integrity as a semi-structured interview can include questions aligned to the original question survey. The semi-structured interviews revealed several interesting case study companies which developed the longitudinal aspect of the study. What was not expected was the shift from the more open questions in the case study companies to the collection of data in a grounded fashion. This shifted the dominance of the method and demonstrated the fluid nature of the longitudinal design (Strauss and Corbin, 1990; van Ness et al., 2011).

The longitudinal design allowed for the findings of the semi-structured interviews to inform propositions for a deeper, more exploratory open set of interviews. Interview participants who had agreed to participate in further interviews beyond the semi-structured interviews, constituted a small set of agreeable participants, initiating a further round of interviews. The timing of the first round of open interviews was particularly important, given Australia's 2009 Black Saturday Bushfires which saw 173 deaths and heightened awareness of climate change impacts. Following this event, the open interviews provided scope to tease out great depth as to the owner/manager's emotions and environmental perspectives. By 2012, Australia had implemented the world's first carbon trading scheme which was later rescinded through a change of government in 2014. This set a rich opportunity for a deeper exploratory examination of environmental issues in these companies. With the increasing effects of climate change in Australia, in 2016 and 2020, participants have been willing to strongly engage their emotions and perspectives with the researcher in a deep investigative discourse. This deeper discourse has significant implications, philosophically, for mixed-method design in sustainable business research.

8.4 Philosophical underpinnings

This fluid nature of the mixed method longitudinal design also has philosophical implications. The mixed-method design was, from the outset, underpinned by a critical realist philosophy. Critical realism (CR) can play an important role in underpinning mixed method research designs that are able to investigate complex phenomena (Allana and Clark, 2018). This is because CR as a meta-theory that diverges from the traditional meta-theories of positivism and social constructivism, with important implications for sustainability research. Sustainability is a complex open system. It involves understanding the casual and generative mechanisms that influence the observable world. This finds, accord with Roy Bhaskar's original tenets that view the world as an open system in direct contrast to the empirically closed and controlled setting of the scientific method (Cruickshank, 2012).

For critical realists, stand-alone quantitative surveys as a methodological approach are characteristic of the dominant positivists who maintain a 'realist' philosophy that recognises that an independent world exists, even if knowledge of that world maybe 'fallible' (Sayer, 1992). Through the positivist's perspective, knowledge is created through independent observation. This approach is criticised by some social scientists purporting to Popper's falsification theory that supports an interdependence of 'facts' (Kvale, 1989; Guba and Lincoln, 1994). Karl Popper's falsification theory recognised that one black swan shatters the illusion that all swans are white became evident in the mixed method findings. The survey findings revealed one particularly interesting finding that not one surveyed company bought green energy. Only through the semi-structured interviews did it emerge that this was due to SMEs being unable to benefit from the discounts offered on large-scale energy purchases favouring larger enterprises. The descriptive statistics alone gave the impression that the sector was not interested in purchasing green energy. Instead, it was found that SME owners/managers were very interested in green energy purchasing. It was only through interviewing the participants and engaging in dialogue that fallibility could be established.

Some social science researchers find accord with this methodological endeavour, recognising that the human dimension of social objects exists in a linguistically constituted and interpersonally negotiated social world where concepts cannot be objectively differentiated and are, thus, concept-dependent (Kvale, 1989; Sayer, 1992; Guba and Lincoln, 1994). Propositional knowledge (rather than hypothesis) is, therefore, 'constructed and expressed in terms of the concepts available in a language' (Sayer, 1992). Post-positivists use these concepts to support a paradigm that is critical of the positivists' absolute objectivity. From the perspective of these 'critical realists' (see Denzin and Lincoln, 1994, p. 109), thought and its object are causally, rather than intrinsically, linked. Socially constructed artefacts may therefore appear to be 'real' but may be nevertheless 'false' (Sayer, 1992, pp. 65–71 and p. 162). CR thus identifies an inadequacy in traditional realist philosophy that does not distinguish between ontology and epistemology. This is known as the 'epistemic fallacy' and is a distinction espoused by the first systemised proponent of CR who introduced his theory in 1975 in his book, *A Realist Theory of Science* (c.f. Bhaskar 1998).

Central to Bhaskar's meta-theory, is a transcendental 'deductibility' (Bhaskar, 2016, p. 36) that permits critical realists to delve beyond a description of observable phenomenon to a description of the underlying cause of relations between individual agents and social structures. Accordingly, through the transformation of observable knowledge to that of taking an alternative guise, CR moves from examining conceivable social forms to those that are inconceivable. This suggests that there must be implicit knowledge of internal relations, knowledge not immediately explicit to the mind, insights that can only be sustained through the transcendence of CR (Sayer, 1992). For Kant, transcendental deductions were about delving down to the *a priori* conditions that explain the events that we experience in the perceived world (Kemling, 2018). The more the researcher drills down into the underlying events and mechanisms that explain the empirical world, the more the researcher finds patterns and themes that inductively create meaning around abstract events. This was an important concern in both the initial design of the mixed method study and the review and re-design as the longitudinal research developed.

The movement, from a structured observation of the empirical world to a semi-structured, and then unstructured exploration of the environmental behaviours of SME owners/managers, began to resemble the emergent collection of data associated with grounded theory. The following account demonstrates how a critical realist perspective has shaped the mixed-method design and uses critical grounded theory to address environmental complexities in SMEs. CR can be viewed as a post-positivist philosophy as it maintains a realist ontology with an interpretative epistemology (Bhaskar, 1998). In this sense, CR recognises that there is a real world that exists but absolute truth cannot exist as everything is open for interpretation. It also can be a driver for reformation of business school research to engage with global challenges such as climate change (Mingers, 2015). In particular, Mingers (2015, p. 328) states that, 'The pluralist character of CR and the need for holism and transdisciplinarity in turn mean that we need mixed-method research to employ together a range of research methodologies, empirical, interpretive and oriented towards practical action (action research).' This is an important aspect that shaped the mixed-method design. In particular, it informs that quantitative data can be collected about the real world but meaning about social actors and me-chanisms that define this world are open to interpretation.

This aspect is particularly useful in researching owners/managers in SMEs as the traditional divide between positivism and subjectivism does not allow for leadership studies to recognise leadership as a fluid interaction between structure and agency. For Kempster and Parry (2014), CR re-presents an opportunity to study leadership as a holistic concept rather than as either structure or agency. This holistic approach also allows researchers to utilise a range of research methods to understand the structures and si-tuational contexts of participating actors and be aware of the interpreta-tions of participants (Smith and Elger, 2014). This is particularly important in the context of SMEs where structure and agency are often holistically situated within the owner/manager's leadership style.

While the initial mixed-method design aimed at explaining the results of a quantitative survey by use of semi-structured interviews, the longitudinal nature of the open interviews allowed the mixed-method design to shift from a more deductive-orientated study to an inductive study. In this study, therefore, deductive reasoning was able to initially guide the research process through propositions emanating from well-established theoretical principles. As the research questions shifted during the research from de-ductive to inductive, the research also shifted from explanation to ex-ploration. This triangulated approach demonstrates the enrichment capability of mixed methods research. This strengthening of the research process by using a survey and semi-structured interviews prior to long-itudinal open interviews is supported by Eisenhardt (1989, p. 536): 'A *priori* specification of constructs can also help to shape the initial design of theory building research. Measure constructs more accurately, may provide for firmer empirical ground for the emergent theory. When several of these constructs did emerge as related to the decision-process, there were strong, triangulated measures on which to ground the emergent theory.'

Figure 8.1 (see page 149) is representative of the iceberg metaphor, whereby empirical observations in the perceived world represents only part of the reality that exists under the water. What is observed in this empirical world is the tip of the iceberg. In the actual world are the supporting mass of ice and more deeply, the generative mechanisms in the freezing water deep below.

8.5 Sequentially mixed-method design

Hanson et al. (2005) describe the importance of concurrence or sequence of data collection when designing mixed method research studies. They ex-plain the key purposes and rationales for integrating different data types within one study. In this study, a phased approach was taken to collecting quantitative and qualitative data. The sequence of mixed-method design is dictated by the objectives of the researcher (Azorín and Cameron, 2010).

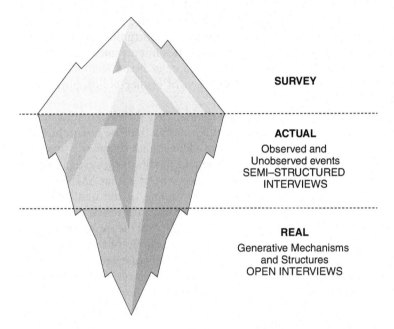

SURVEY

ACTUAL
Observed and
Unobserved events
SEMI–STRUCTURED
INTERVIEWS

REAL
Generative Mechanisms
and Structures
OPEN INTERVIEWS

Figure 8.1 Critical realist mixed method approach.

The objectives included the conducting of a trial of an existing quantitative tool and to use this tool to select participants to explore in more detail about the environmental behaviours in SMEs. It was, therefore, imperative that the first strand of the sequence be a quantitative one.

It was also imperative that the first strand produce quality inferences to inform the next phase. This is specifically important when a sequenced design is used and can significantly influence the quality of inferences of the strand(s) (Teddlie and Tashakkori, 2009; Creswell and Plano Clark, 2011). To ensure quality inferences, the first strand was associated with the following strands (semi-structured, then open interviews) through a cluster analysis undertaken by a specialist statistician who worked with the qualitative researcher to ensure a robust, valid and appropriate selection of participants for the qualitative stage.

8.6 Discussion and conclusion

At the outset, the chapter presents both unique Australian but also common global sustainability challenges, such as climate change and the state of the world's oceans. The inherent complexity that this context represents for sustainability-focused researchers means that appropriate research methods need to be utilised to bring understandings across a holistic set of variables that bring together both objective and subjective elements. A key aspect presented in this study was the awareness of the researcher in recognising both the benefits and limitations of both quantitative and qualitative research approaches and being able to identify opportunities to bring two research strands together into the same study. It is not just methodologically that the researcher must be aware, to eventuate a mixed method research design, but there must also be an awareness of his/her philosophical perspective.

The understanding presented in this chapter that the researcher's stance as a critical realist, then, underpinned what it was that the researcher was attempting to achieve. And this helped define and shape the research questions and drove both the quantitative and qualitative investigations. It fundamentally provided a way of addressing why it is that SME owners/managers tick survey items. Without this coupling of the qualitative investigation to the descriptive statistics obtained from the initial quantitative survey, the researcher could not capture the 'reality' of the owner/manager's mind. Otherwise, the survey alone only captures the tip of the iceberg. For SMEs, specifically ascertaining the way the owners/managers think is the key to unlocking knowledge about the whole business, rather than the fragmented decision-making of larger organisations.

Another key consideration that this chapter presents is that initially, the mixed method research design primarily set out to utilise explanatory, semi-structured interviews to corroborate and confirm initial survey findings. A longitudinal dimension to the study as secondary consideration became a critically important research undertaking. It allowed for the researcher to capture the changing owner/manager perspectives as climate change has increasingly been impacting Australian society and politics.

In conclusion, this chapter shows that researchers who are aware of the research tools, both quantitative and qualitative, that are available to them and are prepared to be creative in the way they design and implement their investigations, can enrich the sustainability field conceptually and methodologically.

8.7 Study implications

The study was funded by a research grant that allowed nine research assistants to be financed to undertake the survey, face-to-face with participants. A statistical analyst was employed to ensure the quality of the statistical analysis. In addition, research was conducted across the entire Greater Melbourne Region and the trial of the survey instrument had already been conducted across the Greater Perth Region in Western Australia. Furthermore, the qualitative research that ensued was conducted longitudinally. This overview of the research requirements demonstrates that mixed methods can be time and cost-intensive, and these considerations should be realistically assessed before designing mixed method research. Solutions for overcoming such restrictions may emerge through working collaboratively with other disciplines, either through an inter-disciplinary or in a transdisciplinary manner. In Chapter 3 of this book, some reported research used web-based surveys which provide an opportunity for researchers to reduce costs and time associated with collecting data. In this study, face-to-face delivery was undertaken to reduce survey bias. With increasingly developed technology, the scope may also be expanded to deliver surveys online, further reducing time and costs.

Sustainability is a holistic and complex phenomenon. This mixed method study has shown that when using the quantitative instrument alone, only a one-dimensional view of this complexity could be observed. Only when the researcher is able to deploy other methodological tools can additional dimensions to this complexity be included within the same study. This can provide the researcher with multiple lenses with which to understand what sustainability is, both in theoretical terms and in terms of informing practice.

Note

1 Swan Catchment Council is now known as Perth Region Natural Resource Management (PRNRM).

References

Allana, S., and Clark, A. (2018). Applying meta-theory to qualitative and mixed-methods research: A discussion of critical realism and heart failure disease management interventions research. *International Journal of Qualitative Methods*, 17(1), 1–9.

ASIC. (2019). AISCs releases 2018 sustainability report activities for planet and people support United Nations sustainable development goals. https://corp.asics.com/en/press/article/2019-05-13-2 Accessed: 30/09/2020.

Askew, D. A., Brady, K., Mukandi, B., Singh, D., Sinha, T., Brough, M., and Bond, C. J. (2020). Closing the gap between rhetoric and practice in strengths-based approaches to Indigenous public health: a qualitative study. *Australian and New Zealand Journal of Public Health*, 44(2), 102–105.

Australian Government. (2014). Australia's fifth national report to the convention on biological diversity. Department of Agriculture, Water and the Environment. https://www.environment.gov.au/system/files/resources/fd293bd1-c8b8-4ef3-9178-315d06a1663d/files/5th-national-report-final_0.pdf Accessed 30/09/2020.

Australian Government The Treasury. (2016). The strength of Australia's financial sector. https://treasury.gov.au/publication/backing-australian-fintech/the-strength-of-australias-financial-sector

Azorín, J. M., and Cameron, R. (2010). The application of mixed methods in organisational research: A literature review. *Electronic Journal of Business Research Methods*, 8(2), 95–105.

Bhaskar, R. (1998). *The possibility of naturalism: A philosophical critique of the contemporary human sciences.* Routledge, London.

Bhaskar, R. (2016). *Enlightened common sense*. Routledge, Abingdon.

Buchholz, K. (2020). Australia is warming faster than global average. Statista. Retrieved August 24, 2020, from https://www.statista.com/chart/20404/mean-annual-temperature-anomaly-in-australia-and-the-world/ Accessed: 30/09/2020.

Cavana, R. Y., Delahaye, B. L., and Sekaran, U. (2001). *Applied business research: Qualitative and quantitative methods*. Wiley, Australia.

Collins, K. M. T., Onwuegbuzie, A. J., and Sutton, I. L. (2006). A model incorporating the rationale and purpose for conducting mixed-methods research in special education and beyond. *Learning Disabilities*, 4(1), 67–100.

Creswell, J. W., and Plano Clark, V. L. (2011). *Designing and conducting mixed methods research* (2nd ed.). Sage, Thousand Oaks.

Cruickshank, J. (2012). Positioning positivism, critical realism and social constructionism in the health sciences: A philosophical orientation. *Nursing Inquiry*, 19(1), 71–82.

Denzin, N. K., and Lincoln, Y. S. (1994). *Handbook of qualitative research*. Sage, Thousand Oaks.

Eisenhardt, K. M. (1989). Building theories from case study research. *Academy of Management Review*, 14(4), 532–550.

Greene, J. C., and Caracelli, V. J. (1997). Advances in mixed-method evaluation: The challenges and benefits of integrating diverse paradigms. *New Directions for Evaluation*, 74, 1–94.

Guba, E. G., and Lincoln, Y. S. (1994). Competing paradigms in qualitative research. In Y. S. Lincoln (Ed.), *Handbook of qualitative research*. Sage, Thousand Oaks.

Hanson, W. E., Plano Clark, V. L., Petska, K. S., Creswell, J. W., and Creswell, J. D. (2005). Mixed methods research designs in counseling psychology. *Journal of Counseling Psychology*, 52(2), 224–235.

Kemling, J. (2018). Peirce's transcendental method: The latent debate between prescision and abduction. *Transactions of the Charles S Peirce Society*, 54(2), 249–272.

Kempster S., and Parry K. (2014). Critical realism and grounded theory. In O. J. and V. S. Edwards P. K. (Eds.), *Studying organizations using critical realism: A practical guide*. (86–108). Oxford University Press, Oxford.

Kenyon, G. (2020). Infections rise as Australia sells water in severe drought. *The Lancet Infectious Diseases*, 20(3). doi:10.1016/s1473-3099(20)30074-8

Kvale, S. (1989). *Issues of validity in qualitative research*. Chartwell-Bratt, Lund.

Mingers, J. (2015). Helping business schools engage with real problems: The contribution of critical realism and systems thinking. *European Journal of Operational Research*, 242(1), 316–331.

Molina-Azorín, J. F., and López-Gamero, M. D. (2016). Mixed methods studies in environmental management research: Prevalence, purposes and designs. *Business Strategy and the Environment*, 25(2), 134–148.

Monárrez, A., Galvan, L., Wagler, A. E., and Lesser, L. M. (2018). Range of meanings: A sequential mixed methods study of how English language learners encounter assessment items on descriptive statistics. *Journal of Statistics Education*, 26(3), 162–173.

OECD. (2019). OECD environmental performance reviews: Australia *2019*. https://www.oecd.org/australia/oecd-environmental-performance-reviews-australia-2019-9789264310452-en.htm Access: 29/09/2020.

Patton, Q. M. (1990). *Qualitative evaluation and research methods.* Sage, Thousand Oaks.

Redmond, J., Walker, E., and Wang, C. (2008). Issues for small businesses with waste management. *Journal of Environmental Management, 88*(2), 275–285.

Sayer, A. (1992). *Method in social science; a realist approach.* Routledge, Abingdon.

Smith C., and Elger T. (2014). Critical realism and interviewing subjects. In O. J. and V. S. Edwards (Eds.), *Studying organizations using critical realism: A practical guide* (109–131). Oxford University Press, Oxford.

Strauss, A., and Corbin, J. (1990). *Basics of qualitative research: Grounded theory procedures and techniques.* Sage, Thousand Oaks.

Teddlie, C., and Tashakkori, A. (2009). Foundations of mixed methods research: *Integrating quantitative and qualitative approaches in the social and behavioral sciences.* Sage, Thousand Oaks.

Tilley, F. (2000). Small firms' environmental ethics: How deep do they go? In R. Hillary (Ed.), *Small and medium-sized enterprises and the environment: business imperatives* (1st ed., 35–48). Greenleaf, Sheffield.

United Nations (2017). United Nations high level political forum 2017. Voluntary National Review Report, India. Report on the implementation of the Sustainable Development Goals. http://niti.gov.in/writereaddata/files/IndiaVNR_Final.pdf Access: 30/09/2020.

Van Ness, P. H., Fried, T. R., and Gill, T. M. (2011). Mixed methods for the interpretation of longitudinal gerontologic data: Insights from philosophical hermeneutics. *Journal of Mixed Methods Research, 5*(4), 293–308.

Verweij, P. (2013). Living Planet Report. *2010/2012* (Issue December). https://wwf.panda.org/knowledge_hub/all_publications/living_planet_report_timeline/lpr_2012/ Accessed: 30/09/2020.

Walker, E., Redmond, J., and Goeft, U. (2007). Bellevue sustainable industry report. https://ro.ecu.edu.au/cgi/viewcontent.cgi?article=8061&context=ecuworks Access: 30/06/2020.

Walley, E. E. L., and Stubbs, M. (1999). 'Green-jacking' – a tactic for the toolbag of environmental champions? *Eco-Management and Auditing, 33,* 26–33.

Welford, R. J. (1998). Editorial: Corporate environmental management, technology and sustainable development: Postmodern perspectives and the need for a critical research agenda. *Business Strategy and the Environment, 7*(1), 1–12.

Workman, D. (2020). *Coal exports by country.* http://www.worldstopexports.com/coal-exports-country/ Access: 30/09/2020.

9 Exploring differences in perspectives regarding mixed methods and transdisciplinary research

A dialogue

Norma Romm and Ralph Hamann

9.1 Introduction

In this chapter, we report on what we experienced as a generative dialogue about mixed methods and transdisciplinary research on business sustainability issues. Our original objective was to jointly interrogate the methodological assumptions and implications of a particular paper (Hamann et al., 2017), which focused on drivers of pro-environmental behaviours among South African winemakers. The paper was entitled 'Why do SMEs go green? An analysis of wine firms in South Africa'. The paper provides an account of the various phases of the project, which together constituted a mixed methods approach to the winery study. Prompted by the editors of this volume, who were aware of this article and wanted us to explore it further as a mixed methods study, we thought that discussing the methodological choices that were implicit as well as explicit in the article would be a useful platform for a broader conversation about mixed methods research and its underlying ontological and epistemological tensions.

Following some email correspondence, we met for a two-and-a-half-hour conversation in March 2019. The first author prepared some key themes for discussion, but the conversation soon developed its own trajectory. We initially assumed that our dialogue would mostly uncover agreements and convergence in our thinking about mixed methods research on organisations and sustainability. However, it soon become clear that there were also important disagreements and divergences, some of which were linked to our differing scholarly backgrounds. We quickly adapted to this and realised that, indeed, these differences in perspective probably make our dialogue more interesting and useful. We believe that our way of developing the dialogue invites you, as reader, to participate in this conversation.

We brought to the conversation our varied research experiences (and our ways of interpreting them), using as the springboard for our discussion, the winery study reported upon in Hamann et al. (2017). We discussed in depth possibilities for conceptualising the philosophical underpinnings of that project in terms of ongoing debates in the philosophy of the social sciences. As we proceeded, we cast new light on such debates, by listening carefully to each other's perspectives and engaging with them. In this way, we could bring our differences to the surface, while also enabling us to see the issues pertaining to the doing of mixed methods research from fresh angles that emerged during the conversation.

Lipinsky (2015, p. 110), citing Greenblatt (2012) – who in turn refers to certain ancient Greek and Roman philosophers such as Xenophon and Cicero – notes that in the dialogical genre of scholarly work, the idea is not to 'present ... thoughts to ... readers as a tract composed after solitary reflection.' Instead, the objective, as elucidated by Cicero, is to:

> present them [thoughts] as an exchange of views among social and intellectual equals, a conversation in which ... there will be no clear victor... The exchange itself, not its final conclusions, carries much of the meaning. The discussion itself is what most matters (Lipinsky, 2015, p. 111).

Lipinsky laments that 'unfortunately, together with the end of Antiquity this genre of scholarly discourse has also come to an end of its popularity and yielded to the scholarly treatise' (p. 111). The 'treatise' provides a 'monographic exposition' in a unified voice (Lipinsky 2015, p. 112). Lipinsky considers the rise of this (monographic) genre of writing as being reinforced through the Enlightenment project, with its urging of scholars to offer an impersonal vision of whatever is being investigated (in this case, the issue of how to regard mixed methods research) rather than considering that people in dialogue can bring to the fore their differing positionalities (and concerns) as part of the emerging dialogue, which becomes part of the academic writing (p. 112). Lipinsky's hope is to revive this form of scientific communication (alongside other forms) and to indicate that what we call 'scientific discourse' can have different 'stylistic features' (p. 112).

Hence, instead of trying to speak in one voice in this chapter, our differing voices (but also the development of our expressions as we engaged with each other) are foregrounded through this (dialogical) genre. We can say (jointly!) that our conception of dialogue with which we both feel comfortable implies a mutual listening to the 'experience[s] on which a point of view is based' (Harris and Wasilewski, 2004, p. 498): 'We can affirm our view, expand our view, or sometimes alter or even give up our current view when we encounter a new one. We can also allow others to have contrastive views as long as they do not impose their views on us and vice versa' (op cit.). Readers will notice that in what we consider to be our generative (fruitful) dialogue, we were not trying to 'impose' views, but to share our understandings as a basis for further development of the conversation between ourselves and with larger audiences (who will read this work).

In our discussion, we recognise that there are still many openings for further deliberation. Kidd and Finlayson (2015, p. 37), in their concluding statements to a duo-ethnographic dialogue (around processes of academic supervision), ask the question: 'How do we end a conversation that has no end?' Similarly, we are not trying to close the discussion about how to regard research (and mixed methods research in particular), but to open new avenues for thinking about the research issues under consideration in this chapter. Since this form of dialogical writing is still unusual in management and organisation studies, apart from some exceptions (e.g., Gehman et al., 2017), our secondary ambition with this chapter – over and above surfacing diverse perspectives on mixed methods research – is to advocate for an opening to more diverse genres of scholarly writing also in management and organisation studies.

9.2 Our dialogue

Ralph: I'm excited about the possibility of developing a chapter in this way, based on our discussion. I think this dialogical format is gaining some traction in academic writing (e.g., Jacobs, 2001; Gergen and Gergen, 2012; Norris and Greenlaw, 2012; Tlale and Romm, 2019), also in organisation studies (e.g., Gehman et al., 2017).

Norma: This is because it is recognised that the issues are not clear-cut. We are looking at answers together; we are busy exploring.

Ralph: I suppose that is particularly appropriate when there is some salient difference between the authors.

Norma: Yes, one does not want to pretend one is offering a univocal piece. One says to the reader [by implication]: Here are different answers; you [as reader] can make your own perspective.

Now, considering the editors' remit asking us to reflect on how you were justifying your methodological choices in your mixed methods research which led to the paper 'Why do Firms Go Green', you chose a survey to start with. Was there any particular reason for choosing a survey and then following this up with case studies? Did the results of the survey influence the case study part of the research or were these two separate things?

Ralph: Let me take a step back. Many studies use some combination of quantitative and deductive approaches, on the one hand, and qualitative and inductive approaches, on the other, and often these approaches are used in some kind of phased stages. The first phase (whether quantitative or qualitative) influences the second one. Often, the inductive phase is conducted first to develop propositions that are then tested in the subsequent, deductive phase, which is pretty intuitive.

But there are also good reasons for the converse and this was made clearer to me recently in conversation with Joel Gehman. A quantitative, deductive study is good to address some or other variance question. In other words, in what way are variables X and Y related to Z, and so on. The quantitative study can build some confidence in the existence of these relationships, based on a statistical test involving a large sample, but it is less likely to provide nuanced insights into the underling mechanisms of these relationships. So, you could show the existence of variance relationships in an upfront quantitative study, and then you can dive into some of the nitty-gritty, idiographic character of these relationships in a follow-on qualitative, inductive study.

In the case of our winery study (Hamann et al., 2017), yes, we conducted a survey first and then conducted comparative case studies following guidance by Eisenhardt (1989), and these were two separate projects with different collaborators. The survey involved samples from the USA, South Africa and New Zealand and it basically confirmed what we had hypothesised: that a key factor influencing whether wine companies will make pro-environmental investments is the personal proclivity of the owner or manager. This is what we had been led to expect from the literature, because wine companies are mostly SMEs and in such companies the owner and main manager often have a high degree of discretion and influence. So, the manager's disposition plays a key role and the other two categories of drivers identified by Bansal and Roth (2000) – competitiveness and legitimacy – play relatively less prominent roles, especially when compared to larger corporations. These arguments were then published in a journal focused on international business (Marshall et al., 2010).

That was all well and good, but I was a bit dissatisfied with this argument. It seemed a bit coarse. I wanted to get closer to the local context and the more fine-grained differences between wine companies. I suppose this betrays my disposition as a mostly qualitative, ideographic researcher. I respect the broad brush of a deductive approach, but I prefer the surprises and the insights that arise in the exploration process, in open-ended conversation with people. What I mentioned earlier about the mechanisms also plays a role in this – our survey showed that some factors are more important than others, but why, at a deeper level, is this so; how is this perceived by the actors in question; what differences may be visible between different actors in between the broad variations highlighted by the survey? These were the questions I was curious about.

To be honest, I was also a bit sceptical about the validity of some aspects of the survey. The response rate had not been great, especially in South Africa. And I was not entirely convinced about the survey instrument itself. The questionnaire was initially developed in the US and even though we put some effort into translating it for the South African context, I am not sure this was entirely successful. It is very interesting to me how easily things get lost in translation. We recently had a workshop including a visiting American academic and many of our students were focusing on 'transformation', by which we mean purposive organisational and social changes to redress legacies of exclusion from colonialism and apartheid. But we only realised some hours into the discussions that our visitor had assumed we meant something quite different with this word, more akin to a generic organisational change process. Beyond this translation process, I was concerned that the questionnaire was preempting quite a lot of what the key variables are, and I wasn't convinced they were the ones. I suppose this betrays my inductive temperament, again.

So, these were my inductive temperament motivations to follow up on the survey with a more inductive, idiographic study, and James Smith was a Master's student who was interested in pro-environment behaviour and he was also interested in wine businesses, so these things came together in developing the second phase case studies.

9.3 On stages, causation and ontologies

Norma: Did stage 1 affect stage 2? You had the data from stage 1 – did they influence how stage 2 was set up?

Ralph: I will answer with a qualified 'yes'. But 'influence' can take a variety of forms. If this had been designed *ex ante* as a sequential staged approach, I guess the findings from the survey would have shaped the qualitative research quite directly. In our case, however, the survey was a bit further at the back of our minds when we designed and implemented the case studies. I suppose part of the reason for this was that I wasn't entirely committed to the survey data and their resulting arguments. So, there was an element of validation involved in the case study research, as well. But there was definitely a clear connection based on the basic questions that we were asking ourselves and asking our research participants.

Norma: I think your case study approach was more about using abduction rather than induction – you were using the literature etc., to help make sense of the data and were not just inducing [theoretical] ideas from what the participants said [in the qualitative research]. And you and James seemed to me to be asking questions in the light of the kinds of variables that you isolated in the original [survey] study.

Ralph: Yes, there was an overlap, but the questions in the qualitative study were definitely a lot more exploratory and open-ended. That's not to say they were not shaped by our reading of the literature. For instance, Bansal and Roth's (2000) three categories of drivers of pro-environmental behaviour provided a kind of basic framework for the case selection and also for data collection and analysis.

As mentioned, I was curious about the way these drivers show up in the specific contexts of different wine businesses, over and above the broad-brush argument that one was prevalent more than others, which we confirmed in the survey. It made sense, at least to me, to use Bansal and Roth's (2000) categories as a kind of point of departure. With this initial framework, our case study analysis showed that there were interesting interaction effects between these drivers. Bear in mind that in Bansal and Roth's (2000) initial analysis, the different motivations for pro-environmental behaviour – that is, ethical responsibility, competitiveness, legitimacy-seeking – were described as acting rather independently of each other. But I felt that this seemed a bit too simple and our case study analysis of specific winemakers in specific contexts underscored and elaborated this suspicion. So, as mentioned, our case studies confirmed what we knew from our survey – that managers' pro-environmental proclivities were vital, but what I thought was more interesting was that some of these environmentally motivated managers combined this sense of responsibility with ways to also enhance their company's competitiveness, while others did not. It was among these managers combining ethical and competitiveness motives, where we saw particularly innovative and far-reaching environmental investments.

So, does this make our analysis abductive rather than inductive? Maybe. I think the term 'abductive' is definitely gaining traction, though it still isn't popping up very consistently in the methodology sections in mainstream journals. I guess it may assert itself in coming years. But perhaps part of the reason why it might not, is because even what we call 'inductive' designs generally involve some iterative back-and-forth between the literature and our data and analysis. The view that grounded theory and so on rely on 'true' induction, where we avoid the use of prior concepts in our analyses, seems less defensible or relevant these days. There are some variations, of course. For instance, Gioia et al. (2012) put more emphasis on staying 'true' to the data than, say, Eisenhardt (1989). But all of these very influential guides on inductive research speak of an iterative back-and-forth between the literature and our analysis. That's the way it should be, given that our research is essentially a conversation with others in our field (Huff, 1999).

Norma: I am hearing lots of things from listening to you. And I am considering how we can extend these thoughts to examine ontological, epistemological, and paradigmatic issues. My first question that I will pose for us to consider, is whether the hypothetico-deductive ontological assumption that there are independent variables which influence dependent variables (you know this vision of the world as made up of causal connections) can be rendered compatible with ideographic thinking in some way. That is, in order to link up this deductive or nomothetic approach such that it is not inconsistent with ideographic approaches, do you think if we speak of 'drivers' instead of 'causes' we break with the view of people's behaviour as predictable? Instead of considering that our location of independent variables helps us to predict people's behaviour [as if people's behaviour can be predicted as we assume of natural objects] if we speak of a driver, are we reconsidering this conception of causality and recognising that what drives people are their *conceptions of what is meaningful?* So in this case, it would be meaningful (important) to get legitimacy (as one possible driver) or important to make a profit as a business person (as another driver) or meaningful to care for nature, for example. So the quantitative and more positivist or postpositivist-geared approach which suggests that behaviour is caused, can then in this way be brought together with the inductive, more interpretivist position that human behaviour is not *caused* as such. So through the word 'driver' as you use it, do we shift the more positivist assumption to a more interpretive one in terms of our ontology (way of seeing the social world)?

Ralph: You raise interesting and challenging questions about these different ontological perspectives emphasising either causes and effects, on the one hand, or meanings, on the other. But our approach to the qualitative research component was not really a fundamental challenge to the ontological assumptions of the survey component. As mentioned, we relied largely on Eisenhardt (1989) in designing and implementing the case studies. Her guidance is quite comfortably within a postpositivist paradigm, where cause-and-effect are important and legitimate things to identify and analyse. She participated in the panel discussion reported in Gehman et al. (2017), and there she was quite explicit about this: 'I used to call myself a positivist. I don't do that much anymore—it's a loaded term. But I also don't cringe at positivism' (Eisenhardt, in Gehman et al. (2017, p. 9)).

Norma: Yes, this was also the position of Glaser and Strauss (1967) who introduced grounded theory as a methodology into social scientific research and suggested that its inductive approach was not incompatible with postpositivism's bent towards relying on empirical evidence to justify theoretical claims. But of course, this has been questioned by more epistemologically constructivist scholars (e.g., Charmaz, 2000, 2006, 2009, 2012; Clarke, 2005; Reichertz, 2007; see also Romm's account (2018, pp. 326–337) of continuing contention among grounded theorists).

It's interesting to hear about your apparent comfort with a postpositivist paradigm. Elsewhere, you seem to emphasise a more interpretivist approach, like in your work on research-practitioner collaboration (Hamann and Faccer, 2018). Aren't you being somewhat inconsistent?

Ralph: Only the dead are consistent! (This is paraphrasing Aldous Huxley.) Jokes aside, I do think it is possible to overemphasise consistency. Perhaps our paradigmatic inclinations should be a bit fluid and can shift over time. I also think that the paradigmatic approach may adapt to the purpose or focus of a particular study. That's where the consistency is important – between paradigmatic assumptions, research objectives, research design and resulting arguments.

Norma: This is what postmodernists suggest when they say that people's identities need not be treated as fixed. Meerwald talks of 'identities as multiple and fluid' (2013, p. 45). Something along these lines also pops up in your work, when you talk of 'hybrid personal identities' (Hamann and Faccer, 2018, p. 246).

However, I am still wondering if in your case studies of wine businesses, you were concerned with what meanings people might give to stewardship. So, for example, some participants suggested they were stewards in the sense of wanting to 'do the right thing'; some people felt it was their 'ethical obligation' to act as stewards; some felt that it was important to leave the land 'the same way we found it', although James did not seem to probe these various expressions of the participants to get more of a sense of how participants might be attributing meaning. But now I am thinking whether what we consider as participants' proclivity to steward-ship is linked to the meanings they attribute (or express that they attribute) to the term, so that it is not a result of independent variables causing them to act in this direction.

Ralph: I am not sure if there is such a distinction. Bear in mind that even in the survey component of our wine research, some of the independent variables were measured in the form of perceptions. This is standard practice in psychology. It relates to the meanings that you have as a manager that, for example, 'I am a steward of the land: it is part of my identity'. In the first phase of the study we considered that this could be measured in a survey. So, it is not such a clear-cut distinction between measuring identity through variables and considering identity as meaningfully created.

Norma: Do you think that because meanings in life that might guide people's actions and/or that they might (*post facto*) attribute to their actions when asked about this are more complex than can be defined through survey research which looks at 'strong predictors' (i.e., some variables being more predictive than others in explaining behaviour)? Can quantitatively-oriented research do justice to the meanings that might become attached to behaviour (or rather, to meanings and behaviour – as expressed in the interview when people are asked to reflect on this and when these are co-explored in the context of the interview)?

In the survey, the respondents are just ticking a box against survey items like 'At our winery, people feel a personal obligation to do whatever they can to minimise environmental harm' or 'We believe that environmental initiatives lead to increased consumer demand'. But in a more open-ended interview, the research participants get an opportunity to reflect more deeply even on their 'identity' (or identities) such as 'I am a steward of the land/I care for the land' and 'I am also a business person'. They can reflect on this during the interview encounter in relation to questions posed. That is, through a dialogical interview they can reflect more on their 'attitudes' and meanings. So, attitudes/meanings that might not have been fully reflected upon can become more formed, as we engage in conversation with people. I see you allude to such dialogical interviews in Hamann and Faccer (2018), but it's not so clear in your winery article what style of interviewing James was using [See Romm, 2010, Chapter 5, and for more detail on dialogical interviewing; see also Denzin, 2001; Gubrium and Koro-Ljungberg, 2005; Tanggaard, 2009; Mitropolitski, 2013].

The implication is perhaps that you may have been able to theorise about interaction effects between different motivations of pro-environmental behaviour only because your research participants could engage in deeper reflection about their motives and identities in your interviews?

Ralph: I think there are two issues that you are raising here: The first issue is whether the fact that the interaction effects between motivations were drawn out during our second, qualitative phase is because this exploratory, inductive type of research is inherently more likely to expose more nuanced relationships. The short answer to this question, in my view, is 'yes'. But we also need to be careful in saying this. It would in principle be possible to develop a more sophisticated model upfront, based on the extant literature, and then to test this model using more complex statistical methods, such as structural equation modelling and not just regression analysis. I suppose it depends on the sophistication of the existing literature and also the researchers' wherewithal. In our case, we felt that the literature did not give us a lot of guidance in creating a more nuanced, multi-layered model that included interaction effects and so on.

Now, your second point has to do with dialogical interviewing and the possibility that such interviews don't just surface meanings, but somehow help shape or form them in the participant, and whether this can be a useful thing in data collection. This is another really challenging question! It also raises again this possible problem of inconsistency, because I realise I have different responses to this question in different projects. A lot depends on my collaborators. I find that two of my American collaborators generally encourage a more postpositivist, removed approach, in which our role in data collection is to influence the data as little as possible. In some of my other projects, my role in the data collection process is more influential and we could even speak of a kind of co-creation process during interviews. For instance, in one of my recent projects, I was working with companies trying to figure out how they could better contribute to community resilience (Hamann et al., 2019). This sense of trying to figure things out together allowed for some fascinating discussions. But there was a clear normative agenda that shaped our interviews and I needed to bear that in mind during data analysis. So, in any case it is important to guard against possible sources of bias and so on.

Norma: Yes, so your American colleagues argue for increased objectivity, but as you know there are also lots of people who do not agree with that, such as the people advocating interactive or dialogical interviewing.

9.4 Pervasive tensions in the academy

Ralph: I suppose there are these tensions that pervade the academy, and I think they also jostle within each of us. During my postgraduate studies, I was quite a fervent anti-positivist and indeed this was also part of the reason I resisted participating in management conferences and journals, which I perceived to be overly positivist, which in turn I associated with an uncritical approach to managerialism. I've become less fervent about all this, and now have a more pluralist, pragmatist, and contingent view on these things. Different approaches line up with different objectives.

In our wine research, we were trying to understand what influences pro-environmental behaviour. Some managers and firms display quite clearly varying degrees of such behaviour. So, a postpositivist study seeking to elaborate cause-and-effect relationships underlying these differences, guided by Eisenhardt (1989), seemed like a fitting approach for this. Part of this approach is to be very vigilant about possible sources of bias, such as social desirability bias, and frankly I've been learning that I didn't pay sufficient attention to such issues in some of my earlier work, and my collaboration with the American colleagues I mentioned earlier has been highlighting this for me.

Some authors have criticised any systematic attempt to reduce social desirability bias as being misguided or fruitless, and as reflecting a naïve belief in having some kind of 'unmediated access' to some objective reality (e.g., Speer and Hutchby, 2003, p. 334). I think that's throwing the baby out with the bathwater. Yes, I think most of us recognise that naïve realism is untenable and that we necessarily rely on our perceptual and conceptual 'lenses' and our language to make sense of the world. But that doesn't mean that we cannot adapt our interactions with people so that they can speak as frankly or directly as possible.

Norma:　We can take the point about social desirability being at play during the interview context and use this as an opportunity to encourage people to reflect; so – in the case of your wine study – they can become more reflective around how they operate in relation to the land. You may want to lead them to think about something. When you ask a question such as 'do you think we are ethically obligated to care for the land'?, they may realise this is something they need to think more about!

Ralph:　There is a good chance that they will perceive that the socially desirable answer to that question is 'yes', so they can just lie to you.

Norma:　This is the same as in a survey where they are asked to tick a box which is offered as a choice, such as: 'At our winery, people feel a personal obligation to do whatever they can to minimise environmental harm'. They may realise that they are expected to tick this box [In the context of studies of racism, Bonilla-Silva and Baiocchi, consider that surveys on racial attitudes have 'become like multiple choice exams where respondents work hard to choose the "right" answers' (2008, p. 139).].

Ralph:　But this also depends on the way the survey is designed. That is one of the problems I had with the scale that I mentioned to you earlier – social desirability bias was one of the concerns. So, this isn't necessarily a problem with survey questionnaires.

Now, in the case of the inductive theorising, we were trying to relate attitudes and identity to people's behaviours. Even if one can indeed influence attitudes and meanings during the course of an interview, this is not what we were looking for. We wanted to try to understand how their "past" or "existing" attitudes might have been related to their behaviours.

Norma: One could also try to be more forward looking: if they get a sense during the interview (as they reflect) that 'I care for the land' this might influence their way of acting in the future.

Ralph: Well, that's an interesting possibility especially if that's part of your study objectives, for instance, if you are doing a kind of action research project, in which you, as researcher, are also an actor involved in facilitating organisational or some other change. Then you could analyse change over time in attitudes and behaviours. But you would have to work very hard at convincing a critical reader at the end of all this that your arguments aren't significantly influenced by your vested interests in the outcomes. I think there are many reviewers whom you'll struggle to persuade about this.

Norma: To me what is important is that we become more conscious that how we ask questions to participants may make a difference to how they come to reflect on the issues. How you ask makes a difference through the words you use and the issues you flag up for attention.

Ralph: Yes. A lot depends on what you ask and how you ask it. I used to recommend to students to develop semi-structured interview protocols with ten or so key questions or themes. I still recommend making such a list, but the actual interview should be influenced as little as possible by this. What this means is that we find one or two generative questions to launch the conversation and ideally, we interrupt the participant very little. One of my collaborators is Ted Baker and he's been encouraging this to good effect. He's recommending to our jointly supervised students to kick off an interview with a question like, 'So, how did you come to start this business?' and then to speak as little as possible. So, we are moving more towards the narrative style of interviewing where we encourage people to tell their stories. This is also because I am conscious of the effect we can have on participants through leading questions and the like.

Norma: It looked to me from reading your mixed methods article that the literature influenced the way in which James asked questions in trying to explore, for example, people's decisions as based on a quest for legitimacy, competitiveness, or a sense of stewardship of the land.

Ralph: Well, bear in mind that what I've been saying about my evolving approach to these things is just that, it's evolving, and I think my guidance to James would be a bit different if he was doing this project now, eight years later. Also, students bring their own dispositions to their projects. Some are happy to have open-ended conversations, while others like to have more structure.

So, if James were embarking on this project now, it's likely I would have recommended a more open-ended interview approach, starting with a question like, 'Please tell me about your environmental practices'. Then they start to talk. They talk about what they do. Sometimes they talk about why they do things and that is what we probe. Then, if necessary, we hone in on stuff. We may ask something more directed like, 'What about government regulations – do they play a role in your approach to the environment?' So, we can still get to more directed questions, but we leave them for the latter parts of an interview.

Norma: So you could also say to the participants: 'What about the role that might be played by people's possibly feeling a connection to the land and acting in terms of this? Would you say that this applies or not in your experience?'

Ralph: Yes, but we'd have to be careful about the phrasing. It is probably awkward for a winemaker to confess that connection to the land isn't really relevant for him. It's a cultural emphasis in the wine industry, so there's likely a strong social desirability bias that can creep in there.

We would also need to check for consistency. If they respond to your question by saying, 'I love nature a lot' but they've said nothing about this during the interview, or they don't reflect this passion in any behaviours, then we would need to be wary of this response. So, I seem to require more consistency from my research participants than from myself!

Norma: To cater for this, I suggest that one can and should explain (and offer enough detail) to readers the question (or set of questions) to which the participant is responding. That is, one can let the reader know how this response came to the fore and how the question(s) you asked may have influenced what was said. So, you can show your reader how the data have become generated through the interaction. It was in this context that the data were generated. Even in survey research, you can tell your reader about possible social desirability effects. As a matter of epistemology you are not then saying to the reader 'this is what we found'. You are saying 'this is what we found based on these questions'.

Ralph: Yes, but I also think we need to assume that our readers know this kind of thing. We write for a specialist audience, after all, and a big part of their specialisation is on methodology. So, we can assume that our readers will anticipate our data to arise from our interaction with participants, and so we need to explain in our methodology section how we tried to make sure that the data are nevertheless reliable or dependable, if you think that the term 'reliable' is too positivist in orientation.

Norma: I think the way in which research results are written up do not lend themselves to readers recognising that the findings [from survey and other research] are a product of an interactive encounter between researchers and research participants.

Ralph: Okay, agreed, there's probably more we can do to explicate the interactions involved in data collection and perhaps in analysis, too. As you know, authors generally provide a rather sanitised version of their research methodology in the eventual article or book. But this is also evolving. Especially in the more demanding journals, there is a remarkable level of depth and detail that reviewers are insisting on seeing, and this is evident also in the published articles. I feel that I am getting better at this and so are my students – I recently read one of my PhD student's draft thesis and it had close to 20 pages just on data analysis, and it was actually interesting to read, to boot!

Norma: But in the case of the mixed methods study on the wine farms, the reader gets the impression that this scale was validated – designed in America and then applied in South Africa – the reader may not know it was not so well adapted. And they may not consider how the choices to tick boxes may have influenced the data generation. It reads as if the scale was a good scale and was 'validated'.

Ralph: Well, yes, the article was not as self-critical of the survey data as I was myself. But I wouldn't say we were being disingenuous or even dishonest about this. After all, the survey findings did provide a platform for the more in-depth exploration in the case studies. And the findings from the case studies complemented – rather than contradicted – those of the survey research. If a more critical view of the survey findings had been substantiated in the inductive study, then the paper would have looked very different.

Norma: Generally, I think we need to be clearer to audiences [of research] and not say 'these are the predictors'. But we can say 'in this context, based on these questions, this is what arose'. This is what allows the knowledge to be more dialogical.

Ralph: Based on what I've said earlier, I think both approaches have their place. As mentioned, I adopt a more pluralist approach.

Some will say that such pluralism implies a postpositivist – and thus naïve – assumption of commensurability between objectivist and subjectivist epistemologies. This is a tricky territory. I think commensurability is sometimes possible and other times it may be less so.

In the case of our wine study, there was no fundamental incongruity in my view, either intuitively or in the analysis and writing of it. I suppose it helped that both the survey and the case studies were broadly speaking within a postpositivist framing. Things might have been more complicated if our inductive component was much more focused on meanings and identities, as you implied above, and if its design was shaped more by guidance by, say, Gioia et al. (2012) than by Eisenhardt (1989).

Norma: I don't think that researchers bring such tensions and decisions sufficiently to the fore in their articles.

Ralph: Perhaps. At the same time, I don't think that we always have to elaborate in great length our philosophy of science. A lot of this is signalled by our general approach and references. So, if I rely very clearly on Eisenhardt (1989), as we did in our wine article, I think this ought to signal to our readers that we are working broadly within a postpositivist paradigm. I don't then have to add a whole sub-section in my methodology section that spells this out.

Norma: When I think of epistemological questions my concern is that I don't want professional researchers to adopt an authoritative voice – in relation to other researchers and also to practitioners when they present their so-called findings. This goes against the spirit of a dialogue in which one invites the reader to engage.

Ralph: I guess you are pointing at postpositivist researchers and especially those with authoritative positions in the academy with this criticism. But even postpositivist researchers recognise the tentative nature of their truth claims, I think, and that their contributions are part of an ongoing conversation. Their tone may sometimes be somewhat annoyingly authoritative, and indeed we need to attend to the tone of our writing, but most accomplished researchers I've had a chance to meet, or even work with, are pretty humble about their knowledge claims.

Norma: Would they write in a dialogical genre?

Ralph: I don't know. There are lots of ways of writing. As mentioned at the outset, I see more and more articles in dialogue format in management journals. The Gehman piece (Gehman et al. 2017) that I've been referring to a lot has this approach.

So, there is a broader move towards a bit more freedom and pluralism in scholarly work and writing, and I think that's a good thing. By the way, this also includes being more open and transparent about twists and turns in our research projects, and to talk more explicitly about the back-and-forth between theory and data – or what you referred to earlier as an abductive approach. For instance, working with Erin Powell and Ted Baker was illuminating not only because of their staunch approach to avoiding biases, as I've mentioned earlier.

It was also refreshing to see how they celebrated the role of surprise in inductive work, which is often emphasised by advocates of abduction (Locke et al., 2008). So, in our final paper, we start by explaining how we went into this research expecting X, but then we found Y, which allows us to argue Z (Powell et al., 2018). This was a core of the article and it was dialogical – we invite people into a dialogue based on what we think are shared assumptions.

Norma: When you say that as a pragmatist you wish to provide 'useful knowledge', how do we decide that it is useful? I am wondering if one would need to check with some participants or stakeholders and ask them if they think your (tentative) findings are valuable, or whether these findings might have interesting practical implications. For example, some actors in the wine industry could build upon your arguments about managers' sense of stewardship and the role of knowledge in this. For instance, they could develop training programmes to address the gap you speak of in the article. So, my question to you is, if you wish the 'knowledge' from the research to be useful, would this be useful to do more theorising or useful for practitioners, or both?

Ralph: We've spoken quite a bit about this metaphor that sees scholarship as conversation. One implication is that any scholarly argument is tentative; it is not the final word. A second implication is that any conversation is characterised by its participants. This is pertinent to your question because the simple answer is 'both', but we also need to bear in mind that scholars and practitioners are two quite different kinds of audience.

We won't get very far, in my experience, if we seek to share the same 'knowledge' in the same way with both audiences. It's taken me quite a long time to learn this and to make some gains in recognising what is useful to practitioners and in what form it can be communicated. My colleague Stephanie Bertels, who founded and directs the Embedding Project, has taught me a lot in that regard.

Norma: And they are not only *audiences* but *participants*.

Ralph: Absolutely. Recognising the difference between practitioners and scholars is just one step. Then, there are different ways to grapple with this difference. I generally aspire to follow Andy van de Ven and Johnson's (2006) advice, which is to see these differences as generative and as an opportunity to co-create knowledge that's 'useful' to both practitioners and scholars. In other words, practitioners and scholars are not just audiences but participants in the knowledge creation process.

In our business school, we've made a commitment to this kind of 'engaged scholarship'. In many projects, we invite practitioners throughout – in the conceptualisation of the study; in data collection; and then in discussing our emerging findings. This is the process we've been following in the project on corporate contributions to community resilience, which I mentioned a bit earlier. But as I've also mentioned, I think this also brings with it some interesting challenges in addressing possible sources of bias.

Norma: So, in the case of your wine study you could in principle go back to industry actors and engage further with them and discuss practical implications.

Ralph: In that particular study, the subsequent interactions with practitioners were quite limited. However, I'm glad to say we're keeping and extending links to these networks. Just two weeks ago we arranged a fascinating field trip to some winemakers and associations and so on. At the end of that field trip we had lunch with some of the practitioners, during which we 'turned the tables', and gave them a chance to ask us the questions!

In some of our other projects, this link back to practice is more direct. For instance, the research on corporate contributions to community resilience has led to a practitioner guide on partnering for community resilience, which is available via the Embedding Project website (https://www.embeddingproject.org).

9.5 Conclusion

As indicated earlier, we are wary of offering a 'conclusion' to this chapter as if we are trying to close the discussion on our ways of conceiving mixed methods and transdisciplinary research. We have pointed to some of the continuing tensions in the mixed methods research community, which also played out in our conversation: we have offered new angles for thinking about them when setting up and conducting research, and when considering relationships with participants, stakeholders and wider audiences (such as readers of the chapter). Transdisciplinary research by definition implies that these relationships need to be given (more) attention (cf. Romm, 2015; Chilisa, 2017; Stokols, 2018), so that the research can be regarded as meaningful to scholarly audiences as well as to participants and stake-holders in 'the field'. We have indicated some of the (varied) ways in which we ourselves have tried to take such relationships into consideration as part of the doing of research. We hope that our deliberations as dialogically developed here can function as a spur for readers to continue (in further dialogue with our text and with others) to engage with the broad question of the role that mixed methods researchers can play in advancing insights and actions in relation to business sustainability, and other themes.

References

Bansal, P., and Roth, K. (2000). Why companies go green: A model of ecological responsiveness. *Academy of Management Journal, 43*(4), 717–736.

Bonilla-Silva, E., and Baiocchi, G. (2008). Anything but racism. In T. Zuberi and E. Bonilla-Silva (Eds.). *White logic, white methods: Racism and methodology* (137–151). Rowman and Littlefield, Lanham.

Charmaz, K. (2000). Grounded theory: Objectivist and constructivist methods. In N. K. Denzin, and Y. S. Lincoln (Eds.), *Handbook of qualitative research* (2nd ed., 509–535). Sage, Thousand Oaks.

Charmaz, K. (2006). *Constructing grounded theory*. Sage, London.

Charmaz, K. (2009). Shifting the grounds: Constructivist grounded theory methods. In J. M. Morse, P. N. Stern, J. Corbin, B. Bowers, K. Charmaz, and A. E. Clarke (Eds.), *Developing grounded theory: The second generation* (127–154). Left Coast Press, Walnut Creek, CA.

Charmaz, K. (2012). The power and potential of grounded theory. *Medical Sociology Online, 6*(3), https://ecrag.files.wordpress.com/2014/02/charmaz-power-of-grounded-theory.pdf Access: 30/09/2020.

Chilisa B. (2017). Decolonizing transdisciplinary research approaches: An African perspective for enhancing knowledge integration in sustainability science. *Sustainability Science, 12*(5), 813–827.

Chilisa, B., Major, T. E., and Khudu-Petersen, K. (2017). Community engagement with a postcolonial, African-based relational paradigm. *Qualitative Research, 17*(3), 326–339.

Clarke, A. E. (2005). *Situational analysis: Grounded theory after the postmodern turn*. Sage, Thousand Oaks.

Denzin, N. K. (2001). The reflexive interview and a performative social science. *Qualitative Research, 1*(1), 23–46.

Eisenhardt, K. M. (1989). Building theories from case study research. *Academy of Management Review, 14*(4), 532–550.

Gehman, J., Glaser, V. L., Eisenhardt, K. M., Gioia, D., Langley, A., and Corley, K. G. (2017). Finding theory-method fit: A comparison of three qualitative approaches to theory building. *Journal of Management Inquiry, 27* (3), 284–300.

Gergen, M. M., and Gergen, K. J. (2012). *Playing with purpose: Adventures in performative social science*. Left Coast Press, Walnut Creek.

Gioia, D. A., Corley, K. G., and Hamilton, A. L. (2012). Seeking qualitative rigor in inductive research: Notes on the Gioia methodology. *Organizational Research Methods, 16*(1), 15–31. doi.org/10.1177/1094428112452151

Glaser, B. G., and Strauss, A. L. (1967). *The discovery of grounded theory: Strategies for* qualitative research. Aldine, New York.

Greenblatt, S. (2012). *The swerve: How the world became modern* [e–book]. W.W. Norton and Company, New York.

Gubrium, E., and Koro-Ljungberg, M. (2005). Contending with border making in the social constructionist interview. *Qualitative Inquiry*, *11*(5), 689–715.

Hamann, R., Smith, J., Tashman, P., and Marshall, R. S. (2017). Why do SMEs go green? An analysis of wine firms in South Africa. *Business and Society*, *56*(1), 23–56.

Hamann, R., and Faccer, K. (2018). Mind the transformation gap. In J. M. Bartunek and J. McKenzie (Eds.), *Academic practitioner relationships: Developments. complexities and opportunities* (234–252). Routledge, London.

Hamann, R., Makaula, L., Ziervogel, G., Shearing, C., and Zhang, A. (2019). Strategic responses to grand challenges: Why and how corporations build community resilience. *Journal of Business Ethics*, *161*(4), 835–853.

Harris, L. D., and Wasilewski, J. (2004). Indigeneity, an alternative worldview: Four R's (relationship, responsibility, reciprocity, redistribution) vs. two P's (power and profit). Sharing the journey toward conscious evolution. *Systems Research and Behavioral Science*, *21*(5), 489–503.

Huff, A. S. (1999). *Writing for scholarly publication*. Sage, London.

Jacobs, J. (2001). *The nature of economies*. Penguin, Harmondsworth.

Kidd, J., and Finlayson, M. (2015). She pushed me, and I flew: A duoethnographical story from supervisors in flight. *Forum Qualitative Sozialforschung / Forum: Qualitative Social Research*, *16*(1), Art. 15. https://www.qualitative-research.net/index.php/fqs/article/view/2217/3753 Accessed: 30/09/20.

Knaggård, Å., Ness, B., and Harnesk, D. (2018). Finding an academic space: Reflexivity among sustainability researchers. *Ecology and Society*, *23*(4), 20. doi.org/10.5751/ES-10505-230420

Lipinsky, D. (2015). Can one write a scholarly paper in a form of poem? Genre changes in academic writing over history. In A. Duszak and G. Kowalski (Eds.), *Academic (Inter)genres: Between texts, contexts and identities* (105–116). Peter Lang, New York.

Locke, K., Golden-Biddle, K., and Feldman, M. (2008). Perspective-making doubt generative: Rethinking the role of doubt in the research process. *Organization Science*, *19*(6), 907–918.

Marshall, R. S., Akoorie, M. E., Hamann, R., and Sinha, P. (2010). Environmental practices in the wine industry: An empirical application of the theory of reasoned action and stakeholder theory in the United States and New Zealand. *Journal of World Business*, *45*(4), 405–414.

Meerwald, A. M. L. (2013). Researcher/Researched: Repositioning research paradigms. *Higher Education Research and Development*, *32*(1), 43–55.

Mitropolitski, S. (2013). Interactive interview: A research note. *Forum Qualitative Sozialforschung/Forum: Qualitative Social Research*, *16*(1), Art. 8. https://www.qualitative-research.net/index.php/fqs/article/view/1963/3740 Accessed: 30/09/2020.

Norris, J., and Greenlaw, J. (2012). Responding to our muses: A duoethnography on becoming writers. In Joe Norris, Richard Sawyer and Darren E. Lund (Eds.), *Duoethnography: Dialogic methods for social, health, and educational research* (89–113). Routledge, London.

Powell, E. E., Hamann, R., Bitzer, V., and Baker, T. (2018). Bringing the elephant into the room? Enacting conflict in collective prosocial organizing. *Journal of Business Venturing, 33*, 623–642.

Reichertz, J. (2007). Abduction: The logic of discovery of grounded theory. In A. Bryant, and C. Charmaz (Eds.), *Handbook of grounded theory* (214–228). London, Sage.

Romm, N. R. A. (2010). *New racism: Revisiting researcher accountabilities.* Springer, New York.

Romm, N. R. A. (2015). Reviewing the transformative paradigm: A critical systemic and relational (Indigenous) lens. *Systemic Practice and Action Research, 28*(5), 411–427.

Romm, N. R. A. (2018). *Responsible research practice: Revisiting transformative paradigm for social research.* Springer, Cham.

Speer, S. A., and Hutchby, I. (2003). From ethics to analytics. *Sociology, 37*(2), 315–337.

Stokols, D. (2018). *Social ecology in the digital age: Solving complex problems in a globalised world.* Elsevier Academic Press, New York.

Tanggaard, L. (2009). The research interview as a dialogical context for the production of social life and personal narratives. *Qualitative Inquiry, 15*(9), 1498–1515.

Tlale, L. D. N., and Romm, N. R. A. (2019). Duoethnographic storying around investments in, and extension of the meanings of, engaged qualitative research. *Forum: Qualitative Social Research, 20*(1), Art 7. https://www.qualitative-research.net/index.php/fqs/article/view/3085/4329 Accessed: 30/09/2020.

Van De Ven, A. H., and Johnson, P. E. (2006). Knowledge for theory and practice. *Academy of Management Review, 31*(4), 802–821.

Part C

Added value, challenges and practical relevance of applying mixed methods in research on sustainability and SMEs

10 Extending the value-added of mixed methods in sustainability research

Elizabeth G. Creamer

10.1 Introduction

More than one author has commented on the under-utilisation of mixed method approaches in research in management and organisation research, including on topics related to sustainability. For example, after a review of the use of mixed methods in management research, Molina-Azorín and López-Gamero (2016), concluded that 'it seems likely that the advantages, possibilities, purposes, designs, and potential of mixed methods research may be unknown to environmental management scholars' (p. 145). In particular, authors of a systematic review in accounting document the relatively low acceptance of mixed methods in business when compared to other fields (Grafton et al., 2011). They, too, concluded that most business researchers are missing the opportunity to leverage the value-added of a mixed method approach.

A common criticism of the mixed method research that exists in management is that many researchers are not acquainted with the body literature about its foundational concepts (Cameron et al., 2015). This extends to the neglect of advanced mixed methods designs and ways to integrate qualitative and quantitative data (Fielding, 2012), including in the most common use of mixed methods in management journals which is for purposes of instrument development (Molina-Azorín, 2011). Sharpening and broadening of methodological skills will go a long way to increasing the rigor of analytical and theoretical reasoning of research in management (Molina-Azorín and Cameron, 2015; Molina-Azorín and López-Gamero, 2016). This chapter explores ways that the integration of qualitative and quantitative data and/or methods can advance the rigour, analytical density, and originality of research about sustainability in management.

10.2 Defining mixed and multi-method research

Despite variations, all definitions of mixed method research point to it as a methodology that combines qualitative and quantitative data or methods with the intent to integrate them in substantive ways. Multi-method research shares the drive to combine data from multiple sources but does so without the intent to integrate them (Bazeley, 2018). The multi-method label extends to situations where multiple qualitative approaches are used, or multiple quantitative approaches are used to promote construct validity. Mixed method research combines the logic from three analytical approaches: a quantitative one (numbers, deductive or hypothesis driven), a qualitative one (words or visuals that provide an exploratory drive at some point in the research process), and an abductive logic that introduces an iterative approach that seeks, seeks to move back and forth between and exploratory and a confirmatory stance. On the other hand, a multi-method approach can embrace the idea of integrating more than one qualitative approach or more than one quantitative approach (Bazeley, 2018).

The methodological orientation of mixed methods is evident in the logic of inquiry that underscores what one of its earliest proponents, Jennifer C. Greene, referred to as a 'mixed method way of thinking'. Greene links a mixed method way of thinking with complexity, writing that its principal purpose is 'generating understandings that are broader, deeper, and more inclusive, and that more centrally honour the complexity and contingency of human behavior' (2007, p. 21). Regardless of their philosophical orientation, most methodologists prioritise the principal value-added of a mixed method approach as its ability to generate a more complete understanding of a complex phenomenon, including of a multi-dimensional construct like sustainability.

10.3 Promoting analytic depth and inference quality

One of the most compelling arguments for the use of mixed methods is the potential to promote sophisticated analytical conceptualisations (Fielding, 2008, 2009, 2012). Rather than restricting its purpose to confirmation or triangulation, Fielding advocates for recognising the value-added of mixed methods in creating inferences or a conceptual explanation with greater analytic density or conceptual richness (2009). Analytic density refers to the potential to build the type of multi-dimensional conceptual understanding of social phenomenon that is essential to the iterative process of building knowledge in a scientific way (Fielding, 2012). The opposite of analytical density, according to Fielding (2009), is the type of tunnel vision that leads an investigator to refuse to engage a hypothesis or theoretical proposition because it is incompatible with his or her preconceptions.

Gibson (2017) explored the value-added of mixed methods with a set of exemplars identified from a systematic review of empirical articles appearing in top-tier journals in management and organisational science. She concluded that the value-added of mixed methods extends beyond its role in triangulating findings in ways that supported convergent validity. She suggested mixed methods often adds value by both triangulating or corroborating findings and elaborating them, often by revealing the multi-dimensionality of a construct or by adding to an existing theoretical framework. Gibson (2017) linked research that produces outcomes that both validate and elaborate conceptual understanding of a construct or theoretical framework with a design that has an iterative phase.

An iterative process differs from one where one step, like data collection, is completed before another is begun. It often loops back. An iterative process 'shifts back and forth between different types of data and analysis to achieve triangulation' (Gibson, 2017, p. 211). It is one where 'insights gained in one phase inform data collected in other phases to expand access and improve "generalizability"' (Gibson, 2017, p. 210). That can be seen, for example, when a finding from one source of data leads an investigator to backtrack to re-analyse data from another. An iterative engagement between the findings and results drawn from the different methods generally requires that an initial plan for a research design be modified (Bryman, 2008).

In a dialogue reported in Chapter 4 in this volume describing the interaction between the first phase that involved a survey and the second that consisted of case studies of wine firms in South Africa (i.e., Hamann et al., 2015), Norma Romm and Ralph Hamann link a dialectical approach to an abductive logic. In a classic qualitative approach to grounded theory, induction assumes that findings emerge exclusively from the data. This differs from an abductive logic that moves back and forth not only between findings emerging from different analytical procedures, but also in light of constructs and theoretical frameworks from the literature that cannot be set aside. In the mixed method study about the views of wine makers' views about sustainability, the abductive logic meant that the phases of the research process where more tightly linked than one might presuppose for a two-phase, sequential design.

One of the early proponents for mixed methods, U.K. author from a school of management, Alan Bryman, argued that the ways mixed methods are utilised in the field is far different from how it was initially intended. Barely 10 years into its growth as a legitimate approach, he argued that the 'public face of mixed method research' (2008, p. 162) and the experience of researchers in the real world are often not the same. Investigators, for example, often set out with the goal to corroborate results from different types of data but find that when the sources of data are brought together, new ways of thinking and connections come to mind. 'The products of mixed methods research are often not predictable,' Bryman maintained. 'In fact, they may be rarely predictable' (p. 163).

10.4 Purpose and contribution

The aim of this commentary is to add to the discussion about the ways that mixed methods can be used to develop or refine a theoretical construct or explanatory framework. Its' purpose is to explore ways that the integration of qualitative and quantitative data and/or methods can advance the rigour, analytical density, and originality of research about sustainability in management. It extracts information about the type of integrative procedures or techniques that have been used to extend inferential validity or analytical density from examples of research in business and management. It further develops the argument for the value added of mixed methods to analytical density by comparing two critical case exemplars reporting on a mixed method project with an iterative phase, with a contrasting case that deployed a sequential explanatory design with a secondary qualitative phase.

The description of each critical case serves several purposes. The first, is to inspire fewer mechanical uses of mixed methods. The second is to inspire the reader to consider ways that one or more of the integrative strategies could be adapted to advance the originality of their own research. The third may be to offer references to primary source material that can be used to bolster the legitimacy of the use of a procedure.

The commentary is linked to discussions about research quality because it illustrates approaches to integration that have been used to extend the strength of inferences and conceptual frameworks. It extends the idea of dialogic mixing (Creamer and Edwards, 2019). Dialogic forms of mixing reflect a methodological commitment to deliberately and thoughtfully interrogate gaps, inconsistencies, and counterintuitive findings between different sources of data, particularly during data analysis. It adds consideration to the use of mixed methods to extend or elaborate existing theory to what I have written elsewhere about the ways it can be teamed with grounded theory to advance theory development (Creamer, 2018b, Creamer, in progress). It also adds to Gibson (2017) by expanding ideas about the implications of an iterative component during analysis in a mixed methods study. This includes highlighting the analytical gains achieved by engaging unexpected and sometimes contradictory findings.

Table 10.1 (see p. 181) provides definition of key terms used in the chapter.

10.5 The author's perspective about mixed methods

The methodological orientation I take to mixed methods is a pluralistic one. It is informed by immersion in a wide body of methodological literature, but more so by long engagement in the real world of practice. Like Bryman (2008), I experienced a gap between what is actually described in articles using mixed methods and the abstract world of textbooks. For my purposes, mixed method articles are the data I analyse. Each article is like a case or an experiment (Eisenhardt, 1989). My perspective is not an abstract one. It has been shaped and continues to evolve by ideas emerging from reading a constant stream of new articles.

The philosophical perspective I take in this methodological commentary is one that resonates with emphasis on a dialectical approach reflected in

Table 10.1 Key mixed method terminology related to research design and definitions

Term	Definition
Abduction	An analytical logic that moves back and forth between an exploratory and confirmatory stance in a way that allows for alternative hypotheses to be generated and tested.
Analytic density	Associated with validity, analytic density refers to envisioning constructs in a multi-dimensional way or to developing or elaborating theory in a way that adds to its conceptual nuance or richness.
Dialectical	Associated with Greene's (2007) 'mixed method way of thinking', a dialectic stance reflects a commitment to engage diverse perspectives.
Dialogic mixing	Dialogic forms of mixing reflect a methodological commitment to deliberately and thoughtfully interrogate gaps, inconsistencies, and counterintuitive findings between different sources of data, particularly during analysis (Creamer and Edwards, 2019).
Embedding	A type of integration when data collection and analysis link at multiple points (Fetters et al., 2013).
Hybrid design	A hybrid design is an advanced mixed method design that contains both sequential and concurrent phases (Schoonenboom and Johnson, 2017).
Iterative	An iterative design includes phases where there is on-going interaction between different sources of data and analytical procedures. It involves a cyclical process with repeated loops as insight from one leads to further exploration in the other.
Integrated visual display	A figure or table that integrates data from different sources in ways that enhance conceptual insight.

the 'mixed method way' of thinking first described by Jennifer Greene in 2007. My principal interest has continued to be approaches to mixed methods that support opportunities for meaningful interaction between qualitative and quantitative approaches during analysis (Creamer, 2018).

Pre-occupation with integration, rather than to design, makes the long-standing practice of categorising examples by a core set of mixed methods designs as the organisational framework less effective than it is in other contexts. There are other implications of my continuing fascination with uncovering examples with unusual strategies for integration. One of it is the tendency to uncover examples where there is an on-going, iterative back and forth between the qualitative and quantitative phases that extends across phases.

The main body of the paper sets out to identify examples of procedures that integrate qualitative and quantitative methods during analysis for purposes of enhancing analytic density. It seeks first to demonstrate that there is a wide range of analytical procedures that can be employed by providing an overview of a cluster of examples of articles in business and management. The section that follows delves more deeply into the topic by exploring the analytical procedures used in two critical case exemplars. Following that, there is a section that considers a contrasting case example that is explicitly related to sustainability. The principal purpose of the critical case to draw out the contrast between mixed method approaches that use an iterative design and those that use a more conventional design that postpones integration until the final step where conclusions are drawn. The chapter closes by exploring the implications of an iterative approach to mixed method research.

10.6 Procedures that integrate qualitative and quantitative methods to enhance inference quality

A number of reviews of the ways that mixed methods has been used in disciplines in the business and management fields offer a good starting point to locate examples of mixed methods research, including those that integrated different methods or sources of data in ways that advanced analytical and theoretical insight (e.g., Grafton et al., 2011; Cameron et al., 2015; Molina-Azorín and López-Gamero, 2016; Gibson, 2017).

A wide range of analytical procedures can be used to integrate qualitative and quantitative methods during analysis for purposes of extending the analytical depth or breadth of the findings. These almost always involve the type of dialogic exchange that occurs when findings from the analysis of one source of data generate ideas about ways to pursue analysis with another source of data. Analytic density can be achieved by strategies that integrate findings from different methods in ways that create the opportunity to discern patterns, detect relationships between constructs, identify conditions that influence the outcome, and that recognise the multi-dimensionality of core constructs.

Table 10.2 (see p. 183) extracts data from a diverse cluster of empirical articles from business and management that integrated qualitative and quantitative data during analysis. It only includes examples where meaningful integration occurred during data collection and analysis. The table

Table 10.2 Examples of procedures that advance inference quality and their contribution in mixed method research in management research

Innovative Procedure	Principal Contribution of the Procedure	Examples
Investigate group differences	Explain non-significant or contradictory results.	Kaplan and Duchon (1988)
Quantify qualitative data	Reveal multi-dimensionality of a construct.	Santiago-Brown et al. (2015); Hamann et al. (2017)
Pursue contradictions with additional analysis	Expand an extant theoretical model by adding constructs to it.	Barley et al. (2011); Gardner (2012); Kaplan and Duchon (1988); Sutton and Rafaeli (1988)
	Elaborate conditions under which a social process occurs and doesn't occur.	Bezrukova et al. (2009)
Case-based analysis	Test relationships observed in cases.	Sharma and Vredenburg (1998)
	Suggest and/or confirm relationships between variables.	Hamann et al. (2017); Sharma and Vredenburg (1998)
Process tracing	Generate ideas about causation associated with a process that is time-ordered.	Gardner (2012); Kaplan and Duchon (1988); Vaast and Levina (2015)
Visual display	Generate hypothesis or theoretical propositions for further analysis.	Gardner (2012); Hamann et al. (2017)

pinpoints the analytical procedure used, the principal contribution of the procedure to analytical insight, and lists a few publications that utilise the procedure.

The transparency afforded by labelling research as 'mixed methods' varied across the entries listed in Table 10.2. Some describe their research as combining qualitative and quantitative methods. Some label their approach as multi-method. Very few facilitated the act of locating examples of research about sustainability that used mixed methods by explicitly including these words in the title or abstract.

The examples highlighted in Table 10.2 integrated methods for purposes of elaboration or expansion of conceptual understanding that is achieved when data from one source informs data collection or analysis in another. The fact that most entries appear more than once in the table reflects that integration often serves multiple purposes in studies using an iterative design.

10.7 Two Case Exemplars that Integrated Methods to Advance Inference Quality

In this section, we put under the microscope two examples from the management literature that expand conventional approaches to mixed methods in several ways. First, they are unusual in that they illustrate mixed method analytical strategies used in the service of what Fielding (2008, 2012) referred to as analytical density. Secondly, they link an iterative design with that outcome. There is an on-going "back and forth" between different methods as new interpretations emerge and are weighed against different sources of data in an iterative design. A third critical distinction highlights the contribution of dissonance to analytical insight. The first two cases pursued dissonance between the different methods with additional, probably unplanned, rounds of data collection and/or analysis.

Table 10.3 (see p. 185) contrasts key elements of the three critical cases, including one that is designated as a contrasting critical case. It identifies the design, integrative strategy used by each, and identifies the contribution of the integrative analytical procedure.

The first two cases used a hybrid mixed method design with an iterative phase. A hybrid design is an advanced design that incorporates both concurrent and sequential phases (Schoonenboom and Johnson, 2017), but is not always iterative. The contrasting case used one of the basic designs where the quantitative and qualitative strands are compartmentalised. Integration for purposes of explanatory insight is not a priority in this study.

I use the same organizational template to summarise information about each of the three case exemplars. The section about each article is organised in three parts: purpose of the research, a description of how integration occurred, and a summary of the analytical contribution of integration.

Case 1: Kaplan and Duchon (1988): *Reconciling conflicting findings by re-analyzing the quantitative data with new constructs introduced during the analysis of qualitative data*

Purpose: It is quite a common experience, particularly in research gauging the outcomes of an intervention, to find that the quantitative results and the qualitative findings point to different conclusions. This was the experience of a pair of collaborators reporting on a pilot study they described as combining qualitative and quantitative methods. This study has an explanatory, hypothesis testing drive. It was designed to explore the relationship between orientation to work and what happens when a new management information system is installed in commercial laboratory settings.

Table 10.3 Integrative procedure, generic label, and contribution to analytical insight for two critical cases in method

Example	Integrative Procedure	Contribution of the Procedure to Analytical Insight
Kaplan and Duchon (1988)	Quantitative data reanalysed with constructs identified in the qualitative analysis.	Confirmed grounded theory model that explained differences between groups.
Gardner (2012)	A case-based mapping activity.	Illustrate how paradoxical results play out in interaction patterns during meetings.

Integrative procedures: Results from an independent analysis of the qualitative and quantitative data conducted by two different researchers were contradictory. The initial analysis of survey data provided no statistical support for the findings from the qualitative data analysis that pointed to strong differences in the work orientation of laboratory team members in different settings. Following the concurrent analysis of the qualitative and quantitative data, the member of team who described her expertise as qualitative, developed a grounded theory model that foregrounded work orientation as a mechanism underlying the differences between attitudes toward the newly implemented management information. In the final phase of analysis, the quantitative survey data were re-analysed with the addition of variables constructed to represent the constructs or themes emerging from the grounded theory.

Contribution of integration to analytical insight: Results of the integration of the qualitative data both confirmed and elaborated findings. The re-analysis of the quantitative data confirmed the grounded theory model developed following the completion of the qualitative phase. It elaborated the conceptual framework by providing statistical support to document the intermediary role of work orientation in explaining attitudes about the implementation of new management software.

Case 2: Gardner (2012): *Leveraging a mapping activity and case-based analysis to explain paradoxical findings*

An example what the author refers to as multi-method research by Gardner (2012) demonstrates ways that a "back and forth" exchange between qualitative and quantitative strands can generate new analytical insight. Most specifically for our purposes here, we examine it to consider the way that a visualization like a diagram that maps interactions can be used to explore paradoxical findings. The description Gardner provides of the analytical procedures could be helpful to others looking for ways to analyse observational data of team meetings.

Purpose: Gardner set out with the purpose that applies to almost any type of workplace team. She sought to explore the link between team knowledge and performance by using what began as an explanatory sequential design but shifted to a hybrid design. Gardner's objective was to unravel the puzzling finding that teams often default to the person, probably more senior, with non-specialised knowledge in the very setting where high performance pressures demand the expertise provided by a team member with specialised knowledge. She added a third, qualitative phase to the project where she used process tracing. Process theory deals with events and the processes that connect them (Maxwell et al., 2015). Gardner drew process diagrams to map the sequence of actions and interactions she observed in team meetings.

Integrative procedures: Gardner (2012) used a type of case-based analysis with a process-oriented mapping activity. Not to be confused with a case study that serves a summative purpose in a final report, case-based analysis is a mixed method analytical strategy that integrates qualitative and quantitative data in a narrative form or through a visualization (Bazeley, 2018). According to Pat Bazeley, an Australian and prolific textbook writer, 'Each case holds data from different sources and different types together, thus cases provide the lynchpin for integration of data' (2018, p. 26).

The maps developed by Gardner (2012) served the same role an analytic memo might serve in a project with a grounded theory component. She recorded each incident of knowledge use and used a symbol system to distinguish between the language used by the general professional experts and domain-specific experts. Each map was annotated to provide data to support her interpretation. In the two examples of maps included in the article, time pressures may have explained why the views of the more experienced, but less technically proficient, member prevailed.

Contribution of integration to analytical insight: Findings from the cross-case comparison of the process maps are not elaborated. Gardner makes that argument that they supported generalizability by confirming findings from the analysis in earlier phases of the quantitative data. There is a lot more this author could have learned by further exploring the data in the process maps.

The third and final critical case by Mahmood et al. (2018) is a contrasting case. It addresses the issue of corporate governance structure and sustainability reporting. It further illustrates just how closely the approach taken to integrating research methods (and often team dynamics) influences the potential to gain analytical depth in a mixed method study.

Contrasting case example with a non-iterative design. Case 3 Mahmood et al. (2018): *Research in sustainability with a non-iterative design*

A mixed methods study appearing in the journal, *Sustainability*, by Mahmood et al. (2018) further magnifies the distinctions between iterative designs and more basics ones. This is the only case where the authors show familiarity with a slice of foundational literature about mixed methods. It's the only case to offer transparency by using the expression "mixed methods" in the title, by explicitly labelling the research design, and by using language to explicitly acknowledge how integration occurred.

This example has the advantage of using a widely recognised, core mixed method design. It aligns an explanatory sequential design with a triangulation purpose. The drive is quantitative and the rationale for integration is triangulation or validation. The purpose, integrative strategy, and outcomes achieved differs markedly for this research than for the two cases previously presented.

Purpose: The aim of the research was to explore the relationship between elements of corporate governance and disclosure sustainability. Results supported research documenting the link between board size, but not gender diversity, and initiatives to report sustainability initiatives.

Integrative procedures: In the "materials and methods" section the authors describe a study with a distinct quantitative phase that was followed by a second, qualitative phase. Integration in this case occurred at a single point and in a procedural, rather than conceptual way. That was at the juncture between the two phases when results from the quantitative analysis were used design the qualitative instrument and to guide selection of participants.

Contribution of integration to analytical insight: The qualitative phase in this study is so secondary as to make it unlikely that it could be published separately. Only a very small number of board members were interviewed in order to validate the quantitative results. The qualitative data were used to illustrate the quantitative findings, but there was no separate emergent analysis. Contradictions between the qualitative and quantitative findings from the different methods were acknowledged but not pursued.

10.8 Discussion

Ten empirical mixed methods articles extracted from a search of the management literature made it possible to generate a list of analytical procedures that contributed to analytic density in ways that elaborate or extend an explanatory framework. These overlap with the four strengths for using mixed methods identified by Gibson (2017): elaboration, generalization, triangulation, and interpretation. A number of procedures have been defined that can be deployed to extend analytical density and inferential validity. These include to: (1) investigate contradictory results by exploring group differences, (2) reveal the multi-dimensionality of a construct, (3) add constructs that elaborate conditions that influenced the social process, and (4) trace causation suggested by a time-ordered process.

Three additional procedures triangulated data in ways that extended generalizability by confirming relationships between constructs and by pursuing hypotheses or theoretical propositions generated by one method with data from another method. My analysis of the ten empirical articles from management add to the results reported by Gibson's (2017) by underscoring the pivotal role dissonance between data sources or between findings and existing theory played in propelling the systematic pursuit of possible explanations.

There are a wide range of implications to using an approach to mixed methods that has an iterative component. Implications extend to study design, the way mixing occurs, the purposes served by mixing, philosophical foundations, and reporting.

1. **Design**

   a. Often contain elements from core designs by combining concurrent and sequential and exploratory and explanatory phases.
   b. Engagement of findings from different methods during analysis often introduces unexpected sources of dissonance that would not likely emerge in studies where data collection and analysis are de-coupled.

2. **Integration**

   a. Methods are integrated at multiple points in the research process, including during analysis.
   b. A principal way that integration occurs during analysis is when findings from the analysis of one source of data informs additional data collection and/or analysis of another. This type of interaction maintains the integrity of the analytical procedures associated with each method.

3. **Purposes Served by Integration**

   a. Integration occurs in more than one way and serves more than one purpose.

4. **Philosophical Implications**

   a. There is often a commitment to engage diverse perspectives.
   b. Qualitative and quantitative methods are considered to share many qualities.
   c. Interpretive approaches are awarded comparable weight in the research process.

5. **Reporting**

   a. The way that qualitative and quantitative analytical procedures are interlocked makes it unlikely that the phases could be reported separately.

10.9 Conclusion

Numerous researchers have offered templates to help those new to the field to imagine how a mixed methods study might be conducted. These can be interpreted in far more prescriptive ways than they were originally intended. To design a study carries dual meaning in that it emphasises both the importance of careful planning and on-going adaptation to the context (Hunter and Brewer, 2015) as well as to the unpredictably introduced by integration that Bryman (2008) observed. The type of original insight that leads others to thoroughly digest an unfamiliar piece of research rests on expertise, skill, and in-depth knowledge of a phenomenon but also the willingness to adapt data collection methods and analytical procedures to meet complexities encountered in the research environment. It also means following a promising lead that emerges when data analysed by different means or feedback from different constituents' complicate matters by communicating a different story when integrated (Creamer, 2018b).

Authors who have reviewed the use of mixed methods in business and management research have questioned how familiar investigators are with the methodological literature about it. One of the consequences of this knowledge gap, especially with the terminology associated with it, makes it unlikely that than an article will ever surface in a literature search of articles using mixed methods. Researchers trying to find a way to distinguish their work and make it competitive in a methodological journal, will benefit by trolling the literature in unfamiliar academic fields for examples of original uses of mixed methods. Examples encountered can spur creative thinking, inspire ideas about how to design an eye-catching visual, and help an investigator develop a repertoire of procedures to construct a nuanced explanation for perplexing findings.

Developing methodological expertise requires reading a breadth of different viewpoints about any method. The expertise to utilise multiple approaches requires that researchers thoughtfully engage with contemporary viewpoints about qualitative, quantitative, and mixed methods approaches. Advancing methodological training through professional development activities, now readily available online, can promote dialogue that bridges disciplinary domains. It builds fluency with a dictionary of the terminology associated with different research methods. Diverse ways to approach mixed methods helps to build knowledge (Fielding, 2008). It contributes to the ability of researchers to develop the confidence about the potential for creativity and new insight when mixed methods are recognised as a methodology that extends well beyond the initial act of collecting qualitative and quantitative data.

References

Barley, S. R., Meyerson, D. E., and Grodal, S. (2010). E-mail as a source and symbol of stress. *Organizational Science*, 22(4), 817–1120.

Bazeley, P. (2018). *Integrating analyses in mixed methods research*. Sage, Thousand Oaks.

Bezrukova, K., Jehn, K. A., Zanutto, E. and Thatcher, S. M. B. (2009). Do workgroup faultlines help or hurt? A moderated model of faultlines, team identification, and group performance. *Organization Science, 20*(1), 35–50.

Bryman, A. (2008). Of methods and methodology. *Qualitative Research in Organization and Management: An International Journal, 3*(1), 159–168.

Cameron, R., Sankaran, S., and Scales, J. (2015). Mixed methods use in project management research. *Project Management Journal, 46*(2), 90–104.

Creamer, E. G. (2018). *An introduction to fully integrated mixed methods research.* Sage, Thousand Oaks.

Creamer, E. G. (2018b). Enlarging the conceptualization of mixed method approaches to grounded theory with intervention research. In E. G. Creamer and J. L. Schoonenboom (Eds.), Methodological innovation in mixed method research. *American Behavioral Scientist, 62*(7), 919–934. doi/10.1177/0002764218772642 Accessed: 30/09/20.

Creamer, E. G. (2020). Visualizing dynamic fully integrated mixed method designs. *International Journal of Multiple Research Approaches, 12*(1), 67–77.

Creamer, E. G. (forthcoming 2021). *Advancing grounded theory with mixed methods.* Routledge, London.

Creamer, E. G., and Edwards, C. D. (2019). Embedding the dialogic in mixed method approaches to theory development. *International Journal of Research and Method in Education, 42*(3), 239–251.

Eisenhardt, K. M. (1989). Building theories from case study research. *Academy of Management Review, 14*(4), 532–550.

Fetters, M.D., Curry, L.A., and Creswell, J.W. (2013). Achieving integration in mixed methods designs-principles and practices. *Health Services Research, 48,* 2134–5610.

Fielding, N. G. (2008). Analytic density, postmodernism, and applied multiple method research. In M. M. Bergman (Ed.), *Advances in mixed methods research* (37–52). Sage, London.

Fielding, N. G. (2009). Going out on a limb: Postmodernism and multiple method research. *Current Sociology, 57*(3), 427–447.

Fielding, N. G. (2012). Triangulation and mixed methods designs: Data integration with new research technologies. *Journal of Mixed Methods Research, 6*(2), 124–136.

Gardner, H. K. (2012). Performance pressure as a double-edged sword: Enhancing team motivation but undermining the use of team knowledge. *Administrative Science Quarterly, 57*(1), 1–46.

Gibson, C. B. (2017). Elaboration, generalization, triangulation, and interpretation: On enhancing the value of mixed method research. *Organizational Research Methods, 20*(2), 193–223.

Grafton, J., Lillis, A. M., and Mahama, H. (2011). Mixed methods research in accounting. *Qualitative Research in Accounting and Management, 8*(1), 5–21.

Greene, J. C. (2007). *Mixed methods in social inquiry.* Wiley, San Francisco.

Hamann, R., Smith, J., Tashman, P., and Marshall, R. S. (2015). Why do SMEs go green? An analysis of wine firms in South Africa. *Business and Society, 56*(1), 23–56.

Hunter, A., and Brewer, J. (2015). Designing multi-method research. In S. Hesse-Biber and R. B. Johnson (Eds.), *The Oxford handbook of multimethod and mixed methods research inquiry* (185–205). Sage, Oxford.

Kaplan, B., and Duchon, D. (1988). Combining qualitative and quantitative methods in information systems research: A case study. *Management Information Systems Quarterly*, 12 (4), 571–586.

Mahmood, Z., Kouser, R., Ali, W., Ahmad, Z., and. Salman, T. (2018). *Sustainability, 10.* doi:10.3390/su10010207

Maxwell, J., Chmiel, M., and Rogers, S. E. (2015). Designing integration in multimethod and mixed methods research. In S. Hesse-Biber and R. B. Johnson (Eds.), *The Oxford handbook of multimethod and mixed methods research inquiry* (223–239). Sage, Oxford.

Molina-Azorín, J. (2011). The use and added value of mixed methods in management research. *Journal of Mixed Methods Research*, 5(1), 7–24.

Molina-Azorín, J., and Cameron, R. A. (2015). History and emergent practices of multimethod and mixed methods in business research. In S. Hesse-Biber and R. B. Johnson (Eds.), *The Oxford handbook of multimethod and mixed methods research inquiry* (466–485). Sage, Oxford.

Molina-Azorín, J., and López-Gamero, M. D. (2016). Mixed methods studies in environmental management research: Prevalence, purposes, and designs. *Business Strategy and the Environment*, 25, 134–148.

Santiago-Brown, I., Jerrarm, C., and Metcalfe, A., (2014). What does sustainability mean? Knowledge gleaned from applying mixed methods research to wine growing. *Journal of Mixed Methods Research*, 9(3), 232–251.

Sharma, S., and Vredenburg, H. (1998). Proactive corporate environmental strategy and the development of competitively valuable capabilities. *Strategic Management Journal*, 19, 729–753.

Schoonenboom, J., and Johnson, R. B. (2017). How to construct a mixed methods research design. *Koln Z Soziol*, 69, 107–131.

Sutton, R. I., and Rafaeli, A. (1988). Untangling the relationship between displayed emotions and organizational sales: The case of convenience stores. *Academy of Management Journal*, 31(3), 461–487.

Vaast, E., and Levina, N. (2015). Speaking as one, but not speaking up: Dealing with new moral taint in occupational online community. *Information and Organization*, 25, 73–98.

11 Addressing the challenge of mixed methods integration through joint displays and clear writing

Timothy C. Guetterman and Jennifer Moss Breen

11.1 Introduction

Mixed methods research is increasingly used in sustainability research in business and other fields and has demonstrated its value in understanding complex problems. The value of mixed methods arises from the intentional integration of qualitative and quantitative research. Integration is best achieved through careful design and giving systematic attention as to how the two forms of research may be combined. The combining of the two research approaches provides for a mixing of the methods whereby opportunities arise such as differentiating the most and least successful enterprises using quantitative data analysis methods and then looking for variation among qualitative themes to identify best practices.

We think of integration as the "What" and "Why" of research, with quantitative data providing the "What" and qualitative data providing the "Why" or "How". For example, researchers used an explanatory sequential mixed methods design to first examine the relationship between governance measures and sustainability reporting and then interviewed board members to 'validate the results of the quantitative study and to provide more depth and more insight into the quantitative results' (Mahmood et al., 2018, p. 7). The mixed methods approach allows for a more rigorous examination of phenomena than mono-method studies.

These mono-methods, while appropriately addressing the researcher's questions, may not capture the complete phenomena. In the area of sustainability, which is a complex problem, mixed methods research becomes highly relevant. For example, quantitative measures might include data about the enterprise or its board members, surveys, or indices, such as the Global Reporting Initiative sustainability disclosure or the "What" (Brown et al., 2009) while qualitative interviews with corporate leaders may shed insight into their thinking and planning for the future, or the "Why" and "How" (Reinecke et al., 2016), such as drivers and barriers to eco-efficiency (Klewitz et al., 2012).

Integration is the central characteristic of mixed methods research (2018), yet achieving integration remains challenging to researchers (Fetters et al., 2013; Fetters and Freshwater, 2015) and practitioners as well as those with direct responsibility of organisational sustainability (Searls, 2005; Rafiei and Ricardez-Sandoval 2020). Writing about integration strategies and presenting integrative mixed methods results appears to be one of the most difficult aspects of mixed methods research. Conveying integrated results, however, is essential to maximize the value of mixed methods research (Yarime, 2017).

Our aim for this chapter is to discuss strategies for integrating qualitative and quantitative research with a focus on visual joint displays as a way to conduct and represent integration. Throughout the chapter, we also stress on how to write about integration, both describing the procedures and reporting integrated results. We hope that by discussing strategies for writing about integration, the process of integration itself becomes more concrete and clearer for both scholarly and business professionals.

11.2 Terminology and language of mixed methods

A common question we hear is how to use the right words, or lingo, to write about mixed methods research. As a newer field in research methodology, we understand the need for researchers and business practitioners to not only understand but to also have the knowledge and skills to apply appropriate mixed methods techniques. As such, Table 11.1 (see p. 194) presents some important mixed methods research terms used throughout this chapter. These terms are meant to provide language, or a toolkit, to be used to write about integrative findings and mixed methods.

As mixed methods is a developing methodology, the terms continue to evolve and agreement among scholars and practitioners using these terms is not unanimous. When using the terms, it is more important to define what you mean rather than to feel bound by any language. However, when writing for certain journals (e.g., the Journal of Mixed Methods Research), remember that standards have emerged when writing, and these terms provide a good starting point. Your organisation or scholarly outlet may have similar or different terms to which you can adapt from the list given below.

11.3 Strategies for integration

Integration refers to the intentional bringing together of qualitative and quantitative research, such that an interdependence among the two is present (Bazeley, 2018). This interdependence is what produces the synergistic effects of integration, or the "What" and the "Why/How". In other words, integration produces something new: 1) meta-inferences that result from integration, 2) data collection tools, 3) samples, or 4) follow-up studies. Authors have described multiple nuanced strategies for integration (Bazeley, 2018; Fetters, 2020). Although numerous strategies exist for achieving integration, here, we will focus on three fundamental strategies for mixed methods integration: merging, connecting, and building.

Table 11.1 Integration terms used in this chapter

Term	Description
Strand	A sole quantitative or qualitative component or phase of research. Example: an organisational employee engagement survey or a qualitative interview study.
Designs	A set of procedures that guides the entire process of research from developing to conducting to disseminating. Example: convergent mixed methods design includes data collection procedures including both quantitative data around key organisational variables or concerns (i.e. sales performance, employee engagement survey data) and qualitative data (i.e. employee focus group data across senior, mid and entry levels concerning workplace diversity, equity, and inclusion efforts).
Integration	Integration is the bringing together of quantitative and qualitative research through which the two become interdependent. Example: following a data analysis plan that combines both quantitative data, such as employee engagement, and its potential relationship with individual perspectives regarding organisational equity, diversity, and inclusion.
Merging	An integration strategy to compare or relate quantitative and qualitative results to produce meta-inferences. Example: Pursuing a data analysis technique whereby direct comparison between employee engagement and perspectives about diversity, equity, and inclusion become the desired outcome from the research.
Building	An integration strategy to use one form of results to inform data collection of another. Example: Utilising results from initial study (perspectives on diversity, equity, and inclusion) to develop a survey to assess strategic goals year over year such that they include previous learnings and with the intent of improving or strengthening in distinct areas.
Connecting	An integration strategy to use one form of results to inform the sampling of another. Example: Adapting current organisational research, based upon previous organisational research, by asking "what else" might be impacting employee engagement? And "who else" shall we seek information from to improve/adapt/or continue our work in the areas of employee engagement, diversity, equity, and inclusion?
Meta-inferences	New results that emerge from the integration of qualitative and quantitative inferences. Example: Concrete, distinct "aha" moments leading to strategic change within the organisation.
Joint displays	A visual way to present the integration of qualitative and quantitative research in a table, matrix, or graphic. Example: Quantitative displays of employee engagement across senior, mid and entry levels within the organisation alongside themes and direct quotes concerning diversity, equity, and inclusion data.

11.3.1 Merging integration leads to meta-inferences

Merging is a strategy that involves comparing or relating qualitative and quantitative results or data in order to produce meta-inferences as an outcome of integration. Meta-inferences are new results that emerge from the integration of qualitative and quantitative inferences (Teddlie and Tashakkori, 2009). Meta-inferences address this general question: What is the added value from integrating the qualitative and quantitative results beyond what either result alone yields? In other words, integration is synergistic, or as some have described, "1+1=3" (Fetters and Freshwater, 2015, p. 115). Our view is that merging can occur in two ways: 1) comparing qualitative and quantitative results, or 2) relating the two in order to examine patterns, or perhaps even discover emerging patterns. Merging data from a business sustainability perspective might include a systemic review of corporate sustainability criteria and outcomes, or quantitative results, with senior leadership perspectives on corporate sustainability and its impact on productivity. These two datasets can bring new insight into the "What" and the "Why" of business sustainability.

Merging by *comparing* quantitative and qualitative data or results entails looking for concordance, discordance, and expansion. As an initial step, it is important to catalog qualitative and quantitative results, perhaps by listing major findings. In the example above regarding business sustainability outcomes and senior leaders' perspectives on corporate sustainability in relation to productivity, our merged data may reveal that though corporate sustainability is a stated goal of the organisation, senior leaders do not prioritise sustainability, often preferring profitability instead. Our research would have revealed discordance. Next, look for similar concepts between the two. You might examine whether themes seem to link to certain key statistical results or whether themes link to major constructs or scales measured. Linking the two then provides a point of comparison to determine concordance, discordance, or expansion. In our example, you might find that different regions prioritise sustainability more frequently than others, and these differences might align with their respective senior leaders' perspectives on the relationship between sustainability and productivity.

While concordance and discordance are straightforward, expansion is the idea that one form of research has concepts that may not have related elements in the other. For example, researchers may have a scale that measures a construct, but qualitative inquiry unpacks the concept into multiple aspects within a business, which is particularly useful for smaller and medium-sized enterprises that do not lend as well to large, generalizable samples. The concepts are still related but the qualitative themes add complexity. In keeping with our example above, perhaps we learn through our quantitative analysis that for corporations, sustainability practices are in place. Yet, our qualitative interviews with senior leaders across the system reveal that regional views and political views create limitations for implementing system-wide sustainability practices. This new finding expands our knowledge of our topic and creates new pathways for future research. These new findings create an opportunity to merge the data and to create meta-inferences, bringing richer insights than keeping the data separate.

Merging by *relating* attempts to look for patterns to generate meta-inferences. This type of integration could involve looking for statistical patterns by themes or looking for qualitative patterns by quantitative results. In the first example, we might explore variation among themes that arise. Assume that a study yielded major themes, and you are interested in a statistical profile of individuals (or cases) for whom that theme was present. Merging in this manner would illuminate statistical differences among themes. From our example, we could split our data by corporate regions to understand forces that may be limiting corporate sustainability requirements, or from a leadership perspective, if one theme related to servant leadership within organisational leaders and another related to transformational leaders, you might look for patterns in the quantitative results. That analysis could address research questions about similarities or differences in an environmental sustainability index between organisations that demonstrate servant (Greenleaf, 1977) versus transformational leadership (Bass and Riggio, 2005) and their additional relationship with productivity as well as compliance.

The opposite approach is to look at qualitative results to explain quantitative variation. A typical approach is to categorise a quantitative variable (e.g., high/low or high/medium/low) and to analyse the data to understand what accounts for variation. For example, researchers might look for what themes arose in the higher versus lower performing organisations on the Global Reporting Initiative index. The research question addressed through this analysis is focused on what distinguishes higher versus lower performing organisations.

11.3.2 Building integration leads to new data collection tools

Building is an integration strategy that leads to new tools for data collection and is common in sequential designs in which one phase leads to the next. In brief, the results of one phase inform data collection in the next (Fetters et al., 2013). Building creates a stairstep type process where each form of data and the findings inform planning the subsequent phases to add to our knowledge about the topic. Building can occur in many mixed methods designs, but what is critical is the systematic use of results to inform data collection tools (e.g., surveys, interview protocols). The data collection plans should flow from the research questions.

In one example of building, the results of a quantitative phase can be used to develop qualitative data collection tools, such as interview protocols or observational protocols, used in a subsequent phase. Systematically using those results is taking advantage of the value of mixed methods. If you are attempting to explain quantitative results in more detail with a follow-up qualitative phase, building helps to ensure that the interview will truly elaborate on key aspects of interest as per your research questions. For example, if you are interested in understanding significant results, interview questions can be constructed around those specific experiences. Or, if the focus is on explaining unexpected results, interview questions should focus on what is not already known to unpack the results.

A joint display (discussed later in this chapter) can help you to link specific results to specific questions, to make the process explicit for a reader. Looking again at the corporate sustainability example, perhaps you learn through a quantitative study that the eastern region of the United States demonstrates greater compliance with corporate-mandated sustainability requirements than the western region. This is puzzling to you, and so you plan to interview senior leaders from each region to learn about regional facets that may be creating disparate results. Through building, you hope to learn if barriers exist, and if they do, how to work with senior leaders from the western region to improve sustainability compliance.

Alternatively, the results of a qualitative phase can be used to develop a survey or to adopt an existing survey. Again, the most important point is to take advantage of the results and use them systematically to maximize the value of mixing methods. This strategy can help to ensure that the survey or instrument is contextually relevant, especially if the initial qualitative phase was conducted with a sample from the same target population as the survey. In other words, the resulting instrument will reflect their specific and context-related perspectives, views, and their language. To implement building at a practical level, we recommend starting with specific qualitative results: codes, categories, or themes as per your qualitative approach. Then, consider which of those qualitative results are relevant to construct or adapt to the instrument. Finally, write survey items or questions for each result, remembering that you may have more than one item for each result.

11.3.3 Connecting integration leads to new samples

Connecting is another integration strategy, and its goal is to generate a new sample. The results of one form of research systematically informs sampling strategies of the other. Most commonly, researchers use results of a quantitative phase to plan a purposeful qualitative sample that will explain results further. The research questions should drive sampling decisions. Thus, the first step is to use the quantitative results of the initial phase to develop research questions for the subsequent phase. The intent could be to explain variation or unusual, typical, unexpected, significant, non-significant, or other results. Then consider who needs to be sampled to best expand and address research questions. From our earlier example, we simply discussed senior leaders. But it is likely that mid-level managers and first-line workers are responsible for implementing mandated corporate sustainability requirements. If so, it is important to learn more about this set of individuals. Results can be matched to a sample that will best allow follow-up. For example, an initial quantitative phase might identify high versus low performance on a sustainability index. A subsequent purposeful qualitative sample could focus on obtaining a mix of high versus low performing organisations to interview, in order to understand what might explain the variation.

11.3.4 Summary of integration

Different integration strategies exist, and three foundational strategies to consider are merging, building, and connecting. Merging involves comparing or relating quantitative and qualitative results. Collectively, building and connecting lead to follow-up studies. Building is the use of one form of research to plan data collection, such as developing interview protocols or surveys. Connecting is the use of one form of research to plan sampling for the other. Mixed methods research studies ideally use multiple integration strategies (Bazeley, 2018). To select a strategy, consider whether there is an opportunity for one strand to inform the other and if there is an opportunity to merge. To determine what specifically to integrate, return to research questions and look for specific ways to link qualitative and quantitative strands. Next, we will review joint displays to facilitate the process.

11.4 Joint displays as a visual integration strategy

Joint displays have increased substantially in popularity as a visual way to present the integration of qualitative and quantitative research in a table, matrix, or graphic. In the past 5 years, numerous conference sessions and articles appearing in journals, including the Journal of Mixed Methods Research, have used joint displays to represent integration. Moreover, methodological articles have been surfacing that showcase the use of joint displays in various disciplines (Guetterman et al., 2015; Younas et al., 2020) and describe how to develop joint displays for different designs (Guetterman et al., 2015; Bustamante, 2017). The emphasis on joint displays is often levied on their value for explicating integrated results to depict the results of merging integration. However, joint displays are also helpful for planning, such as systematically showing how results of one strand of research informed data collection (i.e., building), sampling (i.e., connecting), or other procedures in planning a sequential strand.

11.4.1 A joint display for merging

Joint displays can be helpful for identifying meta-inferences. As a method of analysis in itself, developing a joint display for merging involves linking related quantitative and qualitative results, moving back-and-forth between the two to compare or identify patterns, and identifying meta-inferences. Joint displays can facilitate both comparing and relating, as discussed previously in this chapter. Joint displays provide the consumer of our research with a visual product that speeds understanding of our research results. Joint displays are also useful in the business setting where 'a picture is worth a thousand words', and quick understanding of research findings is extremely beneficial.

Table 11.2 (see p. 200) presents a simple template for a side-by-side joint display for comparing quantitative and qualitative results (Guetterman et al., 2015). This template is meant to be a guide, adapted to your specific project. The first column, domains, is meant to be an organising principle for the joint display and could consist of domain similarity or a theoretical or conceptual model guiding the study. Rows can be used to align similar quantitative and qualitative results for comparison. The cells include the respective results (e.g., a summary of a theme, a key statistic or figure). The final column is most critical and a place for writing about meta-inferences.

Joint displays can also be used for analysis and representation of relating quantitative and qualitative results. Table 11.3 (see p. 201) presents one potential template for explaining variation between high and low performers using qualitative data. The domain column is flexible but meant to be a way to organise the joint display. The next two columns in the template represent levels of a categorical variable. The "performance" column could be high or low scores on any construct or variable and can be extended to more categorical levels. The cells are a way to summarize how higher versus lower performing organisations, individuals, or cases are different or similar in terms of qualitative themes. The final row is a way to present meta-inferences, such as a broadinference about high performers across all domains. Alternatively, meta-inferences could be included as a final column. Presenting a joint display, such as in Table 11.2 or 11.3, in a results section of a manuscript can make the integrated results, and process of integration, explicit for the reader.

11.4.2 A joint display for building

When building new data collection tools, a joint display can help to systematically think about how specific results lead to subsequent data collection questions. In this way, the joint display aids in planning the follow-up data collection. Table 11.4 (see p. 202) presents a template for using a joint display to develop qualitative interview questions based on quantitative results. As with other joint displays, first consider how to organise it, such as by domain or key results. The next two columns are for quantitative results and the related qualitative questions, respectively. In this template, the order of columns follows the sequence of research procedures, with quantitative first and qualitative second. The cells below each

Table 11.2 A side-by-side joint display template for comparing

Domain	Quantitative Results	Qualitative Results	Meta-inferences
The domain is a way to organise the joint display and link related quantitative and qualitative concepts. It could be derived from a theoretical construct or similar concepts. Example: Employee Engagement and Diversity, Equity, and Inclusion.	Use these cells to summarise results. It could include a column graph, scatterplot, or statistical results. Example:	Use these cells to summarise results, such as a summary of the theme or category and perhaps an illustrative quote. Example: 'I feel that I am not 'seen' within our company. I serve on so many teams and everyone seems to know me, but I never get the next position'.	These cells are to write about meta-inferences identified through integration. Example: We learn that some organisational members are feeling highly disengaged because they feel they are not offered opportunities to advance as frequently as others.
{...}	{...}	{...}	{...}
{...}	{...}	{...}	{...}

The Relationship Between Number of Process Indicators and Sustainability Scores

column are to link a specific result of interest or item to specific qualitative interview questions. The link does not have to be 1:1, and mixed methods researchers often write multiple questions to unpack each key result. The final column is a place to indicate the rationale for that specific question (McCrudden and McTigue, 2019). This template could be modified to develop quantitative items from qualitative results. For that modification,

Table 11.3 A themes-by-categories joint display template for relating

Domain	High Performers	Low Performers
The domain provides a way to organise the joint display and can be major themes, categories, or theoretical concepts. Example: Employee Engagement.	These cells are for a thematic summary of high performing organisations, individuals, or cases. Example: We found that highly engaged employees tended to work in more diverse workgroups and collaborations.	These cells can be used for a thematic summary of low performing organisations, individuals, or cases. Example: We found less engaged employees tended to work in less diverse settings.
{...}	{...}	{...}
{...}	{...}	{...}
Meta-inferences	Summarise meta-inferences for high performing organisations.	Summarise meta-inferences for high performing organisations.

switching the two middle columns would be ideal so that the qualitative and quantitative columns follow the flow of research. This type of joint display could appear in a results section, or possibly, a methods section of a manuscript to clearly explicate procedures for building the new data collection tool.

11.4.3 A joint display for connecting

When connecting to identify an appropriate follow-up sample, joint displays can also be helpful in thinking about sampling. Joint displays for connecting also serve a planning purpose, using the result of one strand to plan the sample in the other (Guetterman et al., 2015). For example, assume that researchers used a quantitative survey to categorise enterprises in a typology from business-as-usual to truly sustainable (Dyllick and Muff, 2016). In a joint display, the author can clearly link those quantitative groups (i.e., types) to a specific qualitative sample that will elaborate the results. Table 11.5 (see p. 203) presents a template for a sampling joint display to connect from a quantitative strand to a qualitative sample. Alternatively, you could start with key quantitative results rather than groups, and create a joint display to think through specific sample characteristics. While a joint display is a presentation of the outcome of integration, the process of creating the display can help to step through the cognitive process of integration. This type of joint display might appear in a

Table 11.4 An interview protocol development joint display template to depict building

Domain	Quantitative Results (or Items)	Qualitative Interview Questions	Reason for the Question
The domain provides a way to organise the joint display and can be major themes, categories, or theoretical concepts. Example: Employee Engagement.	Indicate the specific quantitative results or items on an instrument that need explanation Example: Less diverse employees are more engaged that diverse employees.	Write the actual related interview questions to explain the result. Example: 'How can our organisation understand your work experiences and professional goals more clearly?' Note: Should be asked of all employees regardless of their self-disclosed diversity.	Include a rationale for writing the specific question(s). Example: Findings from initial study revealed lower employee engagement from self-reported diverse employees. Asking this question allows the organisation to learn how to improve opportunities for diverse employees, which could improve employee engagement if done well. Additionally, asking this question of all employees can improve overall employee engagement of the organisation.
{...}	{...}	{...}	{...}
{...}	{...}	{...}	{...}

methods section to demonstrate connecting integration as seen in Ivankova et al.'s (2006) study of persistence in higher education. By including a joint display, such as Table 11.5 (see p. 203), the reader will be able to understand the process for selecting the sample.

11.4.4 Advanced joint displays using graphics or images

The process of developing a joint display can be creative. In addition to deviating from the templates, think about other ways to communicate results, such as through graphs, charts, figures, or images. Table 11.6 (see

Table 11.5 A sampling joint display template to depict connecting

Quantitative Groups	Description of Qualitative Sample	Rationale for the Sampling Decision
Indicate the quantitative group (e.g., based on a typology or scores) needing explanation. Example: Senior, mid and entry-level employees.	Discuss characteristics of the purposeful sample, inclusion criteria, exclusion criteria, and sample size. Example: Utilising results from initial study to address concerning results and asking how we might understand employee work experiences and professional goals more fully; Draw random sample from initial study participants and conduct individual interviews to gain greater understanding and determine next steps to improve employee performance.	Include a rationale for the sampling plan. Example: Initial participants agreed to participate in the initial study and offered important insights. Their initial participation indicates their interest in the topic and the organisation. As such, they may appreciate the opportunity to speak openly about their ideas and perspectives.
{...}	{...}	{...}
{...}	{...}	{...}

p. 204) is a variation of the side-by-side joint display for merging for comparison. The variation is that the quantitative results are replaced with an example column graph. Any graph, such as a bar chart, scatter plot, line graph, statistical path model, etc., could appear in place as appropriate for the quantitative results. Although not displayed, the qualitative results could also include qualitative information such as a picture or a visual display of a grounded theory model. Depending on what is depicted, the domain column may not be relevant. The reason for including a graphic or image is because it can simplify what you intend to communicate and reduce text density. As with the other joint displays, this type of joint display would likely appear in the results section.

The joint display is simply another way to communicate how you integrated and the outcome of integration in mixed methods research. Their use is certainly not required, but their visual nature does provide a way to simplify and represent integration for the reader. With all of the templates, it is important to tailor them to your specific project and be creative. To select from the templates, think about the use of the joint display for comparing, relating,

Table 11.6 A graphical joint display template for merging

Domain	Quantitative Results	Qualitative Results	Meta-inferences
The domain is a way to organise the joint display and link related quantitative and qualitative concepts. It could be derived from a theoretical construct or similar concepts. Example: Employee Engagement.	Include a graph or plot of quantitative results. Example: Business Indices (bar chart: Index 1, Index 2, Index 3, Index 4 with Business 1, Business 2, Business 3)	Use these cells to summarise results, such as a summary of the theme or category and perhaps and illustra tive quote. The cell could include pictures, other images, or a figure of a model. Example: 'I feel that I am not 'seen' within our company. I serve on so many teams and everyone seems to know me, but I never get the next position.'	These cells are to write about meta-inferences identified through integration.
{...}	{...}	{...}	{...}
{...}	{...}	{...}	{...}

or planning data collection or sampling. More than one joint display could be included too, as long as they fall within the limits of the publication outlet.

11.5 Writing about integration

Mixed methods research has the potential to add great value to sustainability research in SMEs. However, that value is only realised through meaningful integration (Fetters, 2020). As noted earlier in this chapter, beyond conducting integration, a great challenge lies in communicating about integration. To this point, we have covered strategies for integration, the language of integration, and joint displays that facilitate and represent integration. In this final section, we aim to provide practical advice for writing about integration in proposals and manuscripts, including structures for writing and advice on presenting integrated results.

11.5.1 Where to place the discussion of integration

A clear and constant discussion of integration signals to the reader that you understand that integration is a central component of mixed methods and you have integrated in your research. Drawing from the advice of mixed methods scholars (Bryman, 2006; Bazeley, 2018; Creswell and Clark, 2018), we recommend threading integration throughout proposals and manuscripts for both scholarly and business-related research projects. A substantial integration dialogue might be included in four major sections: 1) introduction, 2) methods, 3) results, and 4) discussion. Of course, the latter two apply to manuscripts rather than proposals.

First, the *introduction section* of a mixed methods study should set up a rationale for integration as a rationale for using mixed methods. The goal of these sentences is to convey to the reader why mixing methods was so important and how the study would be less effective as a mono-method approach. Second, the *methods section* should delineate strategies for integration. Whether you are relying on merging, building, and connecting or more complex strategies (e.g., Bazeley, 2018), the method section needs to clearly detail procedures for integration. A subheading entitled "Integration" or "Mixed Methods Analysis" signals to the reader that you have substantive procedures for integration and can be included, just as you might have subheadings for participants, data collection, and analysis. Third, the *results section* should have a clear paragraph or more to report the outcome of integration in detail. Just as you might have statistical results or qualitative themes, mixed methods results also need to be reported. Historically, mixed methods results may have appeared in a discussion section, but the emerging preference is for reporting integration in results because they are unique outcomes of integrative analysis (Fetters, 2020).

Integration creates something new (e.g., meta-inferences, data collection tools, samples) that needs to be reported. In brief, remind the reader when discussing integrated results and remember that subheadings will also likely be helpful. In the next section, we discuss different approaches to writing mixed methods results.

Fourth, the *discussion section* is an opportunity to again reinforce your attention to integration. With regard to mixed methods research, the discussion presents an opportunity to reflect on the added value of integration (McKim, 2017). Consider and articulate what was learned through mixed methods research or what was created that would not have been possible without integration, thus highlighting the added value of mixing different methods in the study in question.

11.5.2 How to write integrated mixed methods results

Because integrated results are challenging to write, we include specific advice here. A mixed methods results section could be structured in at least two different ways: by method (e.g., quantitative, qualitative, mixed methods) or by key mixed methods meta-inferences (i.e., by mixed methods results) (Creswell and Clark, 2018).

In the first approach, there will likely be separate sections on qualitative, quantitative, and mixed methods results. Ordering the sections that follow the flow of phases in the research may be easiest to follow. In this approach, the mixed methods section should again have a clear sub-heading, such as "Mixed Methods Analysis Results" or similar. Then, the objective is to report the outcome of integrative analysis and clearly present meta-inferences.

In addition to providing a framework for integration, joint displays can help you to conceptualise a writing structure for the integrated mixed methods results. After creating a joint display, you can then provide a narrative description of the joint display to write about integrated results. Simply put, the joint display helps to provide a concrete structure for writing integrated results which can otherwise be nebulous. Just as the "domains" in the first column of many of the templates provided an organising principle for the display, the joint display can also help to organise writing about integrated results. In this example, you might step through domain-by-domain, the integrated analysis and meta-inferences produced.

Another approach for writing mixed methods research results is to present integrated results only by key meta-inferences. The results of separate quantitative or qualitative analysis receive minimal attention. This structure may be particularly helpful in keeping focus on integration or if quantitative and qualitative results will be reported elsewhere in other manuscripts. In this structure, one or more joint displays could also be very helpful in reporting integrated results visually and in giving a way to organise the reporting in both scholarly and business settings.

In our experience of writing, reviewing, and serving as editors, we have continued to observe a lack of integration in proposals and manuscripts. Including more evidence of integration in your writing will serve to distinguish your work and make the value of mixed methods apparent to the reader. We hope this advice of threading integration through the introduction, methods, results, and discussion improves your chances of success.

11.6 Conclusion

Achieving integration is challenging, and writing about integration is perhaps even more cumbersome. Excellent guidance is available on writing mixed methods proposals and manuscripts (Dahlberg et al., 2010), and here we have added a focus on writing about integration specifically. This chapter is intended to spark thinking about integration and provides the language to use when writing mixed methods research. We recommend identifying what integration strategies you will use and considering the use of joint displays as a systematic approach to help with integration. Joint displays should match your integration technique but also give you a chance to be creative. They may be included in manuscripts and mentioned in proposals to make integration explicit for reviewers and readers. Regardless of your strategy, integration should be glaring and obvious in any mixed methods research study.

References

Bass, B. M., and Riggio, R. E. (2005). *Transformational leadership* (2nd ed.). Lawrence Earlbaum Associates, Mahwah.

Bazeley, P. (2018). *Integrating analyses in mixed methods research.* Sage, Thousand Oaks.

Brown, H. S., de Jong, M., and Lessidrenska, T. (2009). The rise of the global reporting initiative: A case of institutional entrepreneurship. *Environmental Politics, 18*(2), 182–200.

Bryman, A. (2006). Integrating quantitative and qualitative research: How is it done? *Qualitative Research, 6,* 97–113.

Bustamante, C. (2017). TPACK and teachers of Spanish: Development of a theory-based joint display in a mixed methods research case study. *Journal of Mixed Methods Research, 13*(2), 163–178.

Creswell, J. W., and Clark, V. L. P. (2018). *Designing and conducting mixed methods research* (3rd ed.). Sage, Thousand Oaks.

Dahlberg, B., Wittink, M. N., and Gallo, J. J. (2010). Funding and publishing integrated studies: Writing effective mixed methods manuscripts and grant proposals. In A. Tashakkori and C. Teddlie (Eds.), *Sage handbook of mixed methods in social and behavioral research.* Sage, Thousand Oaks.

Dyllick, T., and Muff, K. (2016). Clarifying the meaning of sustainable business: Introducing a typology from business-as-usual to true business sustainability. *Organization and Environment, 29*(2), 156–174.

Fetters, M. D. (2020). *The mixed methods research workbook: Activities for designing, implementing, and publishing projects.* Sage, Thousand Oaks.

Fetters, M. D., and Freshwater, D. (2015). The 1 + 1 = 3 integration challenge. *Journal of Mixed Methods Research, 9,* 115–117.

Fetters, M. D., Curry, L. A., and Creswell, J. W. (2013). Achieving integration in mixed methods designs-Principles and practices. *Health Services Research, 48,* 2134–2156.

Greenleaf, R.K. (1977). *Servant leadership: A journey into the nature of legitimate power and greatness.* Paulist Press, New York.

Guetterman, T. C., Fetters, M. D., and Creswell, J. W. (2015). Integrating quantitative and qualitative results in health science mixed methods research through joint displays. *The Annals of Family Medicine, 13*(6), 554–561.

Guetterman, T., Creswell, J. W., and Kuckartz, U. (2015). Using joint displays and MAXQDA software to represent the results of mixed methods research. In M. McCrudden, G. Schraw, and C. Buckendahl (Eds.), *Use of visual displays in research and testing: Coding, interpreting, and reporting data* (145–176). Information Age, Charlotte.

Ivankova, N. V., Creswell, J. W., and Stick, S. L. (2006). Using mixed-methods sequential explanatory design: From theory to practice. *Field Methods, 18,* 3–20.

Klewitz, J., Zeyen, A., and Hansen, E. G. (2012). Intermediaries driving eco-innovation in SMEs: A qualitative investigation. *European Journal of Innovation Management, 15*(4), 442–467.

Mahmood, Z., Kouser, R., Ali, W., Ahmad, Z., and Salman, T. (2018). Does corporate governance affect sustainability disclosure? A mixed methods study. *Sustainability, 10*(1), Article 207. doi:10.3390/su10010207.

McCrudden, M. T., and McTigue, E. M. (2019). Implementing integration in an explanatory sequential mixed methods study of belief bias about climate change with high school students. *Journal of Mixed Methods Research*, 13(3), 381–400.

McKim, C. A. (2017). The value of mixed methods research: A mixed methods study. *Journal of Mixed Methods Research*, 11, 202–222.

Rafiei, M., and Ricardez–Sandoval, L. A. (2020). New frontiers, challenges, and opportunities in integration of design and control for enterprise-wide sustainability. *Computers and Chemical Engineering*, 132, Article 106610. doi: 10.1016/j.compchemeng.2019.106610.

Reinecke, J., Arnold, D. G., and Palazzo, G. (2016). Qualitative methods in business ethics, corporate responsibility, and sustainability research. *Business Ethics Quarterly*, 26(4), xiii–xxii. Cambridge University Press Online. doi.org/10.1017/beq.2016.67.

Searls, D. B. (2005). Data integration: challenges for drug discovery. *Nature Reviews Drug Discovery*, 4(1), 45–58.

Teddlie, C., and Tashakkori, A. (2009). *Foundations of mixed methods research: Integrating quantitative and qualitative approaches in the social and behavioral sciences*. Information Age, Charlotte.

Yarime, M. (2017). Facilitating data-intensive approaches to innovation for sustainability: Opportunities and challenges in building smart cities. *Sustainability Science*, 12(6), 881–885.

Younas, A., Pedersen, M., and Durante, A. (2020). Characteristics of joint displays illustrating data integration in mixed-methods nursing studies. *Journal of Advanced Nursing*, 76(2), 676–686.

12 Applied mixed methods and the added value

Steve Harris, Bradley Pettitt, Ruth Hillary, Aharon Factor, and John Parm Ulhøi

12.1 Introduction

In this chapter, we address the application of mixed methods and indicate where and how it can have practical action to address environmental sustainability within small and medium-sized enterprises (SMEs). The format differs from the previous chapters in that this chapter comprises of three sections.

In the first section of Chapter 12 Steve Harris (Sustainability systems assessment expert at the Swedish Environmental Research Institute), describes how mixed-method approaches have been applied to develop indicators used to assess industrial symbiosis projects and urban development. Next, are the insights from Bradley Pettitt, Mayor of Fremantle, Western Australia, on how the City of Fremantle uses different methods and data to inform their sustainability and low carbon policies and initiatives and how they benefitted from both, quantitative and qualitative data. Before concluding the book, we complement this with an informal dialogue with Ruth Hillary, a leading UK sustainability consultant, where we discuss the added value and challenges of mixed methods. The format of this third section draws upon the format applied in Chapter 9.

12.2 Assessing sustainability and the circular economy using mixed methods

Steve Harris

12.2.1 Introduction

This section describes lessons from using mixed methodological approaches in the assessment of industrial symbiosis and urban development. Industrial symbiosis involves the exchange of resources (material, energy, facilities and even human resources) between companies, but also between companies and other actors such as municipalities (e.g., in district heating schemes). Urban development and industrial symbiosis are, therefore, strongly related. These systems are inherently complex to understand and assess, because they are influenced by a complex flow of resources, economics, policy, culture, human behaviour and relationships. The most pertinent questions for applying and progressing with sustainability, require and greatly benefit from a mixed method approach.

The following sections provide examples and experience in combining quantitative and qualitative assessment methodologies in several consultancy and research projects performed in Europe and Australia.

12.2.2 Industrial symbiosis

Industrial symbiosis has been researched, using both qualitative and quantitative methods. It was first recognised or uncovered in the early 1990s from research into industrial interactions in Kalundborg, Denmark (Baas and Boons, 2004; Harris, 2004). Quantification has focused on the saving of resources (including economic benefits) and reductions of environmental impact, using material flow analysis and life cycle assessment (Martin and Harris, 2018). A large proportion of the research literature is, however, more qualitative, with the aim of trying to understand the development process of synergies and the drivers and barriers to collaboration amongst traditionally separate industries (Harris and Pritchard, 2004; Boons et al., 2017).

An emerging example of industrial symbiosis involves a cluster of SMEs in Sotenäs, a small seaside town on the west coast of Sweden. In one study, we developed a sustainability assessment framework to assess the potential implications of the continued development of industrial symbiosis (Martin and Harris, 2018). This was a combined life cycle analysis (LCA) with a semi-quantitative-qualitative analysis consisting of 13 indicators. These were primarily based on indicators that could measure uplift or impact such as job retention and creation, improvement of a local skills base, impact on research and development, community engagement, impact on costs and sales, etc.

For each of these, a desktop qualitative analysis was made on how these indicators would be affected by increased industrial symbiosis development, combined with a five-point scoring system based on whether the effects were negative, neutral or positive. This was then reviewed and discussed with stakeholders in the region and the analysis updated accordingly. In addition, a projective analysis for 9 indicators was developed that showed how the future increase in further symbiotic exchanges between companies could lead to increases in factors such as jobs, regional GDP, visitors, hotel nights and research and development.

Together, this approach allowed for coverage of a greater number of indicators than relying solely on quantitative LCA environmental indicators. It showed that there were significant environmental performance improvements for the industrial symbiosis scenario with greenhouse gas emissions only 75% of the reference scenario. In addition, the potential uplift effects for the socio-economic indicators were all positive to highly positive. Thus, combining the methodologies illustrated suggested that further industrial symbiosis was largely positive for all indicators compared to the baseline scenario.

12.2.3 Gotland IS park

In an ongoing project on the island of Gotland, Sweden, we are using mixed methods to support the development of a greenfield industrial park based on industrial symbiosis and sustainability principles. In this project, IVL The Swedish Environmental Research Institute works with Gotland Municipality and the Business Development Gotland (Tillväxt Gotland) organisation to help identify the most appropriate development strategy for the new park. The mixed method approach combines several methodologies and approaches and consists of three main stages.

The first stage is the scoping stage that involves a literature review of the development of eco-industrial parks and industrial symbiosis. This is combined with a review of the region and island of Gotland, in terms of its strengths, weaknesses, opportunities and threats (SWOT) for the development. For instance, the island has a population of 60,000, and skills capacity could be an issue (SCB, 2020), as are the energy and water supply. According to Porter (2014), it is more fruitful to build on existing industry capacity and strengths rather than develop a new sector in a region. The

SWOT analysis involved semi-structured interviews with key companies and stakeholders on the island.

In the second stage, we will develop five potential themes based on the potential focus of the park, e.g., industry types and approaches. The aim is to provide a preliminary assessment of the themes to identify what themes are likely to deliver from a sustainability perspective and a socio-economic perspective. The initial themes to assess, based on the first stage, are food industry, mixed SMEs, circular economy, integration with surrounding areas and new industry focus (e.g., electronics). The assessment will be based on a tailored framework: 1) Environmental, based on LCA; 2) Socio-economic indicators, involving quantitative and qualitative; and 3) Strategic assessment – involving indicators on capacity, integration potential, potential for success and integration into island development strategy. The process is an iterative process with relevant stakeholders that include consultation and interviews with existing local SMEs, business development organisation, municipality, universities, and industrial stakeholder groups (SME associations).

In the third stage, the scenarios are reduced to 2 or 3 and the analysis deepened and the modelling data will be enhanced, although using the same framework to assess the options. This will also involve further interviews with existing and potential SMEs. The key to the final assessment will be how to compare quantitative assessment of environmental impacts (LCA), the strategic assessment and the quantitative/qualitative socio-economic indicators. The challenge is then to translate that into an effective and balanced communication package so that the key stakeholders and decision makers, can make a balanced and informed decision.

12.2.4 Urban development

By 2050, 66% of the Earth's population are expected to be living in urban areas (United Nations, Department of Economic and Social Affairs, Population Division, 2014). Meanwhile, 78% of the global energy consumption and more than 70% of greenhouse gas (GHG) emissions are associated with cities (C40 Cities, 2020). It is well understood, therefore, that cities, and urban areas are key battlegrounds in the drive towards sustainability. In the context of this book too, SMEs constitute significant input to urban carbon emissions, especially across city industrial clusters. In this section, the use of mixed methods in an urban development case study is first presented, followed by its use in modelling the implications of low carbon 2050 strategies.

12.2.5 Urban development in Perth, Australia

In an urban development project at East Perth, Australia, we utilised Logical Framework analysis to develop sustainability goals, indicators and targets, with key stakeholders (architects and development authority). This formed the foundation for a sustainability appraisal framework, sustainability assessment and monitoring system. Logical framework analysis was developed in 1969 for the US Agency for International Development (USAID) to aid international development projects (Norwegian Agency for Development Corporation, 1999). Its strength lies in the framework it provides for consultation and reaching consensus on the goals, indicators and targets. The process involves developing agreed goals and then agreeing on the components of a matrix. A simplified example is shown in Table 12.1 (see p. 214). The four main elements of the Logframe, and in this case sustainability conditions are defined as:

1. Goal – the high-level objectives that the project aims to achieve.
2. Outcome – is the impact of the project output, such as the change in the system, stakeholder behaviour or organisation.
3. Output – the intervention of the project. What the project can be held accountable for producing.
4. Inputs – the components that are required for the project to achieve the desired output.

Key city stakeholders, architects and consultants developed the main components of the matrix, containing the above four elements in two workshops. These were then refined by the consultants in an iterative process with the other stakeholders. The process was then adapted to fit within the standard planning process as shown in Figure 12.1 (see p. 215).

In total, seven goals were created, supported by 26 outcomes which, in turn, were supported by several outputs each. These were used as the framework for a qualitative review of the Masterplan in a sustainability appraisal (part 2 of Figure 12.1). The Masterplan document is primarily a descriptive document with a vision, concept, artist's drawings of precincts and buildings and an outline of the planning structure to guide the future development. It also contains some quantitative information such as the land per precinct, number of lots, type of development (e.g., retail, commercial, or residential) and number of residents. The document was reviewed qualitatively to assess and determine whether the objectives of the Masterplan would be likely to move towards or away from the achievement of each of the sustainability outcomes (and hence the sustainability goals). Each outcome was scored, based on this likelihood, using the system as shown in Table 12.2 (see p. 216). Subsequently, this provided an indication of whether the goals themselves will be reached.

This was supported by a sustainability gap analysis which provided a more detailed scoring of each outcome, based on other documentation provided by the development association that included: research performed, consultation processes and events, targets and goals set, and policies and

Table 12.1 Example of a logical framework structure table for an urban development goal

Criterion	Indicator	Targets	Means of verification	Assumption
Goal: Ensure that development has a low contribution towards climate change and is adapted to the impacts of future climate change				
Outcome: (A) • Reduced greenhouse gas emissions and heat gain	• Tonnes of CO_2-e emissions per resident. • Tonnes of CO_2-e emissions per business unit	• 50% less than WA average • 50% less than benchmarked similar business	Electricity, gas and greenhouse gas measurements and surveys	Comparative data exists and quantitative data can be measured
Outputs (A) • Buildings and landscaping that avoids heat island effects and heat gain • Reduced impacts from mechanical ventilation and cooling devices • Increased use of sustainable cooling/heating techniques • Increased energy efficiency across the lifecycle of the development • Increased use of solar renewables and micro-generation units	% of new developments: • Serviced by district cooling • Offices exceed Greenstar 5 rating • Homes exceed Greenstar 4.5 • With solar panels and heating	>60 % of new developments: • Serviced by district cooling • Offices exceed Greenstar 5 rating • Homes exceed Greenstar 4.5 • With solar panels and heating	Surveys and measurements.	Accurate information on predicted climate events
Input: • Resources of people, ideas technology and dollars • Appropriate regulations • Strategy to use reflective materials/low heat absorbent, trees and shade • Strategy to utilise heating and cooling powered by groundwater heat exchanger, and waste heat utilisation • Passive solar design through orientation and shade. • Plans that minimised the need for lighting, water heating, space heating and cooling • Subsidies for solar panels and water heating • Ability for residents to sell micro-generated electricity to the grid	Strategies and plans with % targets	All strategies and plans aim for desired output targets	Assessment and evaluation of strategies and plans against goals and targets	Information is available

strategies put in place to achieve targets. A low score indicated that improvement was needed, whereas a high score indicated that industry best practice was achieved. For example, it was shown that the outcome "socially inclusive and diverse population living and working in the precinct" scored poorly and there should be an increase in social housing. In later phases, the framework also allows for quantitatively monitoring

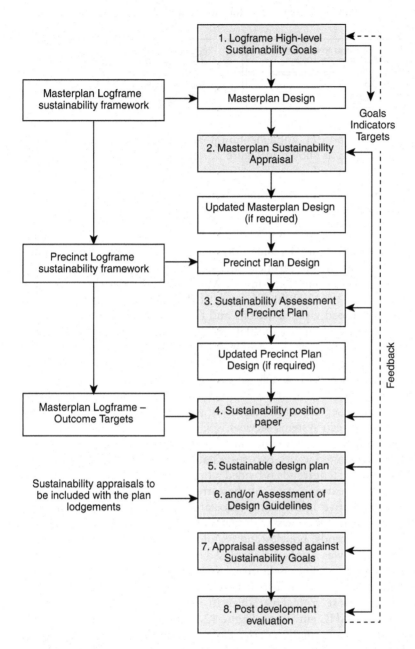

Figure 12.1 Building an urban development framework using logical framework analysis.

Table 12.2 Qualitative scoring system for the sustainability appraisal of the project outcomes

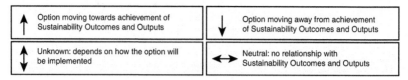

throughout the project implementation and after completion for post-project evaluation as shown in Figure 12.1 (see p. 215).

12.2.6 Understanding the consequences of strategies for low carbon cities in 2050

In the EU project Post Carbon Cities of Tomorrow (POCACITO), mixed methods were used to model and understand potential implications of post-carbon strategies for ten European cities in 2050: Copenhagen, Barcelona, Istanbul, Lisbon, Litoměřice, Malmö, Milan, Turin, Rostock and Zagreb (Harris et al., 2020a, 2020b). For each of the cities, a group of local stakeholders developed visions, actions and targets in a series of three workshops for a post-carbon city in 2050 (PC2050).

The main objective of the sustainability assessment was to assess the difference between a business-as-usual (BAU) scenario and post-carbon 2050 (PC2050) scenario, which were an interpretation of the stakeholder visions and targets. In addition to quantifying and modelling the energy production and use, and GHG emissions, we assessed the consequences for land use change, eco-systems services, socio-economic assessment.

Qualitative data was fundamental to enable and support the quantification and modelling. Twenty-two sustainability indicators were quantified and data on the recent trends provided a time series. Modelling of BAU was based on linear extrapolation of these trends to 2050 but was adjusted based on qualitative information associated with these trends. This was obtained through interviews with stakeholders, literature and reports to understand the trends, policies and ongoing projects that affect BAU. For example, if there was a policy of increased energy efficiency, there needed to be some quantitative or qualitative information that this was being implemented effectively, to adjust BAU accordingly.

Among the most critical variables to model were energy use, energy production and GHG emissions. Figure 12.2 (see p. 217) illustrates how the various data and information was used in the modelling and adjustment of the projections. First, BAU was modelled and then this was adjusted, based on an interpretation of the visions of the city stakeholders on whether targets could be achieved.

In addition to supporting the modelling, the qualitative data and information was critical in the analysis. For instance, a carbon footprint of

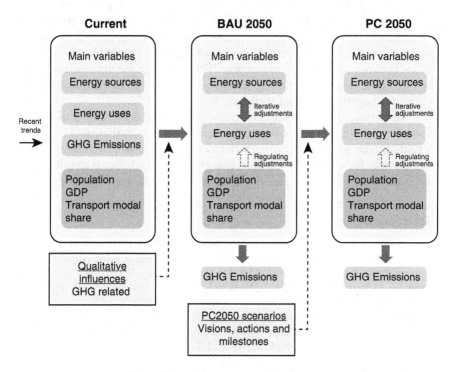

Figure 12.2 Key variables and modelling structure for linear extrapolation of recent trends for the business-as-usual (BAU) and the post-carbon 2050 (PC2050) scenarios (Harris et al., 2020a).

the two scenarios was calculated for each city and the qualitative data helped explain the key differences such as how rising affluence affected the consumption of different product groups, or why energy use was decreasing or increasing.

12.2.7 Summary and research needs

In summary, mixed methods has been vital for performing consultancy and research in the area of sustainability and the circular economy. It allows for the depth of analysis to be extended to include and consider other indicators that would otherwise not be included. A weakness or perhaps lost opportunity, however, is possible in the final analysis in terms of how the two are compared or utilised together. This is typically left to be an afterthought and handled in a discussion but has the potential to achieve more if integration is better planned from the start.

Quantitative information is easier to assemble and communicate, and in most cases, is also easier for the target audience to assimilate. It is also easier to scientifically justify, and to justify for the layman. For the consultant and practitioner, the role of quantitative and qualitative data is rarely considered equal and the importance of applying mixed methods in a scientifically robust way vastly misunderstood and undervalued. There is a tendency also for the researcher and consultant to emphasise the quantitative, because of the communicability. The challenge for the academic field is, therefore, one of continued education, through demonstration of the value and benefits of mixed methods.

In summary, the role of qualitative information is critical, and its importance growing, but its communication remains a challenge. This could potentially be supported through the development of more standardised frameworks for communication, so that the target audience is familiar with the structure, application and importance of a mixed method approach.

References

Baas, L. W., and Boons, F. (2004). An industrial ecology project in practice: exploring the boundaries of decision-making levels in regional industrial systems. *Journal of Cleaner Production*, 12(8-10), 1073–1085.

Boons, F., Chertow, M., Park, J., Spekkink, W., and Shi, H. (2017). Industrial symbiosis dynamics and the problem of equivalence: Proposal for a comparative framework. *Journal of Industrial Ecology*, 21, 938–952. doi: 10.1111/jiec.12468.

C40 Cities. (2020). A global opportunity for cities to lead. C40 Cities. https://www.c40.org/why_cities#:~:text=A%20Global%20Opportunity%20for%20Cities, 70%25%20of%20global%20CO2%20emissions. Accessed: 30/09/2020.

Harris, S. (2004). Drivers and barriers to industrial ecology in the UK. PhD Thesis, University of Edinburgh, United Kingdom.

Harris, S., and Pritchard, C. L. (2004). Industrial Ecology as a learning process in business strategy. *Progress in Industrial Ecology*, 1(1/2/3), 89–111.

Harris, S., Weinzettel, J., Bigano, A., and Källmén, A. (2020a). Low carbon cities in 2050? GHG emissions of European cities using production-based and consumption-based emission accounting methods. *Journal of Cleaner Production*, 248, doi.org/10.1016/j.jclepro.2019.119206.

Harris, S., Weinzettel, J., and Levin, G. (2020b). Implications of low carbon city sustainability strategies for 2050. *Sustainability*, 12, 5417. doi.org/10.1016/j.jclepro.2019.119206.

Martin, M., and Harris, S. (2018). Prospecting the sustainability implications of an emerging industrial symbiosis network. *Resources, Conservation and Recycling*, 138, 246–256.

Norwegian Agency for Development Corporation. (1999). The logical framework approach. In *Handbook for objectives-oriented planning* (4th ed.). NORAD, 1999, ISBN 82-7548-160-0.

Porter, M. E. (2014). "Reshaping regional economic development: Clusters and regional strategy." Mapping the midwest's future, Institute for Strategy and Competitiveness and University of Minnesota, Humphrey School of Public Affairs, Minneapolis, MN, September 29, 2014.

SCB. (2020). Folkmängd i riket, län och kommuner 31 mars 2019 och befolkningsförändringar 1 januari–31 mars 2019. https://www.scb.se/hitta-statistik/statistik-efter-amne/befolkning/befolkningens-sammansattning/befolkningsstatistik/pong/tabell-och-diagram/kvartals--och-halvarsstatistik--kommun-lan-och-riket/kvartal-1–2019/ Accessed: 30/09/2020.

United Nations, Department of Economic and Social Affairs, Population Division (2014). *World urbanization prospects: The 2014 Revision, Highlights; ST/ESA/SER.A/352.* United Nations, New York.

12.3 Building a local authority sustainability framework using a pluralistic methodology

Bradley Pettitt

12.3.1 Introduction

This section looks at how a medium-sized local government, the City of Fremantle, uses research methods to inform their sustainability and low carbon policies and programmes. The approach that the City of Fremantle has taken recognises that sustainability and the low carbon journey is complex, and the City of Fremantle demands for a sophisticated suite of data collection approaches to inform policy and programme implementation. In this context, the section provides insight to the methodology behind the achievement of the City of Fremantle's One Planet certification and its ongoing sustainability practice that is fundamental in driving the City of Fremantle's low carbon outcomes.

The City of Fremantle first became a carbon neutral Council in 2009. It was the second city in Australia to do so after the City of Sydney. The City of Fremantle continues to be an Australian leader in sustainability practices for local government, with One Planet Living helping to guide and document the progress the city is making towards its low carbon goals.

In this section, we show the steps the Council is making towards reducing its carbon emissions and environmental impacts and integrative aspects that influence environmental outcomes, notably community well-being. Set in this context, we first describe how the Fremantle Council is responding to the sustainability challenge. We will also describe the Council's response and show how using quantitative and qualitative data is informing the Council's policy and implementation and how SMEs are integrated into this thinking.

Another feature of this section is that we explain how a suite of initiatives have been informed by mixed methodological data collection and analysis. These initiatives collected physical and quantifiable hard and soft data in the first instance but recognised the limitations of one data type alone. It was recognised that different types of data together was the only way to dig deeper in the community or extend knowledge around sustainability issues. We, hereby, discuss how each of these initiatives benefitted from both, quantitative and qualitative data.

12.3.2 Fremantle in a climate context

Fremantle as a low-lying coastal council will be especially vulnerable to climate change and associated sea level rise. This is one of the reasons it has taken the climate challenge so seriously. Australia, however, is a global laggard in reducing emissions and the State of Western Australia is one of the worst performing states in one of the world's worst performing countries. While WA has only 10% of the nation's population, it contributes 17% of Australia's emissions. But we are seeing poor leadership at a state and national level, leaving leadership in reducing emission increasingly in the hands of local governments and the community and business sector.

Fremantle is well placed to show this sustainability leadership. With more than 30,000 residents, Fremantle is widely regarded as Perth's second city and is home to the state's main cargo port. Fremantle is also ranked as one the state's most visited tourist destinations. Lonely Planet voted Fremantle as one of the top 10 cities to visit in the world for 2016.

Fremantle's unique character is captured not just by its heritage architecture, music, arts, culture, festivals but by its progressive community. Fremantle has developed a reputation for being a leader in a number of key social and environment areas including climate change where, in addition to being the second carbon neutral city in Australia after the City of Sydney, it was the first Australian city to receive One Planet international certification.

12.3.3 One Planet Fremantle

The City of Fremantle has committed to taking this challenge seriously and is using the One Planet Living as a framework. This framework is increasingly being used by organisations, both public and private around the world, to monitor the sustainability of communities. This means being able to measure the complex set of variables that influence individual well-being, and the balanced and sustainable consumption of global resources. One Planet Living as a concept is based on ten principles of sustainability that provide a framework to plan, deliver and communicate sustainable development and guide holistic thinking. It does this using a range of soft and hard data and research methodologies.

The Fremantle One Planet Strategy achieved national One Planet certification in 2014 and international certification in 2015. The national targets outlined in the One Planet Fremantle Strategy 2014/15 to 2019/20 were updated to include corporate and community targets that reflect international certification. Since then, the City of Fremantle has moved to its fourth review of progress under international certification. It uses a range of measures to outline progress towards corporate and community targets for each principal area, detailing key projects and actions undertaken.

One Planet provides a lens through which to view the work of the city and understand how it is tracking to become more sustainable for both corporate operations and the community. As a local government authority, there is naturally some blending of operational and community targets and actions and finding appropriate metrics to measure these. The metrics used are both quantitative and qualitative. This paper looks at some of the metrics used for the target of zero carbon energy as one of the ten principles and look at how these are measured and what methodologies are used, and specifically how they influence and engage with the small and medium-sized enterprises (SMEs).

12.3.4 Zero Carbon Energy – City of Fremantle's Corporate Target

The City of Fremantle has a target to maintain its pledge of carbon neutrality for City of Fremantle corporate emissions to 2020 via a mix of green power purchase options, renewable energy and energy efficiency measures. A plan will be in place for all buildings to be powered by 100% renewable energy by 2025.

The key indicator for this will include carbon emissions from electricity, natural gas, the city's fleet, and refrigerant gases. The data measured included a range of the City of Fremantle's over 70 facilities, including carparks, street lighting, parks and reserves, light and heavy vehicle fleet data, major plant equipment, and refrigerant gases. As you can see, most of the data for the City of Fremantle corporate target is quantitative in nature. The community targets, both setting them and recording them, is somewhat more diverse and complex.

12.3.5 Zero Carbon Energy Fremantle Community Targets

Central to the Zero Carbon Energy community target is that the City of Fremantle will support the community to access a range of green power purchase options, renewable energy and energy efficiency measures and encourage the uptake of renewables through education on and promotion of new technologies, with a goal of City of Fremantle becoming zero carbon by 2025.

The community quantitative data for zero carbon energy is largely sourced from the Clean Energy Regulator website, specifically from the postcode data for small-scale installations. Every month, the Clean Energy Regulator publishes small-scale renewable energy installation data files according to postcode, including installation of small-scale photovoltaic systems and solar hot water heaters. Data from the Clean Energy Regulator reflects residents' attitudes towards and uptake of solar energy.

In addition, there is a range of more qualitative data that the City of Fremantle collects for 'high level, high value and significant impact' issues like climate change (City of Fremantle, 2019, p. 4). For these major issues, the City of Fremantle uses a range of more deliberative community engagement techniques including focus groups, deliberative workshops, face-to-face engagement events and pop-ups at community events. From these events, the Fremantle Council is able to both gauge community sentiment but also harness community ideas and initiatives and record progress on key aspects.

A key example of this was the extensive feedback gained from the Fremantle 2029 Community Visioning Project, which saw almost 1000 people attend deliberative workshops with their vision for Fremantle's future. A more sustainable Fremantle Council was at the heart of this vision with the report seeing Fremantle '... focusing more on becoming a centre for renewable energy, water reuse and green buildings ... and ... known as a sustainable, carbon neutral city demonstrating sustainable housing, walkability, cycling, accessibility, living green shaded walkways and green walls ...' (City of Fremantle, 2014, p. 49).

It is the coming together of the quantitative data on the City of Fremantle's carbon emissions and energy use in conjunction with the qualitative data from these community sessions that the City of Fremantle has been able to drive its leadership on sustainability and low carbon living.

This has enabled the Fremantle Council to continue to drive innovation and ambition in relation to low carbon policies and investment in renewable energy, knowing that it is making investment choices that both have community support and are effective.

The latest *One Planet Fremantle Annual Report* outlines the significant progress made and the value of the mixed methods approach the City of Fremantle has used in its low carbon journey:

> 2019 has seen continued progress in reducing its direct carbon emissions and water consumption, with efficiency measures being the main driver behind a 40% reduction in emissions from electricity compared to 2016.
>
> (City of Fremantle, 2020, p. 7)

12.3.6 Partnering with SMEs

In addition to corporate and community elements, a key element of achieving a sustainable future is in recognising the engagement that Councils must make with their business communities. A key critical community actor includes the hundreds/thousands of SMEs that exist within the auspices of Councils. Across the planet, SMEs accumulate to produce 60% of the world's carbon emissions (Parker et al., 2009) and approximately 50-70% of global environmental impact (Hillary, 2000; Calogirou et al., 2010).

There have been positive low carbon outcomes on the back of a good mix of qualitative and quantitative data. In addition to community targets involving residents, there is the support for Fremantle businesses which are predominantly SMEs.

Key elements of this support have included partnering with the CitySwitch programme which helps office-based businesses to improve their energy and waste efficiency and work towards a carbon positive future. The City of Fremantle has also sponsored the development of the Good Map and showcases sustainable businesses in Fremantle through an awards programme.

More recently, the City of Fremantle has partnered with ClimateClever to better map community and business carbon emissions and refine their targets. This will enable the City of Fremantle to better track the carbon emissions of the Fremantle community and assist them to reduce these through specific programmes. We are already experiencing some innovative partnerships between the City of Fremantle or Fremantle SMEs, including a partnership with businesses on key Fremantle CBD streets to have their shop fronts lit at night with energy-efficient to LED lighting and make streets more appealing and safer.

Inadequate lighting also regularly comes up as a complaint in terms of community perceptions of safety about the Fremantle CBD, and having shop fronts lit at night with energy-efficient to LED lighting makes streets more appealing and safer. The City of Fremantle funds the lighting upgrade for the shop fronts on the agreement that lights are kept on later into the night. Upgrading lighting to LED has substantially lowered costs for businesses as they use 75% less energy than regular incandescent lighting and 85% less energy than halogen lights that are often used in shop fronts. They also last more than 25 times longer, lowering maintenance costs for businesses. The partnership reduces the cost to the business owner in terms of additional electricity charges. It also lowers the carbon footprint of businesses.

These kinds of demonstration projects, linked with a better understanding of the importance of access to more detailed and frequent quantitative data on their energy use and emissions and their outcomes have been important in speeding up the low carbon transition for SMEs in the Fremantle area.

12.3.7 Lessons learnt and conclusion

While there have been some good outcomes along the way, in Fremantle's low carbon journey, some of the key lessons that have emerged include the challenges of ensuring that robust and accurate quantitative data is continually sought to make it relatively easy to identify operational areas for improvement, track emission reductions and demonstrate sustainable outcomes. But, also the importance of inspiring further actions by SMEs beyond BAU is essential. We have seen the value of events like the sustainable buses awards in Fremantle but the ability to measure this and other qualitative outcomes needs to be further strengthened.

As local governments like the City of Fremantle extend further down the low carbon route, the potential for an integrative mixed method research design that better informs SME policy will be increasingly important. This is going to require stronger and deeper collaboration between local governments, SMEs and the university sector, to ensure we have the right policies and implementation strategies to realizing green SMEs. We have seen the beginning of this with a range of Cooperative Research Centre's (CRC's) that the City of Fremantle and West Australian universities have participated in, including the CRC for Low Carbon Living (2019).

But as we move forward towards accelerating decarbonisation, it is clear that we are going to need an approach that better utilises a range of mixed methods, including qualitative and quantitative data from a range of sources in conjunction with collaborations between local government, business, universities and communities. Only then will we be able to adequately meet the climate challenge before us.

References

Calogirou Constantinos, Stig Yding Sørensen, Peter Bjørn Larsen, S. A. et al. (2010). SMEs and the environment in the European Union. Main Report. PLANET S.A. and Danish Technology Institute, Published by European Commission, DG Enterprise and Industry. https://op.europa.eu/en/publication-detail/-/publication/aa507ab8-1a2a-4bf1-86de-5a60d14a3977. Accessed 26/09/2020.

City of Fremantle. (2014). *Fremantle Report on Community Ideas*, https://www.fremantle.wa.gov.au/sites/default/files/Fremantle%202029%20Report%20on%20Community%20Ideas%202013-14_0.pdf Accessed 30/09/2020.

City of Fremantle. (2015). *Fremantle One Planet Strategy 2014/15 – 2019/2020*, https://www.fremantle.wa.gov.au/sites/default/files/sharepointdocs/One%20planet%20Fremantle%20strategy-C-000307.pdf Accessed 30/09/2020.

City of Fremantle. (2019). *Community Engagement Policy*, https://www.fremantle.wa.gov.au/sites/default/files/Community%20Engagement%20Policy.docx Accessed 30/09/2020.

City of Fremantle. (2020). *One Planet Fremantle Annual Report 2019*, https://www.fremantle.wa.gov.au/sites/default/files/One%20Planet%20Fremantle%20Annual%20Report%202019.pdf Accessed 30/09/2020.

CRC for Low Carbon Living (2019). *Exit and Highlights Report 2012—2019 Seven-Year Contribution to Australia's Built Environment Sector*, Sydney. http://www.lowcarbonlivingcrc.com.au/sites/all/files/2019-11-13_exit_report_web_final.pdf Accessed 30/09/2020.

Hillary, R. (2000). Small and *medium-sized* enterprises and the environment: Business imperatives. (1st ed.). Greenleaf, Sheffield.

Parker, C. M., Redmond, J., and Simpson, M. (2009). A review of interventions to encourage SMEs to make environmental improvements. *Environment and Planning C: Government and Policy.* 27(2), 279–301.

12.4 Applied mixed methods research in the context of sustainability and business

Ruth Hillary, Aharon Factor, and John Parm Ulhøi

12.4.1 Introduction

This section is the result of a discussion[1] between Aharon Factor, John Parm Ulhøi and Ruth Hillary, about the application of mixed methods research in a sustainability and business context. The section poses several questions in three broad themes: the added value of mixed methods research, data norms and preferences and the potential of mixed methods to address sustainability.

The decision to take the discursive iterative approach to create this section is to reflect the experimental journey that mixed methods research can take and to capture the complexities confronting the researcher. The journey generated a rich set of ideas and extensive materials[2].

12.4.2 The Discussion

Ruth: Our *first theme* is about the added value of mixed methods research and our reflections on its added value, so the first question is:

> *Do you think that the mixed methods approach, particularly applied in sustainability, has an added value beyond the sort of research that is currently being done?*

Aharon: I think with complexity comes many more variables, many more contexts and different contexts demand different ways or perspectives and ways of understanding that leads to the need for a broader toolkit for researchers to be able to capture many more characteristics. This complexity demands that we hop on board and use more methodological tools to capture the complexity that provides the added value for researchers.

Ruth: The fact is that sustainability is a topic where there isn't overall agreement of what sustainability is. Sustainability is a journey. There are lots of different ideas on what sustainability might be but the great variety of worldviews of what sustainability is and the variables that go into what might be looked at as sustainability as well as its degree of complexity can prevent people from really thinking about the issue and desiring a simple response to it. Therefore, I think the added value of mixed methods research is that it is a way of bringing a lot of variables together, to provide a more nuanced yet straightforward response, but not a simple response, to sustainability.

John: Yes, I guess to me what really entered the equation that somehow calls for or almost requires mixing different methods is that we need to look at sustainability together with human behaviour. Once we look at problems and phenomena that add to human behaviour, the complexity not only increases but also demands that we expand our toolbox with other kinds of techniques to gather data and to ensure that we can actually collect sufficiently nuanced and relevant data and that, to me, is certainly what I would argue calls for considering mixing different methods. If we look at what the quantitative techniques are doing for us in this regard, they help us in evidencing the "what", the "when", the "where" and the "who"; all the tangible aspects of the sustainability/human behaviour phenomenon we are considering. What qualitative approaches or techniques could add to that is to provide an opportunity for us to go more in-depth with understanding this phenomenon in question that is why and how the human agents; the human decisions and behaviour are unfolding as in the sustainability context.

Ruth: In mixed methods research, we bring in human variables much more clearly than in quantitative methods because different worldviews and different perspectives can be captured through using a variety of methods and these methods are more capable of dealing with the multifactorial aspects of sustainability which involve not just the "hard" aspects but the "soft" aspects.

Aharon: You jogged a few things in my head. Mixed methods research offers the chance, if you do the qualitative first in your study before you design a quantitative survey, that instead of designing these surveys with preconceived ideas and assumptions, you can drill down into the insights and better construct your survey and have more informed questions.

Aharon: In the mixed methods study I did in Melbourne, we did a cluster analysis study of 350 small companies to determine from reactive to proactive companies, and one of the items on the Likert scale was that none of the companies wanted to have anything to do with purchasing green energy. I interviewed 14 companies and they said it's very simple: to buy green energy is good for the big businesses because they get a big discount but small businesses get nothing; basically they are treated by the energy provider like households. The quantitative survey didn't capture this, the qualitative interviews did.

Ruth: Yes, I think that the benefits of using mixed methods research in sustainability practices is that we've got the possibility of looking at a variety of variables and this enables us to get a broader perspective; a greater richness therein and it reveals the opportunity of how we can potentially address some of the sustainability issues.

Ruth: In a piece of research I did for DEFRA[3] in the UK, we looked at small companies with less than 50 employees and whether or not they had gained any benefits from implementing ISO 14001. We did a quantitative study to look at the cost savings that they achieved in energy, waste, water and so on, but at the same time, a part of the survey was qualitative interviews which asked the businesses what the broader business benefits were. The business owners found that the emotional response of their employees, to be enthusiastic in the application of saving energy, saving waste, saving water, was really important. Another aspect we found was that staff were prouder to be part of a business that was addressing its environmental aspects. I think these benefits were more multifaceted and richer than even we were expecting to find in the research. It's unfortunate that these types of findings are called the "soft" side of research because that seems to suggest that they are not valued equally as "hard" quantitative data.

Ruth: I think that the examples we've spoken about talk to the plurality of different worldviews that can be captured by mixed methods which can't really be captured in straightforward quantitative methods and this links into our *second theme* which is about data norms, the value ascribed to data and the implications for mixed methods, so the question is:

> What frames one's values and preferences around the qualitative and quantitative data?

John: Sometimes you implicitly or explicitly get the impression that some kind of data, typically quantifiable data, at least by some persons, are seen as more reliable than other data that are not equally easy to quantify. That somehow suggests some kind of hierarchy; that some data are to be challenged less whereas others are from the beginning much more dubious. I mean such misconceptions, which I would like to call them, can be probably more easily kept alive as long as one accepts that there are these two different kinds of techniques to gather data: the qualitative and the quantitative. However, rather than seeing mixed methods as a third category, because if we do that we accept and allow this paradigmatic segregation, I would prefer saying that there should not be such a thing as privileged paradigmatic methods.

Ruth: I think the idea that we've got camps: a qualitative one and a quantitative one, is interesting as the dominant paradigm promoted at the moment is the traditional scientific one which is quantitative and the economic one which is also quantitative. The worldview, driven by the global economy, gives value to quantitative data and that this is somehow more important than qualitative data.

Ruth: Quantitative data presents a comfort to people; to policymakers, regulators, and those in companies, because it appears to present a certainty. This is linked not only to the disciplines that they may have come from: economic, scientific, engineering, but also to the notion that quantitative data seems to give certainty and that introducing qualitative data seems to muddy the waters for people who have their experience in education, life and work dealing with what they think are certainties.

Aharon: I think there's also a cultural thing going on here at multiple levels, and I'll start with it at the national level. When I went to Denmark to do my PhD, I found that they were far more receptive to qualitative research and you see that in the literature, whereas in the US, the culture is really for hard data. Something I've found in the SME environment literature is that Spain has quite a high number of research groups doing qualitative and mixed methods studies, likewise in South America, so there seems to be at the national level some cultural imperative.

Aharon: On a personal level, some people like everything structured and certain and they follow a path in life - that of attaining certainty; for other people, their psychological makeup and their culture and its complexity builds them as persons who like to explore. We teach path dependency; that your historical past dictates your future and launches you into the discipline that then becomes your paradigm and then it's very hard for a person to break out of that.

Ruth: What we're all discussing are the different lenses that we look at information through; what we are comfortable with from our own learnings and how we can be moved out of our comfort zones. There are implications for mixed methods research, the way it's used because of this different type of framing and the associated different values given to data leads to the question:

> *How, then, is the data presented from a mixed methods research project, in such a way that the value of the quantitative isn't seen as greater than the value of the qualitative?*

John: I think a critically important group that drives a lot of research, like the research we are doing, namely applied research, are the politicians. Politicians decide which strategic programmes to launch, and thus, which related fields to increase or decrease funding to, but their horizons are incredibly short. They go from issue to issue; their minds cannot really cope with much complexity, so what they need are very simple answers: very simple results. That's why numbers become the preferred solution or the preferred choice.

John: But until recently, those researchers who were inclined to stick to qualitative research, have not always played their cards right, in that they should have learned from their quantitative colleagues that in order to become more recognised and also much more appealing, they should have cared more about describing in a more rigorous way, how they actually proceeded with their preparation, with the data collection, with analysis so that it becomes much more clear that this is not just some sloppy, quick and dirty kind of interview. At the same time, when they present their results, they should also learn from other kind of data presentation and think in terms of graphical displays. Only then, I think, this unbalanced hierarchical kind of perception might get rebalanced, at least to some extent.

Aharon: I also think it's about the kind of quantitative and qualitative data that are presented to the reader. For example, when researching diversity, policymakers are presented with numbers, but it's the stories that come out of qualitative research that can be really captivating for an audience; so even if you were to have a lot of numbers about diversity in an organisation, sometimes it's that one qualitative story about a diversity issue in the company that captures the whole thing as well.

Ruth: Our societies have become preoccupied with league tables. In the UK, schools are graded in league tables. They're ranked on how well they're doing in exams. That's something that can be easily presented, but actually, the stories behind why a school has its ranking cannot be presented easily in a quantitative league table. In fact, the stories behind the ranking can only be revealed by looking at the qualitative factors related to the ranking. I think that this preoccupation with league tables and quantitative data is something which allows for a simplistic response, but the actual solutions to changing what the quantitative data reveals come from understanding the qualitative context and information.

Ruth: Thinking about understanding context and complex information takes us to our *third and final theme* of mixed methods research and sustainability, which poses the question:

> *What is the potential of transdisciplinary mixed methods research in addressing sustainability?*

Aharon: I came across this paper about institutions formulating the environment in which disciplines interact. One really good example is Massey University. The Vice-Chancellor wanted to have interdisciplinary research and got the Deans together, he metaphorically banged their heads together and got them to speak to each other; soon biology started working with chemistry and so forth. I think, to have this exchange there needs to be some kind of promoter, whether inside the university, inside an institution or the government. I've noticed that in Australia, it's lacking to a certain extent.

John: I think some of the more recent trends we have seen in terms of funding is that funding has moved away from the small individual project and towards the big project. That has a clearer capacity for releasing the potential for mixing methods because these bigger programmes are by definition, more complex. I think the potential for coming up with great ideas for big projects based on an interdisciplinary, transnational approach hasn't been better than now! But having said that, I know that in the end, when you need to disseminate the research, you meet the same silos again, namely, the journals which have not changed a lot.

Ruth: I think that's the point, mixed methods research has the potential to get a richer, more nuanced, iterative set of results which can deliver more abductive, iterative responses to the sustainability issues that we face. But what matters then is how this information is used and whether the results are narrowed into the disciplines and silos that you have talked about. That brings me onto the next question:

> *What are the real challenges and barriers that prevent mixed methods research becoming a norm, and not just for academics but also for academics and non-academics working together?*

Aharon: The challenge is to go up against traditional doctrines of how to generate knowledge. We're finding this out just as we hit the planetary boundaries and as the traditional quantitative scientific approach can no longer make sense of these boundaries. As we move forward, we're going to have to understand human behaviour. We've come to that limit where we have to understand ourselves to make changes if we're going to make the world sustainable.

Ruth: The discussion so far has looked at the disciplines that one would find in the academic arena but one thing we haven't spoken about are the barriers to getting non-academic players into contributing to sustainability research. Rather than academics coming up with information and potential solutions, actually working with non-academics, who at the end of the day are the ones who will potentially provide solutions on the ground to sustainability issues, leads us to the question:

What do you think about working with non-academics, the barriers to doing this work and potential solutions?

John: Some of the funding I have co-raised in the past decade or so, has required that 50% of the funding should come from participating companies. What I experienced from this situation was that practitioners are not interested in how we are creating knowledge but simply solving practical problems. How well we can theoretically explain it afterwards is not really their main concern.

Ruth: For me, the issue is that we need, as a society, more sophisticated and relevant solutions to the problems we face. I think that the application of a variety of methods, which we call mixed methods, and the use of a range of disciplines can only bring forth more nuanced solutions because the diversity of variables and situations, and the uncertainties we are facing require more comprehensive and holistic responses.

12.4.3 Conclusion

The discussion highlights the benefits of applying mixed methods to understanding business and sustainability but it also brings to the fore the challenges that remain in bridging disciplinary cultures. The dominancy in particular of quantification to understanding world phenomena may thwart broader aims of contributing to a more holistic approach to improving sustainable business practice. This dialogue has generated ways forward for sustainability and business researchers to catalyse a change and take up the challenge of being more holistic in their research approach.

Notes

1 Zoom video discussion on 12th August 2020.
2 The discussion was extensive and the transcript is edited as limited space meant many ideas had to be discarded.
3 Department of Environment, Food & Rural Affairs.

12.5 Conclusion

In this chapter, we have explored the added value and challenges of mixed methods research in both, applied and broader settings. In particular the discussion in section 12.4 reveals, that disciplinary boundaries and traditional research approaches decide how decision makers make use of data, and can be a hurdle to researching business and sustainability or can enrich these research endeavours. The potential discussed for applying mixed method research to business sustainability is evidenced in the approaches presented in the Swedish and Australian insights presented in sections 12.2 and 12.3. These two sections show us that if we are to drive sustainability practices beyond BAU, qualitative data must be seen just an invaluably alongside quantitative data. Furthermore, our invited contributors to this chapter agree that the complexity of sustainability needs robust methodologies, and therefore, a need for comprehensively designed mixed methods studies in the field of sustainability and SMEs.

13 Lessons learned

Aharon Factor and John Parm Ulhøi

13.1 Introduction

As an anthology, this book brings together the insights of global scholars with extensive experience in applying mixed methods in the context of sustainability and small and medium-sized enterprises (SMEs). In this chapter, we introduce some key lessons learnt throughout the book about integrating quantitative and qualitative research approaches. This mixing of methods enables the amalgamation of different worldviews and methodological approaches for capturing the dynamics and complexity of sustainability. We begin this final chapter by revisiting sustainability as a complex and transdisciplinary field and then venture to elaborate further as to why mixed methods research (MMR) lends itself well as a research instrument to better understand the field of sustainability and SMEs. The final part of this chapter recognises the importance of reporting the findings and analysis of MMR. Although our focus in this book has been to inform researchers and policymakers about effective ways to research sustainability in SMEs, the lessons learnt and discussed within this chapter also broadly inform us about endeavours to better understand business sustainability.

13.2 Sustainability

While the industrial era has brought great opportunity and wealth to developed countries and aspirations for impoverished nations, it has come with a 'price tag' in terms of increasing destabilisation of ecosystems and uncontrollable climate change impacts, biodiversity loss, agricultural impediment and polluted lands and seas. The book took off by visiting the neo-classical socio-economic *modes operandum* that does not value the natural environment or society other than through quantifiable means and identified with the way that this reductionist approach seeks to solve ecological problems through technology and belief in market liberalisation. In Chapter 1 we further compared this weak sustainability approach with stronger sustainability perspectives. We use this discussion to further explore how this complexity has ramifications for sustainability research.

13.2.1 Weak sustainability

The founding proponent of the weak sustainability approach, Solow (1974), argued that future generations will be sustainable if exhaustible natural capital is optimally converted into reproducible human-made capital. Hartwick's rule (1977) refined this by stating that rents or profits from exhaustible resources should be reinvested into human-made capital as long as the total capital stock does not decline. Weak sustainability, thus, treats natural capital and human capital as interchangeable, as Neumayer (2003, p. 1) states, 'it does not matter whether the current generation uses up non-renewable resources or dumps CO2 in the atmosphere as long as enough machineries, roads and ports are built in compensation'. Nonetheless, the weak sustainability approach does recognise the significant impacts that industrialisation has caused and puts forward ecological modernisation as the elixir to remedy this situation. Ecological modernisation posits that existing technological and instrumentally-focused science can decouple economic growth from environmental impact. The underlying philosophy relies on efficiency gains in resource use, manufacturing and product performance, and the market.

Ecological modernisation has been identified by scholars as a weak response to the sustainability challenge. These proponents point to the continuing degradation of the natural environment and rising CO2 levels at a time when ecological modernisation sits at the centre of the industrial growth policy. This failure is attributed to what is described by Revell (2007, p. 117) as the 'rebound effect' or Giampietro and Mayumi (2018, p. 2) as the Jevons Paradox, which essentially states that increasing efficiencies lower prices, drive consumption and wipe out efficiency gains. The implications mean that tackling sustainability complexities also renders reductivism obsolete (Giampietro and Mayumi, 2018). A recent study by Harris et al. (2020) re-iterates this problem. In effect, this demonstrates that consumption-led economic growth, which is the fundamental driver of economic growth, cannot in the long-term provide sustained development through efficiencies and economic rationale alone.

Ecological modernisation, instead, allows for the continuance of traditional business operations as the conversion of ecological capital to human-made capital assumes interchangeability of one type of capital (ecological) to another (financial). In Chapter 2, it is argued that much of the SME research has focused on weak sustainability within the confines of rationalising natural resources for economic benefit. These are measures such as: regulatory compliance, environmental management practices and technological innovations, all of which often imply technological applications to reduce pollution from the production process. Studies have, thus, tended to focus on market-orientated barriers and catalysts. This has placed the cost prerogative at the centre of decision-making frames, and has shaped and influenced the owner/manager's response to sustainability issues; even when owners/managers are fully cognisant of their impacts on the natural environment and society.

A weak-strong sustainability debate, however, has emerged amongst a range of proponents who identify with a spectrum of weak-strong sustainability behaviours rather than a dichotomy. For some, weak sustainability may be aligned with the prescriptive nature of Solow (1974) and Hartwick (1977), but some other proponents are more accommodative of the need to protect the ecological base that supports the economy (Daly, 2005). This is recognised through attempts to strengthen the ecological modernisation approach such as the industrial ecology approach (Graedel and Allenby, 1995; Allenby, 2011), natural capitalism (Hawken et al., 2005) and (Elkington, 1994, 1997) 'triple bottom line' approach. The focus on a business-as-usual approach tends to discount the significant need for social reform as part of any meaningful long-term sustainable development. In essence, there is a need for recognising a push for a stronger form of sustainability.

13.2.2 Strong sustainability

Other proponents form a spectrum of views as to what constitutes stronger sustainability. A stronger approach to sustainability places a heavier emphasis on maintaining ecological and social capital. Proponents of strong sustainability also argue the case for future generations from an anthropocentric viewpoint but they point to important services that ecosystems provide, to underpin human development and also the lack of knowledge available about natural systems. From a stronger sustainability perspective, natural capital and human capital are *not* interchangeable as certain ecological systems are essential for the sustainability of the planet. If lost, future generations will not be able to sustain themselves. Ang and Passel (2012) identify with two forms of stronger sustainability perspectives, one that places limits on how much ecological substitution is permissible and another more stringent sustainability viewpoint which states that the human use of natural resources can only occur if irreplaceable natural systems are not affected.

While the stronger sustainability perspective that identifies limits to substitution still places monetary value on substitutability, the strongest form does not deem the natural environment to be in the realms of monetisation. This has set up a debate between the proponents of weak and strong sustainability. Although, Ang and Passel (2012) report this debate, they, nonetheless, fail to capture the necessary complexities in achieving sustainable development. They purport that: 'We warn against the reductive nature of focusing only on a stock-flow framework in which a natural-capital stock produces ecosystem services. Concretely, we recommend a holistic approach in which the complexity, irreversibility, uncertainty, and ethical predicaments intrinsic to the natural environment and its connections to humanity are also considered.' (p. 251)

This debate, however, is criticised by a deep ecology worldview that identifies both weak and strong sustainability within an anthropocentric perspective of economic growth, and nature as being supportive of this. From a deep ecology perspective (Dalla Casa, 2012), a steady state dynamic should ensure an equilibrium between humans and nature in an eco-centric manner. Also, from a deep ecology perspective, the way natural and human capital can be interchangeable under a weak sustainability worldview or complementary under a stronger sustainability worldview, does not prevent the overall demise of the ecological system, as suggested by Williams and McNeill (2005, p. 8): 'It is no longer the ability to catch fish that is the limiting factor, it is the fish themselves. It is no longer our know-how and the means of irrigating crops that is constrained, but the amount of water available. It is not the power to pump, but the groundwater in the aquifers; not the number of chainsaws, but the available trees, and so on.'

The limitation, therefore, of the anthropocentric sustainability approach resonates with Bender et al. (2012, p. 314) who describe how anthropocentric perspectives assume a sustainable system of interconnecting economic, political and social elements that do not detrimentally affect the environment. The assumption is that economic growth aligns itself with environmental and social improvement. In this context, sustainability is about human development. This narrative is central to the Bruntland Report's definition of sustainable development that underpins the World Banks frame of what is reality (Mensah, 2019). Alternatively, sustainability, as defined by non-governmental organisations and academics, identifies with sustainability as a concept whereby human actions are embedded in a holistic global system.

In effect, sustainability as a holistic concern becomes a "wicked" problem that needs a 'complex systems' approach (Renn et al., 2020, p. 1). Furthermore, due to the urgency and critical nature of climate change (Bernstein et al., 2007; Levin et al., 2012), one associates sustainability with being a super-wicked problem. This is recognised in a recent book by Kudo and Mino (2020) where they describe how the complex interplay between humans and the ecological systems has been the focus of a newly emerging and growing sustainability science that recognises that ecomodernism needs a new approach that can address complex interrelationships. The use of mixed methods to discuss wicked problems is discussed by Poth and Onwuegbuzie (2015) and specifically point to the need for transdisciplinary mixed methods.

13.3 Lessons learned and implications for research

The chapters reveal important insights associated with the choice and application of mixed methods. Key themes addressed include:

13.3.1 Sustainability, 'Grand Challenges' and mixed methods

Throughout the book, the use of mixed methods has been shown to be an important research tool to better understand the complexities associated with sustainability. For Molina-Azorin (Chapter 4), Bressan (Chapter 6) and

Saindis (Chapter 7), this is also essential to capture some of the properties, the 'grand challenges' that sustainability represents. This is also discussed by Fu et al. (2019) who, in their analysis of the United Nations Sustainable Development Goals (SDGs), purport the need to move from a solely technical focus on sustainable development to a more holistic approach that engages society and its stakeholders. This opens up a plethora of 'grand challenges'. Grand sustainability challenges such as climate change and endemic poverty have also been referred to as wicked problems (Camillus, 2008; Sun and Yang, 2016). During the 1970s, 'grand challenges' arose with aspirations similar to that of the United Nations' 17 SDGs which appear solvable through positive framing but 'are obviously wicked and defy well-defined feasibility.' (Kaldewey, 2018, pp. 167–168). Furthermore, Jarzabkowski et al. (2019, p. 120) suggest that, 'Grand challenges are large-scale, complex, enduring problems that affect large populations, have a strong social component and appear intractable' and include issues represented by the UN SDGs such as climate change and poverty.' The authors present a discussion around the systemic nature of issues considered to be 'grand challenges' and represent a growing recognition by business sustainability researchers that sustainability is a challenging and complex phenomenon (Porter and Derry, 2012; Schaltegger, 2018).

The challenge is demanding in the area of sustainable management as researchers traditionally have focused on the corporate organisation, relevant players and value creation activities; rather than identifying with the holistic nature of sustainability science (Schaltegger et al., 2013). Sustainability research recognises that a more holistic approach to sustainability draws together researchers from different disciplines to tackle its complexities. This means that sustainability management research needs disciplines to work interactively rather than purely as a multidisciplinary approach, whereby disciplines work singularly on the same phenomenon. This interaction between academics results in the mixing of different paradigms, theories, and methods in a combined manner for the common purpose of building new knowledge about a phenomenon. The mixing of paradigms, theories and methods have the potential to occur at multiple points throughout the research investigation as Creamer (2018) shows in her analysis of a fully mixed method approach to complex social dynamics. This important dynamic is captured in our discussion about abduction.

With this comes a shift from traditional scientific and technical realms of academic enquiry to sharing knowledge with multiple stakeholders beyond academic spheres such as industry and government. This transdisciplinary approach is postured by Popa et al. (2015) as necessary when a traditional reductionist scientific approach may not be feasible when the topic, typically of practical concern, becomes sufficiently complex (Popa et al., 2015), especially when grand challenges demand more integral approaches that capture the cultural underpinnings of society (Bergendahl et al., 2018, p. 310).

Sustainability research poses a new challenge for management researchers as the integration of worldviews beyond their discipline of training also brings new ontological and methodological considerations into the research process. Nonetheless, the complexities associated with sustainability demand new ways of knowing and transdiscplinarity provides sustainability management researchers with a new way to knowledge creation. Although there are challenges, sustainability management researchers, however, are 'only beginning to explore the potential of transdisciplinarity' (Schaltegger et al., 2013, p. 227). Encapsulating the need for interdisciplinary and transdisplinary research towards sustainability, academic organisations such as the Swiss Network for Transdisplinary Research[1] and Massey University[2] demonstrate how interdisplinary and transdisplinary approaches are gaining traction as researchers recognise the importance and complexity of sustainability research. This new research approach offers sustainability management researchers with opportunities to understand sustainability as a real-world phenomenon. In sustainability science, Brandt et al. (2013) point out that transdisciplinary research has important implications for the integration of methods, the research process and knowledge production, practitioners' engagement, and in generating impact.

13.3.2 Paradigmatic pluralism

The different chapters reflect a common sentiment that mixed methods philosophically allows researchers to make different assumptions about the realities of the world around us. This means that researchers may not necessarily be constrained by individual paradigmatic enquiries that may occur within singular methodological enquiries, i.e., positivist or interpretivist approaches. Instead, the global chapters show that researchers may go through a necessary learning process that better enables them to answer their research questions based on more flexible ontological assumptions.

This mixing of methods also implies paradigmatic plurality. Some researchers believe that crossing paradigmatic boundaries is possible. This means that researchers must cross the bridge of opposing worldviews that traditionally separate disciplines. Hamann, in Chapter 9 ,however, reminds us that this may not be without problems. Researchers, for example, may strongly frame their research approach based on their academic training and culture of their disciplines (Aliyu et al., 2014). Hamann, in Chapter 9, meanwhile reveals that only by mixing predictive and interpretivist approaches of sustainability can the researcher more fully understand the phenomenon. A more pragmatic approach is, therefore, suggested by some authors such as Shannon-Baker (2016) who describes how mixed methods align diverse groups and individuals into the research process and this is a more pragmatic approach that allows for the sharing of one language and an understanding of the plurality of worldviews. This is an important debate as mixed methods have been acknowledged to allow for researchers to better tackle the 'grand challenges of society' resulting from increasing environmental, social, economic and political turmoil. In Chapter 4, Molina-Azorin describes how these problems call for relevant theoretical and methodological renewal to address these threats.

The researchers in the international chapters show how mixed methods permit engagement with these issues through a more pluralistic paradigmatic approach which, as Hamann (Chapter 9) indicates, is criticised by some in the academic community as being post-positivist, and thus a naive assumption of commensurability between objectivist and subjectivist epistemologies. Molina, for example, explains how the paradigm wars have led to a pacifist view towards MMR. Not only does the pacifist view lend itself to the belief that paradigms are commensurable, but as Creswell and Plano Clark (2018) describe it, this new approach has gained traction among researchers. This is central to the approach of the five global chapters presented in Part 2 of the book. Especially for these researchers, a pragmatic approach allows them to address their research questions from different ontological and methodological considerations.

13.3.3 Mixed methods and abduction

The researchers describe how constructing theory through this more pluralistic approach has enabled them to bring together inductive and deductive logic through a process of abduction. Hamann (in Chapter 9) describes his experience with being able to venture 'back-and-forth' between data sets, and that today's scholars are more open to this approach. This is critical in sustainability research. In Factor's study (Chapter 8) of Melbournian-based SMEs too, a critical realist approach allowed for abduction to understand why SMEs were not purchasing green energy. The deductive approach showed that amongst a range of environmental behaviours, purchasing green energy was not a behaviour demonstrated amongst the population studied. Only through reflection of the inductive analysis of the supporting interview data and further interviews and analysis was Factor able to ascertain that this was due to only large businesses getting the benefit of energy discounts, due to economies of scale. Without this process of abduction between different quantitative and qualitative data sets, this analysis would not have been possible.

Being open to moulding the research process to the needs of the research is especially important in sustainability research. Gagnon's study (Chapter 5) reveals that through two studies (Gagnon, 2012; Gagnon and Heinrichs 2016), the sequential process is directed by the needs of the research and the research question. In the 2012 study, Gagnon uses a QUAL-QUAN design to better understand the behaviours of sustainability entrepreneurs and in the 2016 study, a QUAN-QUAL-QUAN approach is used to investigate sustainability behaviours of food entrepreneurs. The researcher, here, shows the adaptable nature of both the researcher and the research question. Importantly too, the 2012 study informs the 2016 study. Using these two different sequential studies, the researcher was able to capture broadly and explore deeply the complexity around sustainable entrepreneurship. Gagnon also helps identify how mixed methods develop the field of sustainability and SME research. The survey results, for example, might not have strongly linked the interaction between sustainable orientation, cognition and sustainable practice; however, the qualitative thematic analysis identifies a positive interrelationship between these three aspects.

Other scholars (Tashakkori and Teddlie, 2010) have discussed somewhat more complex applications of mixed-method designs where a more iterative approach is taken. This allows the mixing of methods to dig more deeply and extend enquiry. Given the complexities and transdisciplinary nature of sustainability research, this offers mixed method researchers approaches that can answer more challenging sustainability questions. Further, as also described in the regional studies section of Chapter 3 (Heras and Arana, 2010), the Basque Region of Spain uses a sequential Qualitative-Quantitative-Qualitative design to follow up as part of a grounded theory (Heras and Arana, 2010). Meanwhile, Tang and Tang (2016) and Factor (Chapter 8) have delivered their mixed methods over time to strengthen the validity of data collection.

13.3.4 MM *design, sustainability and SME research*

This chapter has emphasised that sustainability is a complex and holistic phenomenon. In an attempt to better represent this universality, the chapter has also shown that academic researchers need to embrace other disciplines, worldviews, data collection methods and data analysis techniques beyond their norms. In this section, we revisit Chapters 3 to 10 to explore how researchers in the sustainability and SME field have applied and designed their mixed methods approaches to integrate this dynamic. The design of these mixed method studies also reveals implicitly that academics as well as practitioners need to draw on inter-disciplinary and transdisciplinary knowledge if they are to purposefully address sustainability challenges.

Typically, there are three types of mixed-method designs that have been used by researchers in the sustainability and SME field. These have been: (i) Convergent-Parallel Quantitative and Qualitative study, (ii) Sequential-Quantitative study, followed by Qualitative study (QUAN-QUAL), and (iii) Sequential-Qualitative study, followed by Quantitative study (QUAL-QUAN). The mixed-method design that many researchers may be most conversant with, is the use of the convergent mixed-method design. Creswell and Creswell (2018) describe how novice researchers in mixed methods may think of this approach first as it allows for both quantitative and qualitative studies to occur simultaneously, and allows for the integration of methods for the results after analysing both data sets. This approach has been taken up by Cloquell-Ballester et al. (2008) in an early

European mixed method study in the field (c.f. Chapter 3). More commonly, sustainability and SME mixed method researchers seem to have a preference for sequenced mixed method research designs whereby quantitative and qualitative strands inform the development of the subsequent strand (Tashakkori and Teddlie, 2010). The many permutations of this sequential approach are described by Bernstein et al. (2007). Furthermore, Creswell and Creswell (2018) discuss these permutations in accordance with the relevance of the research question and approach.

In the early development of the field, the approach used was a QUAN-Qual design. These early studies recognised that a qualitative component can be used to explain 'specific results from the quantitative phase' (Creswell and Plano Clark, 2018, p. 234), and it continues to be used by researchers in the sustainability and SME field. A QUAN-Qual design, in particular, may have appeal for researchers with quantitative strengths or scholars in disciplines newly open to qualitative methods (Creswell and Creswell, 2018). As Bryman (2007) learned in his interviews with mixed methods researchers who had tendencies to follow a positivist quantitative approach, many had not trained in qualitative studies. Nonetheless, a qualitative second stage also allows researchers to expand upon and develop their findings (Greene et al., 1989). For example, Hamann describes, in Chapter 9, how 'the existence of variance relationships can be demonstrated in an upfront quantitative study, allowing to dive into some of the nitty-gritty, idiographic characters of these relationships in a follow-on qualitative, inductive study.' Quantitative large samples, instead, do not allow the researcher to delve down into underlying themes in such fashion. A second qualitative stage in a QUAL-QUAN design has been shown in this book to:

- Strengthen the limitations of the first phase where quantitative data such as insufficient explanation from modelling and survey weaknesses provide a need to elaborate, confirm and corroborate findings (e.g., Chapters 5, 8 and 9).
- Strengthen an explanatory investigation (Creswell and Plano Clark, 2018) that can be particularly useful in developing consistency in exploring the same phenomenon through using the same data instrument used in both phases of the sequential design (Chapter 7).
- Use expert opinion as a qualitative component that can be used to strengthen the development of their quantitative component or confirm quantitative findings. Ghadge et al. (2017) and Fernández-Viñé et al. (2010, 2013) ,for example, use a quantitative study before soliciting expert opinion to corroborate findings (This is discussed in the regional studies section of Chapter 3).
- Bring a qualitative dimension to a field traditionally favouring a quantitative approach (Chapter 7).
- Improve on the general low frequency responses that have been reported by SME researchers (Chapter 9).

While the QUAN-QUAL Design has taken the lead role in developing mixed methods in sustainability and SME research since the 1990s, more recently (López-Gamero et al., 2008) there began a new wave of research using a sequential QUAL-QUAN approach (QUAN-QUAL and QUAL-QUAN is a generic approach and the researcher can remove the capitalisation of each stage to denote a less dominant supportive strand). The aim of the researchers taking this approach was to explore the field so that a more robust and valid set of variables could be tested using a quantitative methodology. Even more so, the focus of many of these studies was to use the qualitative component to inform the development of the quantitative questionnaire. This was particularly shown by Molina and Bressan in Chapters 4 and 6, respectively. In Chapter 6, Bressan used a four-phased Qual-QUAL-QUAL-quan study. Meanwhile, in Molina-Azorin's Chapter 4, while the Spanish group's traditional focus in management research was quantitative, realisation that environmental management research needs a qualitative dimension led first to the publication of Molina-Azorin's paper described in Chapter 3 and later, the QUAL-QUAN-QUAL designs in two mixed methods studies (see Chapter 4). A Quan-Qual design has been shown in this book to:

- Develop theory through explanation (Greene et al., 1989).
- Allow for survey design and development

13.3.5 Methodological reporting

Methodological reporting of the research approach is an important aspect of conducting mixed methods research. The methodological sections of research publications should provide the author's philosophy of science and methodological considerations for conducting the mixed methods study, and demonstrate how these have an impact on the chosen research design. This section investigates how key journal papers that have published the work of mixed methods researchers have approached this consideration.

As a pioneering study, Petts et al. (1999), in particular, provide a comprehensive methodological reasoning for their mixed methods research approach. They spell out clearly for the reader in their methodological section, why and how they chose the mixed method study. Then they present a full account of how they undertook and integrated the study. As such, they provide an early exemplar for the explanation of their methodological rationale in their methodological section. Only a few papers have, ever since, provided such a rich description of the methodological rationale for using and implementing a mixed method study (López-Gamero et al., 2008; Coles et al., 2016; Sainidis and Robson, 2016), while some researchers provide partial insights to their mixed method study. For example, researchers such as Worthington and Patton (2005, p. 201) describe 'a hybrid methodology' and Fernández-Viñé et al. (2013) offer terminology for a 'stepwise method', suggesting to the reader that a mixed method approach has been used but it does not provide a detailed account within the context of being a mixed method study. Another important aspect to reporting methodology is the need to mention the mixed-method design in the abstract. This is rarely undertaken by authors but some have used the following terms in the abstract: 'both a quantitative and a qualitative approach' (Worthington and Patton, 2005, 'exploratory sequential mixed method' (Wang et al., 2019, p. 526) or 'a mixed method approach' (Hosseininia and Ramezani, 2016, 2016, p. 1).

13.4 Graphical display of methodology

Plano Clark and Sanders (2015) and Ivanko and Wingo (2018) discuss the importance of graphically communicating your mixed method research design with your intended audience. Although this is not commonly practiced in SME and sustainability mixed methods research, some mixed methods researchers in this field have presented useful examples as to how to present their methodology graphically. This is particularly useful in publishing their work, as not all readers may be conversant with mixed methods nor the use of sequentially designing a study. More specifically, the design of mixed method research may use two parallel data collection exercises which bring the data and/or findings together in a convergent manner. Creswell and Creswell (2018) describe this type of approach alongside sequential data collection approaches whereby either a qualitative or quantitative phase precedes the other.

   This section is presented in three parts to depict how each of these mixed methods research designs have been represented in the field of SME and sustainability research.

13.4.1 Convergent mixed-method design

In their study, Cloquell-Ballester et al. (2008) use a convergent mixed methods design to aid in the selection process of environmental training programmes for SMEs. On the left-hand side of Figure 13.1 (see p. 245), they use a quantitative survey and statistical analysis to capture the demand for environmental training courses, and on the right-hand side, they use qualitative investigations using expert insights into the supply of training courses. At the end of the parallel processes, they draw individual conclusions and then integrate the methods using indices and a multicriteria procedure which then informs programme design. Determining that the demand and supply are in balance is, therefore, essential in ensuring the organisation's long-term performance. In addition to Figure 13.1 (see p. 245), they also present a Gannt chart, mapping out across the calendar year, all activities regarding the research process (including human resource and production activities).

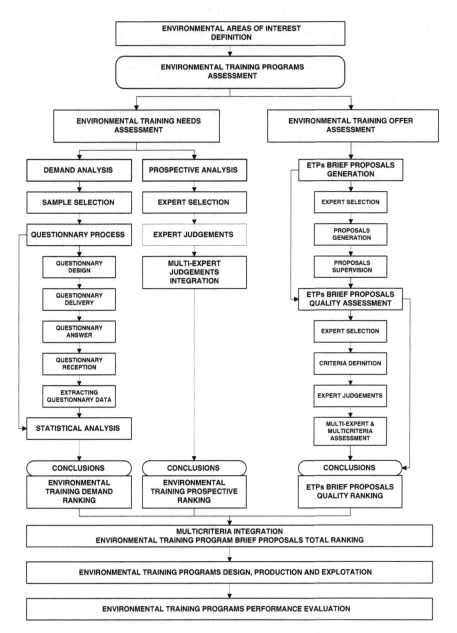

Figure 13.1 'Methodological Layout' by Cloquell-Ballester et al. (2008, p. 509).[3]

13.4.2 Sequential QUAL/QUAN design

Bressan depicts his four-stage research process in Figure 6.1 (Chapter 6, p. 108). It provided an early insight into the powerful tool that illustrations can provide in demonstrating a sequential process. Now that we have made this journey through the book, we look at some notable use of illustrative modes that Wang et al. (2019) and Liston-Heyes 2016 have used to communicate, in a simple manner, their mixed methods design and implementation.

Wang et al. (2019) investigate construction waste management design in Shenzen, China. The authors communicate with the reader through a co-ordinated approach. They embed the terminology 'exploratory sequential mixed method' in the journal article's abstract, and then proceed to further inform the reader what that means through a graphical representation. They describe that: 'The research process is divided into three steps, qualitative sampling, quantitative sampling, and data analysis' (Wang et al., 2019, p. 528). Figure 13.2 illustratively represents this process. The qualitative first stage allowed the researchers to scan secondary data sources and conduct semi-structured interviews with experts. This provided input for their quantitative survey.

Liston-Heyes and Vazquez Brust (2016) deploy another exploratory se-quential mixed methodology. In similar fashion to Wang et al. (2019), they wanted to know more about 'environmental reactivism' in Argentinian SMEs before being able to design a large-scale survey. Figure 13.3 (see p. 247) shows how they used an exploratory investigation in the first phase to build an ' "environmental reactivism" construct and in operationalising the data col-lection.' (p. 367)

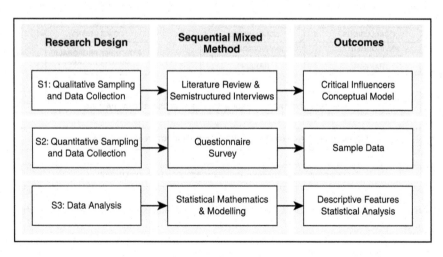

Figure 13.2 The sequential research process diagram adapted from Wang et al. (2019, p. 528).[4]

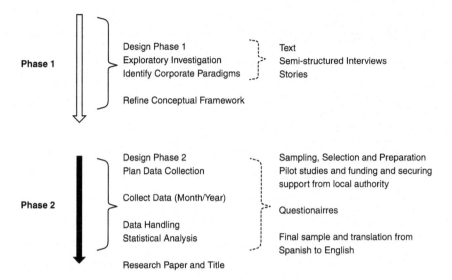

Figure 13.3 Exploratory sequential mixed methodology adapted from Liston-Heyes and Vazquez Brust (2016, p. 368).

13.4.3 *Sequential QUAN/QUAL design*

In Chapter 7 (p. 122), Saindis presents a detailed illustration of his QUAN/ QUAL design. One mixed method study, in the academic literature that also shows that the QUAN/QUAL approach can be displayed simply is demonstrated by Ghadge et al. (2017). Ghadge et al. (2017, p. 2001), uses a 'descriptive research methodology' with a quantitative first stage that conducted a 'systematic data collection approach' allowing for a rigorous data analysis of prospective environmental uptake by Greek dairy SMEs. This provided a descriptive account of the influencers of environmental practice but not the barriers and catalysts. A deeper analysis was undertaken, therefore, by means of a second stage set of qualitative interviews with some respondents from the survey. The simple display of the research process is shown in Figure 13.4 (see p. 248).

13.5 Further reflections on lessons learned

In reading published studies, based on mixed methods research (MMR), relevant and sufficient details about the methodological choices made and procedures followed should be communicated to the reader. There is, however, a lack of this kind of communication by researchers, especially about what they have found to be particularly advantageous from applying MMR. This book, hopefully, fills some of that void. As editors, we have not

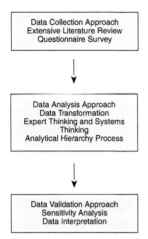

Figure 13.4 Descriptive research approach by Ghadge et al. (2017, p. 2002).[5]

only asked for the sharing of the co-contributors' experiences, but to clarify further, we have also made an *a priori* selection of some of their studies and asked them to reflect upon the added value of MMR in their studies.

Although the interest in mixed methods in SME sustainability studies took off in the UK, Chapter 3 documents that this trend is no longer geographically limited to specific countries or regions. The studies and experiences discussed and communicated in this book address this development. So what are some of the more recent lessons that we can draw from this work? Taking off from Chapter 4, the authors share some interesting learnings from their many years of experience with MMR. Contrary to the idealised picture, most scholars recognise from their general methodological priming in business and social sciences, that the research question and the nature of the problem faced are expected to 'dictate' the 'right' research method(s). In a practical situation, however, researchers tend to be influenced much by the specific methods that they are very well familiar with. As a result, the methods we are comfortable with may, thus, affect (limit) the questions that researchers end up choosing to answer. This, of course, has a bearing on doctoral education, as science can and should not in any way be limited by the lack of methodological competence. So, when wrestling with complex topics like sustainability and SMEs, which often will need a combination and integration of different methods, there is a message for the scientific community to not only be open towards such designs, but to also be capable of executing and integrating mixed methods research. Further, in addition to this important barrier to mixed methods, as pointed out by Molina et al. in the book (see Chapter 4), journal editors and reviewers also need to adjust and reflect upon the adequate competencies required to review MMR.

From the early stages of the editors' discussions of this book, a need for deeper reflection and discussion of what may motivate researchers to undertake an MMR project in the first place, and what some of the important learnings and added value of mixed methods are, when applied to sustainability and SME context. Gagnon (in Chapter 5) noted in his work that the MMR allowed for revealing tensions between the different (QUAN and QUAL) analyses. QUAL methods, for example, provide an abundance of data, which in turn can lead to more depth. Conversely, he argues, QUAN methods offer immediate structure for the data at hand. Although the order of the different methods can vary from study to study, Gagnon finds that doing a QUAL study before a QUAN study offers some obvious advantages. The researcher, for example, can benefit from increasing the possibilities of capturing a larger part of the different themes and structures at play, including possible anomalies. Taking up an empirical validation of a QUAL study, in turn, allows for a thorough development of research propositions to be tested in the following design (QUAN). He further identifies four key themes that cut across his experiences with MMR. First, prior knowledge is useful and needed to inform the specific choice of methods. As already stressed by Molina et al. (Chapter 4), research questions themselves also affect the methods chosen. The third theme relates to the subject population (e.g., students versus 'real-life' representations) and how the latter influences the methods chosen. Divergence between the findings from the different studies, Gagnon points out, can be a challenge. These situations, however, invite for stepping back from the analysis to reflect upon and question assumptions. Such activity can lead to a deeper level of discovery when researching complex topics.

Integrating QUAL and QUAN methods, Bressan points out in Chapter 6, can help strengthen the validity of studies and overcome potential bias and skewed results which can emerge when qualitative and quantitative designs are done in isolation. Having reflected upon his own previous work, he found that MMR has provided the flexibility needed to prepare and execute a study on environmental sustainability and SMEs, in light of the dynamics and idiosyncrasies of such firms, while at the same time capturing important developments and details of the investigated situations. Doing research in the context of sustainability and SMEs, he has learned, often involves layers of increasing complexity. Relying entirely on quantitative or qualitative methods may, therefore, not be sufficient to capture all the trends and details of situations. Moreover, MMR offers the possibility of giving more emphasis/weight to either the qualitative or the quantitative component, depending on features of the field and which data collection method is best suited to address the study's goals and purpose, as well as the adaptability needed for studying the peculiarities of SMEs and sustainability within the embedded community.

The combination and integration of data sets, collected by means of QUAN and QUAL methods, may, however, also have ontological as well as epistemological implications. Based on the UK studies, Sainidis (Chapter 7) used pragmatism to engulf both objective and subjective knowledge produced in his studies. When using such designs, however, you need to keep in mind the importance of integration. This in turn implies, for example, that the discussion of results derived from the two independent sets of quantitative and qualitative data need to show evidence of true integration and nesting of data so as to avoid the study turning into two separate research reports. Moreover, as an MMR study, focus needs to be directed with regard to avoiding bias towards one or the other ontological position. When carefully and thoughtfully practiced, MMR can offer an obvious opportunity for the collection of rich and powerful data. Combining and integrating methods need not be restricted to cross-sectional studies.

In Chapter 8, Factor reports about sequential and longitudinal MMR studies on sustainability and SMEs in Australia. From these experiences, Factor, among others, acknowledged that cluster analysis data from the survey instrument is useful for selecting relevant participants for a deeper qualitative investigation through semi-structured and open-ended interviews. The longitudinal design allowed for the findings of the semi-structured interviews to inform propositions for a deeper and more exploratory open set of interview participants who had agreed to participate in further interviews beyond the semi-structured interviews, with a small set of agreeable participants initiating a further round of interviews.

In tackling the philosophy of science implications from integrating QUAN and QUAL methods, critical realism was used. Adding longitudinality became a critically important research choice, as it allowed for the researcher to capture changing owner/manager perspectives as climate change has increasingly been impacting Australian society and politics.

Apart from building on one of the co-author's (Hamann) previous studies in Chapter 9, the dialogue between the chapters two experienced users of MMR (Romm and Hamann) helps clarify that as regards MMRs, we should be prepared for nuances rather than black and white issues. With reference to another informed dialogue, Hamann emphasised that quantitative, deductive study is well suited for addressing variance questions. QUAN studies can help build confidence in the existence of these relationships, but it is less likely to offer nuanced insights into the underlying mechanisms of these relationships. Adding a QUAL study allows for diving into some of the nitty-gritty, idiographic characters of these relationships in a follow-on qualitative, inductive study.' From the dialogue, it is also evident that language draws on the affinity from ontological differences associated with the different worldviews dominating QUAN and QUAL methods as well as the pervasive tensions present in the academy, which also affect the actual repertoire of methods that the researcher considers. The dialogue additionally reveals new emergent trends towards seeing scholarship as conversations, thereby indicating that knowledge is not fixed but 'moves' around among audiences who may also be participants.

Returning to the added value from employing MMR, Creamer (Chapter 10) discusses ways to extend the value-added potential of MMR in sustainability and SME studies, and how to create meaningful interaction between QUAN and QUAL methods and data. In so doing, she addresses different ways in which the integration of qualitative and quantitative data and/or methods can advance the rigour, analytical density, and originality of research about sustainability in SMEs. A clear distinction is also made between multi-method research and mixed-method research. Regardless of their philosophical orientation, Creamer emphasises, most methodologists appreciate MMR's ability to generate a more complete understanding of a complex phenomenon, as is the case of a multi-dimensional construct like sustainability. One of the most compelling arguments for the use of mixed methods, the chapter further points out, is the potential to promote sophisticated analytical conceptualisations. Advancing methodological training through professional development activities, Creamer stresses, can promote dialogue that bridges disciplinary domains.

Integration of MMR refers, as pointed out by Guetterman and Breen (Chapter 11), to synthesis of the 'what' from QUAN approaches with the 'why and how' from the QUAL approaches. As easy as integration may sound, they argue that it often remains a challenge to researchers. Some challenges in preparing MMR relates to the proper use of the 'right' words so as to secure clarity. Integrating MMR data implies meta-inferences, new results that emerge from the integration of qualitative and quantitative inferences. Achieving integration, Guetterman and Breen argue, is a challenging endeavour. Writing about integration may, however, be more cumbersome. While the authors note that useful and fine guidance is available on how to write mixed methods studies, less guidance is available on writing about integration specifically. Chapter 11 has filled some of that void by introducing, among others, different strategies to employ when preparing MMR studies. A few examples include the determination of which integration strategies to use and the consideration whether (or not) to use joint displays as a systematic approach to help with integration.

13.6 Conclusion

The use of mixed methods is both applicable and highly relevant in studies of sustainability and SMEs. Combining different methods implies that the investigator cannot stay within a discipline-defined methodological comfort zone. Based on the evidence provided in the book, we conclude that conducting mixed-method studies involves acceptance of having more than one paradigm-defined 'disciplinary matrix'. This not only implies the acceptance of 'room for paradigmatic differences', but it further implies that the methodological 'priming' of future scholars needs to go beyond the 'preferred choices' defined by traditional paradigmatic constraints of the discipline in question.

The experiences reported in the book have also shown that combining and integrating methods may affect the research problems and research questions as well as the process of reasoning. It can open and/or widen the research focus and allow for including different kinds of research questions (helping to describe and understand the scope, extent and/or rationale behind the phenomena at play.

Adequately applied, it holds promises of capturing more nuances of complexed scientific problems in dynamic environmental, economic and social contexts. Trying to understand how and why SMEs adapt their behaviours in relation to increasing environmental, social and economic concerns is an example of complex settings that calls for the application of mixed methods. Increasingly, the literature in the field reflects the acknowledgement of this complexity and diversity. The social and economic dimensions, in particular, bring not only additional complexity into sustainability, but allow for considering sustainability behaviour within a continuum of weak and strong sustainability.

Last but not least, the use of mixed methods has implications for how researchers report and display their methodology. Rigour, systematics and transparency do not only apply to quantitative methods. Taking into consideration that the vast majority of researchers within their fields are 'mono-method-driven', the audience cannot be expected to be fully up to date with such design. In consequence, the researcher can use and/or expand the graphical display of critical information and details associated with their mixed-method research design.

Notes

1 http://www.akademien-schweiz.ch/en/index/Portrait/Kommissionen-AG/td-net. html Accessed 29/09/2020.
2 https://www.massey.ac.nz/massey/initiatives/sustainability/strategy/strategy_ home.cfm Accessed 29/09/2020.
3 Note: Permissions Granted Elsevier.
4 Note: Permissions Granted Adaptation Elsevier.
5 Permissions granted by Elsevier for reproduction under CC BY licence.

References

Aliyu, A. A., Bello, M. U., Kasim, R., and Martin, D. (2014). Positivist and non-positivist paradigm in social science research: Conflicting paradigms or perfect partners? *Journal of Management and Sustainability*, 4(3), 79–95.
Allenby, B. (2011). Thoughts on industrial ecology, emerging technologies, and sustainability science. *Sustainability Science*, 6(2), 119–122.
Ang, F., and Passel, Van S. (2012). Beyond the environmentalist's paradox and the debate on weak versus strong sustainability. *BioScience*, 62(3), 251–259.
Bender, H., Judith, K., and Beilin, R. (2012). Sustainability: a model for the future. In H. Bender (Ed.), *Reshaping environments: An interdisciplinary approach to sustainability in a complex world*. Cambridge University Press, Cambridge.

Bergendahl, J. A., Sarkis, J., and Timko, M. T. (2018). Transdisciplinarity and the food energy and water nexus: Ecological modernization and supply chain sustainability perspectives. *Resources, Conservation and Recycling*, *133*, 309–319.

Bernstein, S., Cashore, B., Levin, K., and Auld, G. (2007). Playing it forward: Path dependency, progressive incrementalism, and the super wicked problem of global climate change. 48th Annual Meeting of the International Studies Association. Chicago.

Brandt, P., Ernst, A., Gralla, F., Luederitz, C., Lang, D. J., Newig, J., Reinert, F., Abson, D. J., and Von Wehrden, H. (2013). A review of transdisciplinary research in sustainability science. *Ecological Economics*, *92*, 1–15.

Brunton, M., Eweje, G., and Taskin, N. (2017). Communicating corporate social responsibility to internal stakeholders: Walking the walk or just talking the talk? *Business Strategy and the Environment*, *26*(1), 31–48.

Bryman, A. (2007). Barriers to integrating quantitative and qualitative research. *Journal of Mixed Methods Research*, *1*(1), 8–22.

Camillus, J. C. (2008). Strategy as a wicked problem. *Harvard Business Review*, *86*(5), 98–106.

Cloquell-Ballester, V. A., Monterde-Díaz, R., Cloquell-Ballester, V. A., and Torres-Sibille, A. del C. (2008). Environmental education for small and medium-sized enterprises: Methodology and e-learning experience in the Valencian region. *Journal of Environmental Management*, *87*(3), 507–520.

Coles, T., Dinan, C., and Warren, N. (2016). Energy practices among small and medium-sized tourism enterprises: A case of misdirected effort? *Journal of Cleaner Production*, *111*, 399–408.

Creamer, E. G. (2018). Enlarging the conceptualization of mixed method approaches to grounded theory with intervention research. *American Behavioral Scientist*, *62*(7), 919–934.

Creswell, J. W. (2009). *Research design: Qualitative, quantitative and mixed methods approaches* (3rd ed.). Sage, Thousand Oaks.

Creswell, J. W., and Creswell, D. J. (2018). *Research design: Qualitative, quantitative, and mixed methods*. Sage, Thousand Oaks.

Creswell, J. W., and Plano Clark, V. L. (2018). *Designing and conducting mixed methods research* (3rd ed.). Sage, Thousand Oaks.

Dalla Casa, G. (2012). Deep ecology as a philosophical basis of degrowth. 3rd Degrowth conference for ecological sustainability and social equity. Venice.

Daly, H. E. (2005). Economics in a full world. *Scientific American*, *293*(3), 100–107.

Elkington, J. (1997). *Cannibals with forks: The triple bottom line of 21st century business*. Capstone, Oxford.

Elkington, J. (1994). Towards the sustainable corporation: Win-win-win business strategies for sustainable development. *California Management Review*, *36*(2), 90–100.

Fernández-Viñé, María Blanca, Gómez-Navarro, T., and Capuz-Rizo, S. F. (2010). Eco-efficiency in the SMEs of Venezuela. Current status and future perspectives. *Journal of Cleaner Production*, *18*(8), 736–746.

Fernández-Viñé, María B., Gómez-Navarro, T., and Capuz-Rizo, S. F. (2013). Assessment of the public administration tools for the improvement of the eco-efficiency of small and medium sized enterprises. *Journal of Cleaner Production*, *47*, 265–273.

Fu, B., Wang, S., Zhang, J., Hou, Z., and Li, J. (2019). Unravelling the complexity in achieving the 17 sustainable development goals. *National Science Review*, 6(3), 386–388.

Gagnon, M. (2012). Sustainable minded entrepreneurs: developing and testing a values-based framework. *Journal of Strategic Innovation and Sustainability*, 8(1), 9–25.

Gagnon, M. A., and Heinrichs, P. A. (2016). Food entrepreneur sustainable orientation and firm practices. *International Journal of Food and Agricultural Economics* 4(4), 11–28.

Ghadge, A., Kaklamanou, M., Choudhary, S., and Bourlakis, M. (2017). Implementing environmental practices within the Greek dairy supply chain Drivers and barriers for SMEs. *Industrial Management and Data Systems*, 117(9), 1995–2014.

Giampietro, M., and Mayumi, K. (2018). Unraveling the complexity of the Jevons Paradox: The link between innovation, efficiency, and sustainability. *Frontiers in Energy Research*, 6, 1–13.

Graedel, T. E., and Allenby, B. R. (1995). *Industrial Ecology*. Prentice-Hall, Upper Saddle Valley.

Greene, J. C., Caracelli, V. J., and Graham, W. F. (1989). Toward a conceptual framework for mixed-method evaluation designs. *Educational Evaluation and Policy Analysis*, 11, 255–274.

Hamann, R., Smith, J., Tashman, P., and Marshall, R. S. (2017). Why do SMEs go green? An analysis of wine firms in South Africa. *Business and Society*, 56(1), 23–56.

Harris, S., Weinzettel, J., Bigano, A., and Källmén, A. (2020). Low carbon cities in 2050? GHG emissions of European cities using production-based and consumption-based emission accounting methods. *Journal of Cleaner Production*, 248, 1–13.

Hartwick, J. (1977). Intergenerational equity and the investing of rents from exhaustible resources. *American Economic Review*, 67(5), 972–974.

Hasan, M. N. (2016). Measuring and understanding the engagement of Bangladeshi SMEs with sustainable and socially responsible business practices: An ISO 26000 perspective. *Social ResponsibilityResponsibility Journal*, 12(3), 584–610.

Hawken, P., Lovins, A.B., and Lovins, L. H. (2005). *Natural capitalism: The next industrial revolution*. (10th ed.). Earthscan, Abingdon.

Heras, I., and Arana, G. (2010). Alternative models for environmental management in SMEs: the case of Ekoscan vs. ISO 14001. *Journal of Cleaner Production*, 18(8), 726–735.

Hitchens, D., Clausen, J., Trainor, M., Keil, M., and Thankappan, S. (2017). Competitiveness, environmental performance and management of SMEs. In S. Schaltegger and M. Wagner (Eds.), *Managing the business case for sustainability: The integration of social, environmental and economic performance* (274–290). Routledge, Abingdon.

Hosseininia, G., and Ramezani, A. (2016). Factors influencing sustainable entrepreneurship in small and medium-sized enterprises in Iran: A case study of food industry. *Sustainability*, 8(10). doi:10.3390/su8101010

Ivanko, N., and Wingo, N. (2018). Applying mixed methods in action research: Methodological potentials and advantages. *American Behavioral Scientist*, 62(7), 978–997.

Jarzabkowski, P., Bednarek, R., Chalkias, K., and Cacciatori, E. (2019). Exploring inter-organizational paradoxes: Methodological lessons from a study of a grand challenge. *Strategic Organization*, 17(1), 120–132.

Kaldewey, D. (2018). The grand challenges discourse: Transforming identity work in science and science policy. *Minerva*, 56(2), 161–182.

Kudo, S., and Mino, T. (2020). *Framing in Sustainability Science*. Springer, Singapore.

Levin, K., Cashore, B., Bernstein, S., and Auld, G. (2012). Overcoming the tragedy of super wicked problems: Constraining our future selves to ameliorate global climate change. *Policy Sciences*, 45(2), 123–152.

Liston-Heyes, C., and Vazquez Brust, D. A. (2016). Environmental protection in environmentally reactive firms: Lessons from corporate Argentina. *Journal of Business Ethics*, 135(2), 361–379.

López-Gamero, M. D., Claver-Cortés, E., and Molina-Azorín, J. F. (2008). Complementary resources and capabilities for an ethical and environmental management: A qual/quan study. *Journal of Business Ethics*, 82(3), 701–732.

Mensah, J. (2019). Sustainable development: Meaning, history, principles, pillars, and implications for human action: Literature review. *Cogent Social Sciences*, 5(1), 165–531.

Mertens, D. M. (2016). Advancing social change in South Africa through transformative research. *South African Review of Sociology*, 47(1), 5–17.

Neumayer, E. (2003). *Weak versus strong sustainability. Exploring the limits of two opposing paradigms*. Edward Elgar, Chelmsford.

Petts, J., Herd, A., Gerrard, S., and Horne, C. (1999). The climate and culture of environmental compliance withinin SMEs. *Business Strategy and the Environment*, 8(1), 14–30.

Plano Clark, V. L. , and Sanders, K. (2015). The use of visual displays in mixed methods research: Strategies for effectively integrating quantitative and qualitative components of a study. In M. T. McCrudden, G. Schraw, and C. Buckendahl (Eds.), *Use of visual displays in research and testing: Coding, interpreting, and reporting data* (177–206). Information Age, Charlotte.

Popa, F., Guillermin, M., and Dedeurwaerdere, T. (2015). A pragmatist approach to transdisciplinarity in sustainability research: From complex systems theory to reflexive science. *Futures*, 65, 45–56.

Porter, T., and Derry, R. (2012). Sustainability and business in a complex world. *Business and Society Review*, 117(1), 33–53.

Poth, C., and Onwuegbuzie, A. J. (2015). Special issue: Mixed methods. *International Journal of Qualitative Methods*, 14(2), 1–4.

Renn, O., Chabay, I., van der Leeuw, S., and Droy, S. (2020). Beyond the indicators: Improving science, scholarship, policy and practice to meet the complex challenges of sustainability. *Sustainability*, 12(2). 578 1–6.

Revell, A. (2007). The ecological modernisation of SMEs in the UK's construction industry. *Geoforum*, 38(1), 114–126.

Rothenberg, S., and Becker, M. (2004). Technical assistance programs and the diffusion of environmental technologies in the printing industry: The case of SMEs. *Business and Society*, 43(4), 366–397.

Sainidis, E., and Robson, A. (2016). Environmental turbulence: impact on UK SMEs' manufacturing priorities. *Management Research Review*, 39(10), 1239–1264.

Schaltegger, S. (2018). Linking environmental management accounting: A reflection on (missing) links to sustainability and planetary boundaries. *Social and Environmental Accountability Journal*, 38(1), 19–29.

Schaltegger, S., Beckmann, M., and Hansen, E. G. (2013). Transdisciplinarity in corporate sustainability: Mapping the field. *Business Strategy and the Environment*, 22(4), 219–229.

Schoonenboom, J., and Johnson, R. B. (2017). How to construct a mixed methods research design. *Kolner Zeitschrift Fur Soziologie Und Sozialpsychologie*, 69, 107–131.

Shannon-Baker, P. (2016). Making paradigms meaningful in mixed methods research. *Journal of Mixed Methods Research*, 10(4), 319–334.

Solow, R. M. (1974). Intergenerational equity and exhaustible resources. *The Review of Economic Studies*, 41, 29–45.

Sun, J., and Yang, K. (2016). The wicked problem of climate change: A new approach based on social mess and fragmentation. *Sustainability*, 8(12). doi:10.3390/su8121312

Tang, Z., and Tang, J. (2016). The impact of competitors-firm power divergence on Chinese SMES' environmental and financial performance. *Journal of Business Ethics*, 136(1), 147–165.

Tashakkori, A., and Teddlie, C. (2010). *Sage handbook of mixed methods in social and behavioral research*. Sage Publications, Thousand Oaks.

Wang, J., Yu, B., Tam, V. W. Y., Li, J., and Xu, X. (2019). Critical factors affecting willingness of design units towards construction waste minimization: An empirical study in Shenzhen, China. *Journal of Cleaner Production*, 221, 526–535.

Williams, J. B., and McNeill, J. M. (2005). The current crisis in neoclassical economics and the case for an economic analysis based on sustainable development. U21 Global Working Paper. doi.org/10.2139/ssrn.1606342

Worthington, I., and Patton, D. (2005). Strategic intent in the management of the green environment within SMEs. An analysis of the UK screen-printing sector. *Long Range Planning*, 38(2), 197–212.

Index

Note: Boldfaced page numbers refer to tables. Page numbers followed by *f* refer to figures.

Printed in the United States
by Baker & Taylor Publisher Services